CURRENTS IN JAPANESE CINEMA

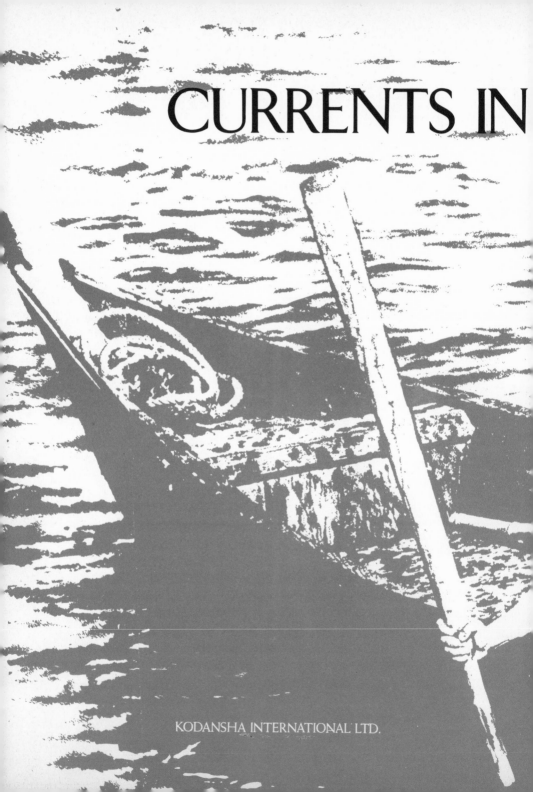

CURRENTS IN

KODANSHA INTERNATIONAL LTD.

JAPANESE CINEMA

Essays by **Tadao Sato**

Translated by Gregory Barrett

Publication of this book was assisted by a grant from
The Japan Foundation.

Jacket photo and photo on p. 240 courtesy
Kawakita Memorial Film Institute.

Distributed in the United States by Kodansha Internation-
al/USA, Ltd. through Harper & Row, Publishers, Inc.,
10 East 53rd Street, New York, New York 10022.
Published by Kodansha International Ltd., 12–21, Otowa
2-chome, Bunkyo-ku, Tokyo 112 and Kodansha Interna-
tional/USA, Ltd., 10 East 53rd Street, New York, New
York 10022 and 44 Montgomery Street, San Francisco,
California 94104. Copyright © 1982 by Kodansha Inter-
national Ltd. All rights reserved. Printed in Japan.
LCC 81–84801
ISBN 0–87011–507–3
ISBN 4–7700–1005–2 (in Japan)
First edition, 1982

CONTENTS

PREFACE

Tradition and Reform
in the Japanese Cinema

The Japanese film industry began around the year 1900. Only some three decades had passed since the Meiji Restoration of 1868, when Japan ceased being a closed feudal country on the outer fringes of Asia. Although a modern, Westernized nation was already in the making, the feelings of the population were slower to change, and both literature and drama were still steeped in traditionalism. Modern Western forms of drama were still at the experimentation level, supported by a small faction of intellectuals. Since film had its origins as an entertainment form for the masses, it drew heavily on traditional drama and literature for material, especially from Kabuki and *kodan* ("historical tales"). The former usually concerned a samurai giving up his life out of loyalty for his lord, and the latter a samurai avenging the death of a parent. Thus early film contained a paradox: it was a new means of expression but what it expressed was old. In primitive cinema, themes had to be kept simple, thereby earning the long-lasting scorn of intellectuals who found its subjects outmoded and infantile, and its producers uncultured and uncouth.

The novelty of cinema, however, primarily excited children, and when they grew up some of them wondered if new themes could be expressed through the new medium. And in the 1920s these youths began making films. At that time Japanese society looked down on this occupation, considering it mere socializing with the masses, and sons who entered the film world were quickly disowned by their upper- and middle-class parents. This did not deter these young men, however, who were obsessed with this Western medium and with liberal ideas. Thus began the battle between the old and the new.

This battle had reverberations in the world of literature and drama. Whereas new, Westernized ideas could be realized through the support of a small number of intellectual play lovers and readers, the cinema, on the other hand, had to cater to the populace at large, conservatives and intellectuals included. While this condition resulted in compromises, frustrations, and the abandonment of ideals, it subsequently gave rise to new ideas that appealed to a sufficiently wide audience, which cannot be said for similar reform movements in literature, where the use of difficult language raised a permanent barrier before the masses. The film world, on the other hand, like the entertainment world of feudal times, had a close connection with the *yakuza,* gangsters, whose language was easily understandable. From its inception the *yakuza* figured both in its management and its employees, and this low-class image deterred many a graduate from entering its ranks until the 1930s.

Besides the *yakuza,* studios were filled with ambitious young men who only had the benefit of a primary education but were possessed with a keen desire to learn. One of them was Kenji Mizoguchi (1898–1956), who made his directorial debut in 1923. Another was Teinosuke Kinugasa (1896–1982), who made Japan's first avant-garde film in 1926, the masterpiece *A Crazy Page (Kurutta Ippeiji)*; he had run away from home to join a troupe of itinerant actors and became a star of the popular theater. Still another was Hiroshi Inagaki (1905–81), winner of the Grand Prix at the 1958 Venice Film Festival for *The Life of Matsu the Untamed (Muho Matsu no Issho)*, who had to help support his family as a child actor and only learned to read and write in dressing rooms.

8

In the 1930s college graduates began entering the film world. Some were forced to leave college after their arrest for participating in the communist movement during the years of the depression. Unlike most enterprises, motion picture studios usually did not discriminate against them, perhaps because the rightist *yakuza* sympathized with fellow trouble-makers. Then, too, they may have been welcomed simply because there had been few graduates in the industry before. Or, again, it could have been due to the lax standards in hiring applicants. In this way did some of motion pictures' brightest directors—Akira Kurosawa, Tadashi

Imai, Satsuo Yamamoto—enter the film world. In the 1950s, too, when graduates from top universities flooded the studios trying for assistant director jobs, their number included several activists, among them Nagisa Oshima, Shinsuke Ogawa, and Noriaki Tsuchimoto, the latter two being pioneers of the antiestablishment documentary film movement. By the 1930s the reputation of film—as a result of the masterpieces produced then—had improved so considerably that university graduates were clamoring for the privilege of working with master directors with the minimum formal education.

The film world of the 1930s was probably the most diverse society in Japan—the self-educated, rightists, leftist intellectuals, graduates—and studios became a sort of marketplace for sounding out the ideas of the intellectuals and the feelings of the common populace. Always groping for new modes of expression, the responsiveness of film to both intellectual movements and popular sentiments created fads that were sometimes difficult to account for.

One example was the fad for the so-called tendency films in 1930–31. Although Marxist thought was prevalent in book form until then, tendency films disseminated its ideas to the populace at large. This fad, along with other leftist movements, was completely suppressed by the government. Then, in 1931, with the occupation of Manchuria leading to war with China, filmmakers, as suddenly as before and without the slightest trace of embarrassment, created a new fad for films that glorified militarism. Among their number were several directors who had been making leftist films. Thus, the battle between old and new had its extremely erratic side. Yet however wildly cinematic modes of expression may fluctuate, film is still rooted in the consciousness of the common people, where ideas do not change so easily.

Japan had cast off feudalism to embrace modernism with such haste and vigor that repercussions of the battle between old and new were being felt at all levels of society. However, as the movements in the film world have been the most active and lively, it is through film that we will witness the clearest tremors of that battle.

TADAO SATO

Tokyo, 1982

TRANSLATOR'S INTRODUCTION

In 1956 Tadao Sato drew the public's attention with the publication of his first book, *Nihon no eiga* (*Japanese Film*), for which he won the 1957 Critic's Award presented by *Kinema Jumpo*, the leading film magazine. Since then he has published sixty-five books on film—including volumes on Mizoguchi, Ozu, Kurosawa, and Oshima—and on other aspects of popular culture, such as comic books (*manga*) and television, and on education. Most of the essays in this collection are taken from *Nihon eiga shiso-shi* (*The Intellectual History of Japanese Film*), published in 1970 and reprinted seventeen times.

The publication of *Nihon no eiga* altered the course of film criticism in Japan by introducing a new approach. Until that time film critics could be roughly divided into two types, the ideologues and the aesthetes. The ideologues judged a film by sociopolitical standards (usually "modernism," democracy, or communism) and, accordingly, criticized a Mizoguchi work on the self-sacrifice of women for its feudalism. The aesthetes, on the other hand, would praise the same film for its atmospheric effects, its acting, and so on. Both types of critics were college graduates, who, in a country as academically oriented as Japan, constitute the élite class.

Tadao Sato, unlike them, never went to college and began writing film reviews while working as a telephone repairman. He felt that understanding the sentiments of a film was more important than its ideology or its conformity to aesthetic standards. A large number of readers shared his view and felt that Sato was better suited to understanding the sentiments of the people than the college-educated intellectuals.

Sato's success also swept aside biases toward certain film genres, for he reviewed films that were beneath the dignity of the ideologues and aesthetes, for example, melodramas, slapstick comedies, and *chambara,* or swordfighting, films. He felt that such works were significant because they reflected the feelings of the common people, and it was the critic's task to consider the implications they aroused. Nowadays these genres are taken seriously by most Japanese film critics, and some even find value in some of the soft-core pornographic films currently produced in abundance.

Given Sato's background and approach to film, he can be called the common man's ally; however, as he is a firm believer in progress, he can also be critical of sentiments that he regards as *hoken-teki,* or feudalistic. Like many Japanese intellectuals he uses the word in a derogatory fashion to refer to pre-Meiji period ideas and sentiments that continue to exist today, especially feudal sentiments that emphasize submission to one's superiors. While he is similar to the ideologues in this respect, he believes that new ideas can only gain wide currency if their expression is synchronized with the sentiments of the common people. In other words, the ideas cannot be forced down people's throats by a few intellectual leaders. Until the invasion of television in the 1960s, cinema, to him, was the best forum for the introduction of new thought.

Sato's antifeudalistic stance leads him to assume an ambivalent attitude toward the traditional culture of Japan and, in this respect, he differs from Western critics such as Donald Richie, Joseph Anderson, Paul Schrader, Audie Bock, or Noël Burch. All of them discuss Japanese film in terms of traditional aesthetics and concepts, particularly Zen Buddhism, looking upon tradition positively as a repository of alternate modes of thought and perception that present a stimulating challenge to Western thought. Sato, on the contrary, favors popular culture over traditional in his treatment of Japanese film. While Sato appreciates the beauty inherent in traditional forms, he firmly rejects their feudalistic contents, perhaps as a result of his own youth when traditional concepts were used to inculcate submission to the state and even resignation to death on the battlefield. Moreover, as most of Japan's aesthetic heritage was fostered by the upper classes, it is not necessarily a reflection of the sentiments of the common people of the past nor of the average Japanese today.

Sato's interest in the sentiments of the average man and his own belief in human progress add a second dimension to his approach to film criticism. The essays in this collection are just as much about modern social history as they are about film, for films mirror social developments and reflect how sentiments change or become further entrenched. This second dimension may leave him open to criticism on methodological grounds. It seems that in the West, due to semiology, film criticism is becoming more and more of an academic discipline, and Sato's social concerns could be considered external to the study of the mechanics of film. However, while semiology has its adherents in Japan, its disciplinarian approach is not prevalent at present. Sato can be as analytical in regard to cinematic technique as the structuralist Noël Burch, but he regards structural analysis as only one factor in a comprehensive approach that includes a critical evaluation of social concerns. At any rate, it is the reader who will benefit from Sato's comprehensive approach, for not only will he obtain film evaluations that make interesting comparisons with those of Western critics like Richie but he will also receive a rare view of modern Japanese history.

In Japan, as in the West, most histories are written with an emphasis on politics and economics, and since the leaders in these fields take the spotlight, the view is usually from the top looking down. The combination of Sato's concern with the sentiments of the common people and his interest in intellectual thought presents a view of history that can be best described as at a gut level.

GREGORY BARRETT

Tokyo, 1982

ACKNOWLEDGMENTS

In this work the translator makes the following acknowledgments: to Peter High for his first draft of some of the material in this volume and his translation of part of Chapter 5, which appeared as "War as a Spiritual Exercise: Japan's 'National Policy Films,'" in *Wide Angle*, vol. 1, no. 4 (1977); and to Paul Andrew's translation of "On Kenji Mizoguchi," in *Film Criticism*, vol. 4, no. 3 (1980).

Most of the essays in this volume are taken from *Nihon eiga shisoshi*, which is also referred to as *A Theoretical History of Japanese Film*, or as *Thought and Image in Japanese Film*, or as *History of the Intellectual Currents in Japanese Film*. Part of Chapter 6 and the Ozu section of Chapter 9 were taken from the author's *Nihon eiga no kyosho-tachi* (*"The Masters of Japanese Film"*), while the section on eye behavior in the films of Ozu and Naruse, Chapter 9, was taken from his *Katei no yomigaeri no tame ni—homu dorama-ron* (*"For the Revival of the Home—Essays on Home Dramas"*). This appeared in *Cahiers du cinéma*, April, 1980, as *"Le Point de regard,"* translated by Jean-Paul Le Pape.

The author has also updated and rewritten some of these essays. Chapters 1, 2, 12, and the Preface are new essays especially written for this publication, as is the Chronology in Appendix I.

Stills were selected by the author and are courtesy of the Japan Film Library Council, Tokyo.

Both the author and the translator wish to thank Donald Richie for all his help and useful suggestions.

13

NOTES: In the first reference to a film, the Japanese title is given in parentheses after the title in English; all subsequent references have only the English title. The Index contains a listing of all films under both their Japanese and English titles.

All personal names follow the Western order, i.e., with the surname last.

1

The Two Leading Men in Japanese Film

Maple Viewing (*Momijigari*, 1899), the oldest extant print of a Japanese movie, is a filmed performance of a Kabuki play with the same title. It was originally made only to record the performances of the most famous Kabuki actors of the day, Danjuro Ichikawa and Kikugoro Onoe, although after some years it was given a public showing. At that time film was considered a low-class show, inappropriate for appearances by the proud leading stage actors. However, since Kabuki was the most popular form of drama, early film producers considered using its actors and filming its repertoires just as they were, and so they scouted for suitable second- and third-ranking actors.

For a Kabuki actor, the label "second-ranking" or "third-ranking" does not necessarily denote that his performances are poor. In the feudalistic Kabuki world, only the natural or adopted son of a top-ranking actor affiliated with a famous school can ever aspire to play the main role at a leading theater. Consequently, ambitious actors who lacked suitable connections abandoned Kabuki and turned to the film world, where they could earn more than the leading Kabuki actors. In this way the forms of Kabuki, along with its two types of leading roles and even its *onnagata*—actors who played female roles—were introduced into early cinema.

The actor who plays the main lead in Kabuki is called *tateyaku* ("standing role") and, as a rule, he heads the troupe. The characters he plays are noble, idealized samurai, warriors who are not only victorious in fights but also sagacious men, with a strong will and determination to persevere. However, because men of this breed were educated according to Confucian morals, which placed no value on romantic love, such a character was never permitted to place his love for his wife or sweetheart above loyalty toward his lord. This was one of the fundamental principles of Bushido, the code of behavior of the warrior.

Although the Bushido code and the Western code of chivalry were both idealized forms of conduct in which honor and courage were esteemed, in one important aspect they differed significantly. In the Western code loyalty toward the lady one worshiped was valued more highly than loyalty toward one's lord, and medieval tales of chivalry abound in love triangles involving a knight and the wife of his lord or in a knight's rebellion against the lord to protect the honor of the lady in question. Such situations may lie at the root of the concept of Western individualism, where not even the nation can obstruct the rights of the individual. On the other hand, such situations were impossible in the tales of Bushido. There, a noble samurai (performed by the *tateyaku*) would sacrifice his wife and children out of loyalty toward his lord and, despite his inner pain, would watch them die without betraying the slightest emotion.

Such were the heroes in Kabuki, and the stylized forms of a *tateyaku* performance were refined through the centuries to present an ideal image of the samurai, an image, however, that was not meant to entertain these ascetic warriors themselves—at best seven percent of the population of feudal Japan—who looked

16

upon Kabuki as gaudy, even erotic entertainment and refrained from frequenting its theaters. Kabuki's main source of support was the merchant class in the cities of Edo (modern Tokyo) and Osaka, and it developed according to their view of the world.

While the merchant class recognized the *tateyaku*'s samurai as an ideal of manhood, the audience, especially women, was not completely satisfied simply because the *tateyaku* never fell in love. The wives and daughters of these merchants, as well as the geisha who catered to them and the women who ran the geisha houses and restaurants, held another ideal—a man who could whisper sweet words of love. Accordingly, Kabuki evolved the *nimaime* ("second"), so named because the actors playing the role were given second billing to the *tateyaku*.

The *nimaime* had to be handsome, though not necessarily strong, pure in heart, though not necessarily clever. The purest type of *nimaime* was called *tsukkorogashi* ("feeble") because he gave the impression of a frail, helpless fellow who would fall over if nudged. The character played by the *nimaime* was always kind and gentle toward the heroine, and when circumstances drove her to suicide, he gladly died with her. The *nimaime*'s big scene is the *michiyuki*, when he walks together with the woman to the place where they are to commit suicide. This scene is the climax of his performance and is filled with emotional facial expressions and grand gestures. Ironically, however, it is often his own imprudence or carelessness that prompts her decision, for he then becomes socially unacceptable and she loses all hope of a happy marriage with him.

The fact that the *nimaime* could never be as strong or as wise as the *tateyaku* may be a manifestation of the inferiority complex of the merchant class toward the samurai. Ideally, in feudal Japan parents chose marriage partners for their sons and daughters, and the couple concerned had no say in the matter. Although the samurai rigidly maintained this system, the merchants, craftsmen, and farmers were not so strict, and farmers were relatively free to choose their wives. However, as the moral conduct of the ruling samurai class was held in such esteem, even though the other classes might sympathize with those who did not adhere to this strict code, they could not approve of them. Noble human beings were those strong, sagacious samurai played by the *tateyaku*. *Nimaime*,

17

on the other hand, played characters who fell in love with geisha and prostitutes and who, as a result of misconduct, such as misappropriating their master's funds, committed suicide with such women. Thus, no matter how handsome they were, it was difficult to call them exemplary men. However, as they could love and as they showed romantic love to be something beautiful, many of them outdid the *tateyaku* in popularity and even respect.

The presence of these two completely different types of leading men in one play probably constitutes a tradition found only in Japanese drama. The hero of a Western drama, as a rule, is not only strong, intelligent, and active, but is also, if not a winner in love, a manly character who can act passionately for love. This tradition was carried into movies, and Rudolph Valentino, Jean Gabin, Gary Cooper, Clark Gable, and Laurence Olivier all achieved fame playing such classic heroes. However, there were also exceptions. John Wayne and Burt Lancaster played roles similar to the *tateyaku*'s, for they portrayed characters who were strong and reliable but not suited to love scenes. On the other hand, Gérard Philippe and Marcello Mastroianni played *nimaime*-type roles, since they were seldom strong but enthralled audiences with their love scenes. Nevertheless, these two types are never so clearly separated in Western drama as in Kabuki.

The two types of leading men in Kabuki were inherited by Japanese movies and continue to appear in them even today. The first superstar Matsunosuke Onoe had been a *tateyaku* and the head of a second-ranking Kabuki troupe that primarily toured the provinces. Until 1926 he dominated the period drama genre, meaning films set in history before the Meiji Restoration of 1868. He was discovered by the manager of a Kabuki theater in Kyoto, Shozo Makino, who became Japan's first film director. At first Onoe's film performances were straight from the Kabuki repertoire, but Makino soon realized that a combination of Kabuki material with a swordfighting climax and simple heroic tales from *kodan* (historical stories recited by a storyteller) would be more suitable for films than the complicated plots of Kabuki plays. The resulting action thrillers were popular with audiences then, who were mainly children and youths, and Onoe continued playing the strong samurai in over one thousand films from 1908 to 1926.

18

When the reign of Matsunosuke Onoe ended in the 1920s, Tsumasaburo Bando, Denjiro Okochi, and other actors appeared to take up his mantle, and they continued to be popular right into the 1950s. Like Onoe, most of them had been second-ranking Kabuki actors specializing in *tateyaku* roles. Although at times these new stars and their young directors made films based on original scripts or adapted from modern novels with more complex themes and plots, the samurai remained the center of their dramas and their performance was still that of a *tateyaku*.

The fact that the only Japanese film actors to achieve an international reputation today belong to that type further demonstrates the appeal of the *tateyaku*. One such actor was Sessue Hayakawa, who became a star in the 1910s by presenting a faithful imitation of the *tateyaku* performance in American movies. Like the loyal samurai who allows his own wife and children to be killed, Hayakawa hardly ever changed his facial expression and showed his intense inner emotions only by slight eye movements. In the West this was considered an original acting style and quite a departure from the conventional grandiose gestures employed as a means of filling the silent screen. Later it led French film theorists to conclude that a close-up of a slight change in facial expression was the most powerful means of cinematic expression.

Another actor, Toshiro Mifune, who became famous through Kurosawa's samurai films in the 1950s and 1960s, is also a classic example of the *tateyaku*. Since his debut in 1947 he has appeared in approximately one hundred and twenty films; however, as far as I remember, he has only played three or four love scenes, in which he was so terribly miscast that they are a clear case of the exception proving the rule.

Although neither Hayakawa nor Mifune had any connection with Kabuki, they had unconsciously assimilated the facial expressions and bearing of the *tateyaku*, appearing like the samurai of old in their performances. To the modern Japanese this frequently seemed anachronistic and overtheatrical; however, in Western eyes these actors became splendid representatives of the samurai tradition.

Despite the appeal of the *tateyaku*, women viewers in the early days of cinema, like their counterparts in feudal Japan, needed a romantic interest. This was supplied by the contemporary drama genre, meaning films set after the Meiji Restoration of 1868 which developed around the *nimaime*. As period drama evolved from Kabuki, so contemporary drama evolved from Shimpa. Shimpa, a new drama form with contemporary plots, came into being around 1890 as a potential replacement for Kabuki, whose feudalistic forms were no longer capable of reflecting the mores of a modernizing Japan. However, Shimpa's early form—consisting of the *tateyaku*, the *nimaime*, and the *onnagata*, or female impersonator, roles—was inherited from Kabuki. From 1900 to the mid-1920s Shimpa was the most popular form of drama. However, because of its antiquated forms, it was replaced in the 1920s by a new school, *shingeki* (modern drama). With texts and techniques directly imported from the West, *shingeki* primarily aimed at realism and became the mainstream of Japanese drama from the 1930s on.

The first contemporary drama films were made at Nikkatsu's Tokyo studio in the 1910s with Shimpa actors, including *onnagata*, playwrights, and directors, and they were simply film presentations of the Shimpa repertoire. The great majority of Shimpa plays are love tragedies, the most common subject matter being stories about handsome but undependable *nimaime* and the sweethearts who suffer on their account. Sample plots are: a geisha is loved by a rich young man, but they cannot marry simply because she is a geisha; a pure-hearted country girl loves a youth who so yearns for life in the city that he abandons her while she is pregnant, returning after having become a failure.

A major innovation took place in the early 1920s when actresses took over the roles of the *onnagata*. This departure from tradition occurred in contemporary drama because, unlike the *tateyaku*-dominated period drama, the love scenes were central, and no matter how adeptly the female impersonators were made up, they appeared grotesque in film when their Adam's apples showed in close-ups.

The first to notice this discrepancy were the intellectual youths who frequented foreign film theaters. In those days of strict sexual segregation, theaters that showed foreign films were the only places where young men could gaze at the faces of beautiful women, "real" women who possessed immense sex appeal. When these intellectuals started making movies in the 1920s they not

20

only abandoned the primitive method of simply shooting a stage play from start to finish, using instead the more cinematic method of a series of short takes, but also did away with the *onnagata*.

Considering the tenacity of tradition, the complete changeover to actresses occurred within the short span of a few years. After success in contemporary drama actresses were also adopted in period drama. At first *onnagata* were simply the result of a governmental ban against using actresses in the seventeenth century, when Kabuki began, since actresses also worked as prostitutes. However, this abnormal practice soon came to be accepted and developed into a highly stylized artistic form. The *onnagata* was said to be more erotic than a real woman because his performance emphasized the elements that men thought characteristic of femininity, such as gentleness, frailty, shyness, coquetry. Still, his acting was only a crystallization of the consciousness of bygone days, and since he was limited to a few set, exaggerated types of women, his disappearance gave Japanese film the chance to proceed in the direction of realism, for actresses could better express the problems of contemporary women. This gave some directors the opportunity to create new heroines, which in turn affected the delineation of the *nimaime* character.

One of the first film actresses was Kumeko Urabe, still an amateur when she appeared in Minoru Murata's *Seisaku's Wife (Seisaku no Tsuma,* 1924), a film which marked the appearance of a new, forceful heroine. The story of this masterpiece in early contemporary drama is as follows.

Seisaku, an earnest youth, is expected to become a future village leader. One day Okane, a young woman with an unfortunate past, returns to the village. She had once been the mistress of a rich man in a far-away town, and is thus spurned by all the villagers except Seisaku, who does not hold her past against her. Consequently, she falls madly in love with him and the two get married, much to the consternation of the villagers, who think he has been debauched by her. When the Russo-Japanese War begins, Seisaku enlists as a soldier. He is wounded and returns home, but when his wounds are healed and he is ready for the front again, Okane, unable to bear the thought of being left an object of prejudice in the village, blinds Seisaku with a hairpin to prevent his going. She is arrested and sent to prison. Upon her release some years later, Okane apologizes to the embittered Seisaku and then commits suicide by jumping into a river. When Seisaku learns of her death, the grudge he bears her for blinding him turns to love and pity, and he sorrowfully drowns himself in the same river.

Seisaku is an earnest youth, handsome and kind, but he is not strong enough to make the woman he loves happy, and the most he can do for her is to follow her in death. Thus, Seisaku is clearly a role for the *nimaime*. Although Murata worked in *shingeki*, not Shimpa, the brilliant re-creation of the *nimaime*-type lead in his film is one example of how strong tradition can be. However, the forceful heroine, who committed the terrible act of blinding a soldier about to go to the front, was a definite break with tradition, and because of her action, *Seisaku's Wife* can be viewed as Japan's first antiwar and antimilitarist film, in spite of its weak *nimaime*-type lead.

Kenji Mizoguchi, a young colleague of Murata at Nikkatsu studio, where *Seisaku's Wife* was produced, made similar films. Two of his masterpieces, *Osaka Elegy* (*Naniwa Ereji*, 1936) and *Sisters of the Gion* (*Gion no Shimai*, 1936), were about unfortunate young women who were capable of decisive action, thereby outshining their undependable *nimaime*-type men. However, before Mizoguchi could advance that far, he had first to transcend his own background. Born to a poor family, he was forced to work at an early age, but either through his ego or his lack of volition, he could not hold down any job for long. Whenever he was out of a job, his older sister, a geisha who became the mistress of an aristocrat, bolstered his spirits and helped him find a new job. When he went to a fine arts school to study painting, she even sent him money. In short, Mizoguchi himself was a weak and undependable young man, protected by an unfortunate woman full of love for him, and, because of his good looks, was pursued by scandal when prostitutes and the like fell in love with him.

Mizoguchi's own *nimaime*-type character resulted in his making movies centering around the *nimaime* at Nikkatsu, which specialized in Shimpa films. Eventually, however, he succeeded in creating modern, realistic films within the fundamental structure of Shimpa by not sentimentalizing the *nimaime* characters and

22

criticizing their defects of personality and thought. While portraying them as worthless fellows unable to make their women happy, at the same time he endowed his heroines with strong characters. The *nimaime* were flustered by the heroines' violent stance on discrimination against women, which was so different from Shimpa heroines, who always pined after the *nimaime* and went together with him toward their tragic finale. Mizoguchi's heroines stopped pining, pushed the weaklings aside, and advanced on their own. At these times they had an appeal that had not existed in former heroines.

One example is the heroine of *My Love Burns* (*Waga Koi wa Moenu*, 1949), although her male lead was not a *nimaime* type. The film is based on the autobiography of Eiko Fukuda, a female revolutionary in the latter part of the nineteenth century, who falls in love with and marries Kentaro Oe, the leader of an antigovernment movement. Although Oe's democratic views mark him as politically progressive, he retains the feudalistic attitude toward women and feels no qualms about taking a mistress. When Eiko learns of this she loses hope in him and furiously attacks him; after their divorce, she goes on to fight for women's rights.

In the conventional dramaturgy of Japanese theater and cinema, the political leader Kentaro Oe should have been played commandingly by a *tateyaku* type of actor. However, Mizoguchi cast Ichiro Sugai—an actor who often played villains—in the role and portrayed Oe as an enemy of women, a man who only puts on the grand airs of a *tateyaku*. Here Mizoguchi, who sides with women as the victims of discrimination, attacks both the weakness of the *nimaime* and the arrogance of the *tateyaku*. Thus, although he started out making Shimpa films, he eventually destroyed that world from the inside.

Despite this, contemporary drama as a whole did not change much and in the more popular films the *nimaime* was still treated sentimentally and the heroine still pined at home. In 1938 *The Compassionate Buddha Tree* (*Aizen Katsura*), a love melodrama involving a nurse and a doctor, who is the son of the owner-administrator of a big, modern hospital, broke all previous box-office records. As the heroine is both a widow with a child and a nurse, the young doctor's parents will not permit their marriage. Although she stops working at the hospital and he leaves home with the intention of marrying her, various misunderstandings and accidents keep them apart. Since the audience is constantly kept on tenterhooks by the lovers' near-encounters that are foiled by chance, this kind of film was called *sure chigai* melodrama —*sure chigai* literally meaning "to brush past someone," that is, just missing meeting someone.

The hero and heroine do not force the issue but wait for the day his parents will allow their marriage. Thus, they can be kept apart indefinitely, and the story was so popular it became a trilogy with repeatedly broken rendezvous. The pining heroine was played by Kinuyo Tanaka (who would later play the fighter for women's rights in Mizoguchi's *My Love Burns*). Her romantic lead, Ken Uehara, was the most popular *nimaime* actor of contemporary drama in the 1930s. A classic example of the weak, gentle beau, he certainly did not give the impression of a man who would overcome all obstacles to win the woman he loved.

After World War II another classic *sure chigai* melodrama, *What Is Your Name?* (*Kimi no Na wa*, 1953) broke the previous box-office record set by *The Compassionate Buddha Tree*. Its male lead, Keiji Sada, who thereafter became extremely popular, usually had an apologetic expression on his face, as if he were chastizing himself for his lack of drive to make the woman he loved happy. From the 1960s on *sure chigai* virtually ceased production because of the social changes incurred by a soaring economy, and forebearance and sentimentality were no longer regarded as noble attributes.

24 As we have said above, contemporary drama developed with its Shimpa-like *nimaime,* and period drama with its Kabuki-like *tateyaku*. Although there were some exceptions (such as period drama star Kazuo Hasegawa, who was a *nimaime* type, and some *nimaime* actors who became *tateyaku* types as they aged), in general this division held and was reinforced by geographical location. Ever since the establishment in 1912 of Nikkatsu, which maintained one studio in Kyoto for period dramas and one in Tokyo for contemporary dramas, the other major film companies—Shochiku, Toho, Daiei—followed suit, and until around 1960 they all showed a new double feature with one film from each genre at their theaters every week. Kyoto, with its old architecture, was the center of traditional culture, while Tokyo was the vanguard of Westernized

culture. Thus, period and contemporary dramas developed with completely different actors, actresses, scriptwriters, and directors. When Toho began shooting both genres at its Tokyo studios in the 1940s the situation started to change. Finally, all distinction was erased in the 1970s, when period drama lost its popularity, and even Kyoto studios became almost entirely involved with contemporary drama. Still, the sense of competition between Kyoto and Tokyo film-makers in the two main genres was a driving force behind developments in Japanese film, especially when directors made crossovers into different genres.

Mizoguchi is one example. Born in Tokyo, he learned the dramaturgy of Shimpa at a Tokyo studio. When his studio was destroyed by the Great Kanto Earthquake of 1923, he was forced to go to Kyoto, where he continued his work. He feared that Kyoto's traditional atmosphere would affect his progressive films, but the opportunity to work in Tokyo did not arise. And so he eventually made one of his greatest contemporary dramas, *Sisters of the Gion,* in Kyoto. In it Mizoguchi denounced the survival of old traditions in modern times, thus stimulating a trend toward realistic films in Tokyo studios, which tended to imitate modern American movies as an escape from reality.

Another example is Kurosawa, also born in Tokyo, who specialized in making contemporary drama films at a Tokyo studio. In 1948 a strike forced him to move to Kyoto, where he filmed his epoch-making period drama *Rashomon* (*Rashomon,* 1950). At that time, Kyoto's period drama productions still relied heavily on the absurd, outmoded, stylized mannerisms of Kabuki, but Kurosawa's *Rashomon* showed no Kabuki influence, and its success afforded other directors opportunities to try similarly ambitious experiments.

New developments also occurred on some occasions when a *tateyaku* actor appeared in a contemporary drama, for he possessed an aura of dignity the *nimaime* lacked. On the other hand, in the *tateyaku*'s own genre, this bearing often obstructed progress. A *tateyaku*'s majestic demeanor was reared on years of experience playing such noble roles, and even offstage a Kabuki *tateyaku* behaved much like a feudal lord. Thus, second-ranking Kabuki actors who turned to period drama demanded special treatment from studio personnel. With the exception of a few major directors, no one could tell them what to do, and since they assumed they knew their public best, they would never abandon a pose or facial expression that had proven popular in the past, and even forced their own formulas on scriptwriters and directors. Therefore, the vast majority of period drama pictures did not vary greatly from Kabuki and were merely cherished vehicles of feudalistic thought. The story of the samurai who sacrificed his family out of loyalty toward his lord was ubiquitous in the 1910s and the 1920s, and in the militaristic 1930s the theme of loyalty was purposefully tied to the nation. Although feudalistic themes were prohibited by the U.S. Occupation forces from 1945 to 1952, period drama was revived in its original form as soon as the Occupation was over.

The movie-going public supported period drama stars who played strong, loyal samurai. While Japan appeared as an extremely dangerous, brutal nation to the West, both militaristic and aggressive from 1900 to 1945, in Japanese eyes it was the Western imperialistic powers that were dangerous and brutal, for they had colonized most of Asia up until the end of the previous century. The Japanese believed that Japan was the only nation in Asia resisting them, and, therefore, Japan had to be strong. Consequently, they applauded these period drama *tateyaku*, seeing them as idealized images of strong Japanese. Viewed in this light, the resurrection of period drama after the Occupation was probably not so much a restoration of feudal thought as a continuation of the old fear—namely, that postwar Japan's weakness would continue unless the will and pride of the samurai was preserved.

26

As Japan rose to become one of the world's most affluent countries in the 1960s, the Japanese gradually shook off their old inferiority complex toward the West. As a reflection of their new standing in the world, period drama declined and only a few were produced in the 1970s. They were still made for television, but the days when they constituted almost half the total movie production had passed.

Two popular *tateyaku* stars who made crossovers from period drama to contemporary drama in the 1940s were Tsumasaburo Bando and Denjiro Okochi. Tsumasaburo Bando, a period drama star since 1924, was cast in Inagaki's contemporary drama *The Life of Matsu the Untamed* (*Muho Matsu no Issho*, 1943), giving the best performance in his entire career. Playing a ricksha man, he exhibited a pride not inferior to that of a samurai, which was an innovation then because such spirit had not previously been associated with the poverty-ridden, uneducated lower classes. Although Inagaki won the Venice Grand Prix with his 1958 remake of this film, with Toshiro Mifune in the lead, Mifune's performance did not even approach Bando's.

Denjiro Okochi became a period drama star around the same time as Bando. In one of Hiroshi Shimizu's masterpieces, *Mr. Shosuke Ohara* (*Ohara Shosuke-san*, 1949), Okochi played a powerful landowner who, in the liberal land reforms of the Occupation, had to turn most of his land over to his tenant farmers for virtually no compensation. Incidentally, these were the biggest democratic reforms in postwar Japan, but they were enforced without the slightest turmoil. In fact, their success probably prevented a revolution because through them poor tenant farmers could hope to become affluent, independent farmers. Unlike the landowners who had meekly borne their downfall, the unperturbed Mr. Shosuke Ohara never lost his composure and concealed the tragedy of his ruin with rich humor. Only a top-ranking *tateyaku* like Okochi, who had played strong, reliable samurai for years, could have given such a splendid performance.

Actors nurtured in contemporary drama usually played modern Japanese who, out of a sense of inferiority, discarded the traditional life-style for a more Western one, and thereby became mediocre and imitative. Furthermore, they were often *nimaime* types who were permitted to assume a weak and undependable attitude. Consequently, although many of these contemporary drama actors were superb at expressing delicate psychological nuances, it was hard for them to assume the grand demeanor of period drama stars like Bando and Okochi or to play a character like Mr. Shosuke Ohara, a man who could take sweeping reforms in his stride.

Bando and Okochi preserved the good side of the samurai-like personality in the postwar era. At that time many Japanese were disillusioned by the prewar excesses committed in its name and considered it useless and ridiculous, thereby becoming so humble and servile that they lost their old pride. Novelist Yukio Mishima was so revolted by this loss that his 1972 *harakiri*, the samurai way of committing suicide, can be viewed as an act of a man who grew up in an age of too much samurai spirit reacting negatively against an age with too little.

Kurosawa was a director who not only preserved the positive side of the samurai-like personality but also achieved a major reform in Japanese film when he skillfully combined the majestic *tateyaku* character and performance with stories that had universal appeal. Before Kurosawa non-Japanese audiences found the *tateyaku* in films too overbearing, unlike in Kabuki, where his role, along with that of the *nimaime*, could be viewed as a mode of classical Japanese theater. Most of the previous *tateyaku* characters were men who were strong and noble out of feudal loyalty and duty. This was not the case with Kurosawa's *tateyaku*, for Kurosawa himself had rebelled against such feudal concepts by participating in illegal communist activities as a youth. However, as the son of a soldier, he affirmed the ideal of samurai strength, and these two sides to his personality eventually led him to create a new ideal of Japanese manhood.

The core of the theme that Kurosawa ceaselessly pursued was probably "manliness," in the sense of a strong man trying to live bravely to the very end. This can be seen in all his films except for *The Most Beautiful* (*Ichiban Utsukushiku*, 1944) and *No Regrets for Our Youth* (*Waga Seishun ni Kui Nashi*, 1946), where women took the lead. Even these heroines, however, were brave in a manly sense and had a stronger sense of responsibility than many men.

The first element in Kurosawa's "manliness" is simply physical strength. In *Sanshiro Sugata* (*Sugata Sanshiro*, 1943), *Sanjuro* (*Tsubaki Sanjuro*, 1962), and *Dersu Uzala* (*Dersu Uzala*, 1975), for example, strong men act admirably with pride. Whether their strength lies in judo, a quick draw of the sword, or the abilities forged through the hardship of life in a Siberian forest, Kurosawa's heroes all have a powerful desire to make themselves strong by continuing to train in some skill or technique. In Kurosawa's films, even a character who at first sight appears mediocre and insignificant can be transformed into a strong human being. This strength is spiritual rather than physical, and this forms the second element of Kurosawa's "manliness." *Ikiru* (*Ikiru*, 1952) is a fine example. The main character is a mediocre bureaucrat approaching old age, a man who leads a humdrum existence, going about his job out of force of habit. "You can't call this living," he is told. When this official learns he has cancer and has only six months to live, he eventually finds a purpose in life by working for the benefit of others and goes to his death contented.

In order to portray such characters of strength, Kurosawa persistently created forceful cinematic images and thus brought to film a novel version of the majestic performance of the *tateyaku*. If it was merely a matter of the main character appearing strong, the film would be no more than an action movie or a lecture on nobility no matter how much he raged, or how much spirit and sense of justice he had. The strength of Kurosawa's characters is overwhelming not only because of their nobility but also because the film images are permeated with power and majesty. There is no single scene that appears to be shot haphazardly or whimsically and all his cinematic images are packed tight with no slack.

Powerful scenes cannot be produced without impassioned acting, and Kurosawa's thoroughness in forcing intense performances out of his actors paid off. In this respect he is exceptional, and only Mizoguchi, in a certain number of films, can be compared with him. However, while Mizoguchi squeezed all he could out of his actors and actresses at the expense of scenic depictions ("You can't make a flower perform"), Kurosawa made not only the players perform but also the wind, rain, and fog.

In *Rashomon* the pelting rain itself is as eloquent as an actor at evoking feelings seething in the breast of the director. It is a rain of rage and also of holy water that washes away the sins of human beings. In *Yojimbo* (*Yojimbo*, 1961), the dry wind that shrouds the post town in dust seems to be murderous in its intentions. In *Throne of Blood* (*Kumonosujo*, 1957), after the main character loses his way in the fog and rides aimlessly on horseback in the forest, the fog suddenly lifts to reveal his castle, an expression of his suddenly coming to his senses after wandering in the darkness of his heart. Kurosawa could have used artificial smoke for the fog, but to show it clearing up he needed real fog. So, on the slopes of Mt. Fuji he had his camera crew wait for days to shoot the fog actually lifting from the castle set.

Kurosawa even went so far as to make the sun perform. In *Stray Dog* (*Nora Inu*, 1949), the midsummer heat becomes an important element in the drama, and the intense sun is like a leading actor. The hand-held-camera shot of it through the reed blinds of the black market stalls is riveting. The sun is also a leading player in *Rashomon*. While the heroine (Machiko Kyo) is resisting the embraces of the bandit in a grove, she opens her eyes wide and stares at the powerful beams of sunlight, a realistic mirroring of her agitated state of mind.

2
The Influence
of Foreign Films

One quality that distinguishes modern Japan lies in the fact that both traditional culture and imported Western culture coexist, whether ingenuously or awkwardly. The two are mixed, however, in such a complicated fashion that it is difficult even for the Japanese to distinguish between them.

As I explained in Chapter One, the two main genres of Japanese film are period drama, which started from Kabuki and developed more sophisticated themes, and contemporary drama, which began with Shimpa and developed a more modern realism. Although competition between these two genres, and the subsequent crossover made by actors and directors from one genre to the other, was a fundamental force behind its development, the influence of foreign films is also a major factor to consider. As the West was literally far away, foreign films presented a stimulating and rare opportunity for Japanese to make contact with Western civilization, and Western ways of life were a continual source of surprise and envy, particularly for young intellectuals opposed to the feudalistic anachronisms of their own society. In these films they felt they could actually see free human beings and a free society, where women were appealing simply because of their activeness, unlike Japanese film heroines who usually behaved like obedient dolls.

Foreign films have been imported since the very early days of Japanese cinema and their influence on Japanese film-makers was considerable. In the 1920s some Japanese films were modeled after German expressionist films, and films from Denmark and Germany stimulated the development of a domestic, everyday kind of realism. In the 1930s respect for the psychological realism of French films encouraged film-makers to inject a delicate psychological nuance into their work. Even Soviet films of the 1920s and 1930s, which were either heavily cut or banned on account of strict political censorship, had a large following among enthusiastic students, who filled in the gaps through books and magazines. Thus Eisenstein's montage theory came to exert a strong influence on the leftist "tendency films" (*keiko eiga*) popular around 1930, and resulted in a fad for an extreme style of editing. The neorealism of Italian films also had a certain, though not necessarily strong, effect, since their subject matter of social problems and their documentary style had already been experimented with in Japanese films of the 1930s.

However, the films that had the most profound influence on the Japanese public and film-makers alike were the prewar American films. Although Japanese scholars and statesmen had more esteem for the civilizations of Germany, England, and France than that of the United States, many youths detested the oppressive atmosphere of their authoritarian society and longed for the liberal spirit seen in American movies. Until around the late 1940s it was common practice to model Japanese films on prewar American hits, especially Ernst Lubitsch's *The Marriage Circle*, 1924, Frank Borzage's *Seventh Heaven*, 1927, F. W. Murnau's *Sunrise*, 1927, Edmund Goulding's *Grand Hotel*, 1932, Josef von Sternberg's *The Docks of New York*, 1928, and Frank Capra's *Lady for a Day*,

32

1933. Even Kurosawa claimed he got his idea for the love story of *One Wonderful Sunday* (*Subarashiki Nichiyobi*, 1947), depicted amid the bombed-out ruins in Tokyo right after the war, from an old D. W. Griffith film.

It was not merely the glamor or the affluent life-style of prewar American movies that attracted the Japanese audience. What they envied most were the heroes and heroines, who were ordinary people, the love stories, and the American freedom of spirit.

The initial influence came from the popular American "Bluebird" movies of the 1910s, one of the many labels used by Universal Studios in its sales distribution. Although regarded as B-grade and now almost forgotten in America, these sentimental love stories that portrayed the daily life of poor but honest people appealed to the Japanese because of their homeliness and lyricism, and because of the similar social conditions shown. America, like Japan, was then undergoing rapid industrialization, and the films portrayed the unease of the farmers as well as the spiritual beauty of their lives in contrast to the iniquity of the cities. Eventually, Japanese film-makers of the 1920s and 1930s, influenced by these and other foreign films, turned to comedies and tragedies about farmers and average city-dwellers, a definite advance on the samurai period dramas and Shimpa melodramas.

One such director was Yasujiro Ozu, who, ever since he set eyes on Thomas H. Innes's *Civilization* (1916), became so absorbed in American movies that he failed to enter college and got a job with a studio. Since most of the films he had seen were American, his first film in 1927 as well as some later works were based on ideas from American movies. With *Passing Fancy* (*Dekigokoro*, 1933) and *A Story of Floating Weeds* (*Ukigusa Monogatari*, 1934), influenced by *The Champ* (1931) and *The Barker* (1928), respectively, Ozu established a new film genre which accurately portrayed the life of Japan's lower classes.

In those days Japanese audiences preferred American love stories because of their optimism and cheerfulness, so different from European films, where the themes were more gloomy. The inevitably happy ending was both a source of hope and envy, and a refreshing contrast to Japanese films with their tragic endings, since romantic love was regarded as immoral and frowned on.

What the American spirit of prewar films meant to the Japanese was probably best summarized by the great director Man-saku Itami (1900–46). In 1940, a year before the outbreak of the Pacific War, he wrote "The Life and Education of Movie Actresses and Actors" ("*Eiga haiyu no seikatsu to kyoyo*," from *Itami Mansaku zenshu,* vol. 2), an essay on outside influences on Japanese film. In those days it was said that the Japanese were being contaminated by American movies, and Americanism was pronounced as a source of frivolity and irresponsibility, a claim which Itami bravely refuted.

"The first thing we learned from American movies was a fast-paced life-style . . . the next, a lively manner and a readiness to take decisive action. Lastly, we learned to take an affirmative, purposeful, sometimes even combative attitude toward life, and to value dearly our pride as human beings, fearing no man—in short, their first-class, tough philosophy on how to get on in the world.

"[The latter was] the strongest and best influence on us . . . It was also the moral upheld by all the main characters in their narrative romances and probably represents the American spirit at its best."

(This declaration was certainly courageous in 1940, in the midst of an ultra-nationalistic campaign. Itami added the fol-lowing, mentioning the dangers of servile adulation of the power-ful groups who ran Japanese society as they pleased.)

"Unless chronic vices are destroyed one by one, a healthy nation cannot be born. Moreover, I think that it was American movies that first gave us the opportunity to reflect upon our ingrained customs and manners. In any American movie I can hear some-one crying out: Young man, be dauntless! Have more pride and backbone! Subordinates, don't be servile! Don't flatter!"

The influence of American films even affected the dichotomy of the *tateyaku* and the *nimaime,* and this can be seen in Ozu's early films, where the young, cheerful heroes belong to neither type and where the love scenes are portrayed with a sense of humor. In period dramas the *tateyaku* were always dauntless men, lacking neither pride nor backbone, but the *nimaime* of contem-porary dramas were too often sad and spiritless. Thus audiences came to idealize actors who were strong and active and could also play love scenes, men who combined the positive sides of the *tateyaku* and the *nimaime*. In response to this demand the following contemporary drama stars arose: Denmei Suzuki in the 1920s, Shuji Sano, Shin Saburi, and Den Ohinata in the 1930s, and Yujiro Ishihara and Tatsuya Nakadai in the 1960s.

Of these Nakadai is probably the best example of this synthesis, particularly in Masaki Kobayashi's major work, *The Human Condition* (*Ningen no Joken*, 1959–61, 6 parts, running time: 9 hours), where he plays a man who undergoes an odyssey of suffering because he refused during World War II to slave-drive Chinese prisoners in Manchuria and treated them humanely. As a result he was sent to the most trying fronts and detained in a Soviet P.O.W. camp after the war, from which he escapes, to die in a desolate, snowy terrain. In adverse situations this strong, samurai-like man remembers his beautiful wife and, by calling out her name, is able to endure his suffering. Nakadai's performance was a revolutionary transformation of the traditional Confucian dictum that a noble man does not love a woman.

To claim that this synthesis of the *tateyaku* and *nimaime*, which occurred in 1959, was due to postwar influence of American films would be inadequate. The Occupation authorities, in order to pave the way for democracy in Japan, prohibited period dramas depicting feudalistic thinking and ordered films with liberal, "enlightened" themes, even encouraging kissing scenes. American movies, too, were imported in great numbers. However, this conscious attempt at Americanization was only partially successful and not completely necessary since after the Occupation the feudalistic period drama was reinstituted. Even during the Occupation, leftists, who had been banned from making films with a social theme due to the cold war, continued to make them. Love stories had been encouraged by the authorities, but filmmakers wanted to produce them anyhow, even before they had been restrained by the militarists from 1930 to 1945.

A good example is Mansaku Itami, who wrote the script for the best movie of 1943, *The Life of Matsu the Untamed*, the story of a ricksha man who, at the request of the widow of an army officer he knew, helps to raise her son. Eventually, however, he realizes his love for the widow and one day (in a scene cut by the censors) reveals this to her, with the result that he is forced to leave for this breach of propriety. This theme of the platonic love of a man of low social standing for a noble lady is rare in Japanese theater and literature before 1910 and is clearly the outcome of American and European movie influence. Thus, it can be inferred that if not for the militarists, love stories would have developed smoothly in prewar Japanese films and the postwar "guidance" of the Occupation authorities was not crucial.

The influence of postwar American films, while not crucial, was certainly considerable. During the Pacific War from 1941 to 1945, when no new American movies were imported and the showing of old ones prohibited, schoolchildren were taught that Americans were inhuman devils. Thus, in 1946, when American films were seen again, the boys and girls of that generation were shocked to find that Americans were human after all and seemed to have higher ideals and to be happier than the Japanese. In order to use such films as lessons in democracy, the U.S. authorities regulated their showings in Japan during the seven years of Occupation, and only those exhibiting the positive side of America were shown. Films that took up social problems were not imported, such as *Gentleman's Agreement,* which dealt with prejudice; *All the King's Men,* whose main character was a political demagogue; *The Ox-Bow Incident,* about lynching; *The Grapes of Wrath,* in which the poverty of farmers was depicted. Moreover, from 1941 to 1952, when the Occupation ended, most Hollywood movies glorified democracy and the good qualities of the American way of life, so obviously Japanese youths then thought of America as the ideal country, a veritable heaven, economically, politically, and spiritually. While a leftist minority assumed an anti-American stance, the vast majority believed that their former enemies were now their most respected friends.

36

I was about fourteen when the war ended. A year later, when I saw the American movies *His Butler's Sister* and *Madame Curie,* I was able to accept our defeat for the first time because I learned that Americans were not devils, and I realized that Japan had suffered a moral defeat as well. Around this time Japanese directors, and actors and actresses, who had been connected with militaristic propaganda films during the war, were now making democratic ones at the behest of the Occupation forces.

After 1945 Americanization advanced at an alarming rate. The government was democratized and the economy eventually surpassed America's in some areas. One reason why this came about so quickly is that thirty years ago Japanese boys made the startling discovery, through movies, that any American could own a car and a refrigerator, and they endeavored to catch up.

However, Americanization was by no means total. Even though the young Yasujiro Ozu mainly watched American movies and based some of his own films on American models, his works eventually bore no resemblance to them whatsoever, and he became an original film-maker who can be considered purely traditional. Similarly, although modern Japan appears to be extremely Americanized on the surface, in reality, it is still a society with a completely different structure. The dichotomy of the two types of heroes also remains tenaciously. In films the *tateyaku* type of character still enjoys great popularity, the only difference being that the samurai is now replaced by a Mafia-type gangster. The handsome, irresponsible *nimaime* type remains the current favorite in television love stories and soap operas. Therefore, Japanese movie fans, who are almost entirely young men who prefer the *tateyaku* type, are completely different from television audiences, who are mainly women. As women stopped going to movie theaters, their idol, the *nimaime*, ceased to exist in films.

In spite of repeated attempts, from the 1930s to 1950s, to produce a hero who synthesized the *tateyaku* and the *nimaime* as in American films, the popularity of television only served to perpetuate this division.

3
Developments in Period Drama Films

1. NEW HEROES

38 Over one hundred period dramas were produced every year from the 1910s through the 1950s, with the exception of the 1940s due to World War II and the Occupation. These tales of revenge and loyalty centered around the old *tateyaku*-type hero and preserved feudalistic sentiments and antiquated institutions. However, in addition to Kurosawa's new postwar heroes mentioned in Chapter One, a few new prewar hero types arose who were not loyal toward their masters and who were central to reformative period dramas.

THE NIHILISTIC HERO: In 1923 Rokuhei Susukita's script for the film *Woodcut Artist* (*Ukiyoe-shi—Murasaki Zukin*) gave birth to a new type of hero. Unlike the noble *tateyaku* type portrayed by Matsunosuke Onoe, the hero of this film was a rebellious young samurai, cynical and rowdy. Moreover, the swordfighting scenes, under the direction of Bansho Kanamori, bore no relation to Onoe's balletic movements inherited from Kabuki but were modeled on American action movies, with speedy action and fast cutting. Critics called Susukita's heroes "nihilistic outlaws," and when the new star Tsumasaburo Bando began playing them in 1924, the image of the suffering rebel alienated from his times became firmly established.

The first director to raise this genre to an avant-garde art form was Daisuke Ito (1898–1981), who combined adept storytelling with a rapid succession of images brimming with beauty and pathos, and the impassioned performance of his favorite lead, Denjiro Okochi. The most representative works portraying the nihilistic hero were Ito's *A Diary of Chuji's Travels* (in three parts, *Chuji Tabi Nikki*, 1927) and Masahiro Makino's *The Street of Masterless Samurai* (*Ronin-gai*, 1928, original script by Itaro Yamagami). The outlaw heroes of these films shared the common trait of being unable to make a respectable living and were thus driven to extreme destitution. However, when cornered, they turned on their pursuers, be they policemen or evil retainers of the shogunate.

Apart from the influence of American action movies, these new hero types were also the result of new developments in earlier works of theater and popular literature. Lively, realistic swordfights and a quasi-revolutionary outlaw had already appeared in 1919 in Shojiro Sawada's *shinkokugeki* ("new national drama") production of *Chuji Kunisada* (*Kunisada Chuji*). Then in 1920 Kaizan Nakazato's voluminous popular novel *The Great Bodhisattva Pass* (*Daibosatsu Toge*) was adapted into a play and performed by Sawada's troupe. The main character, Ryunosuke Tsukue, became the archetype of the nihilistic hero and, like the outlaw Chuji Kunisada, appeared subsequently in several movies.

Both Nakazato and Sawada had participated in movements, dating from the Meiji period (1868–1912), that encouraged the import of modern European thought. The former had experienced setbacks as a socialist, and the latter belonged to *geijutsuza* ("The Artistic Troupe"), which was heavily involved in the arts reform movement. Driven underground by Japanese society, their members sought new ways of reaching the masses. One of these was the popular historical novel, in which Nakazato excelled, and another was Sawada's reform of popular theater. When the two converged in the theatrical adaptation of *The Great Bodhisattva Pass,* a new swordfighting drama, or *chambara,* was created and the play was an instant commercial and critical success in 1920. One main reason for its success then—it ran for three years—was its accurate portrayal of the anguish of the times, reflected in the dark, gloomy atmosphere and violent scenes of slaughter.

In those days when throngs of unemployed filled the streets and leftist ideas agitated the minds of the young, only a handful of young scriptwriters and directors were dedicated leftists, and none of the period drama stars originally had any connection with the leftist movement. However, the theme of rebellion of the oppressed appealed to them because they were concerned about the self-assertion of the alienated, especially since their occupation caused them to be looked down on as social outcasts, in much the same way that entertainers were traditionally disdained in Japan. Therefore, their new period dramas can be considered as a passionate appeal to and protest against the public at large, and the nihilistic outlaws and misunderstood heroes as their own reflections.

Although at times these young film-makers braved the censors with an openly ideological film, they were more strongly attracted to the rebel who was something of an anarchist, such as Ryunosuke Tsukue, the antihero of *The Great Bodhisattva Pass.* He appealed to them because during the turmoil and upheaval preceding the Meiji Restoration of 1868, he sided with neither those who wanted to restore the authority of the emperor nor the forces that upheld the shogunate. He was simply a wanderer dedicated to his skill as a swordsman. Similarly, when struggles between leftists and rightists were common in the 1920s, these nihilistic film-makers sided with neither and lived solely for their craft.

THE FREE SPIRIT HERO: In 1932, in the face of social and governmental oppression, nihilistic and leftist tendency films ceased to be made. The underground Communist Party had just about dissolved and leftist writers recanted their views in works explaining their conversion. However, some liberal period dramas were produced then. Despite the government's conservative policy of "increasing economic wealth and strengthening the military" (*fukoku kyohei*), which prevailed from the latter part of the nineteenth century until 1945, many of the generation who came of age in the relaxed years of the Taisho Democracy (1912–26) were liberal, and some openly flaunted their liberalism by making films critical of militarism and feudalism in the 1930s.

Examples of this, dating from 1932, are *Peerless Patriot* (*Kokushi Muso*) by Mansaku Itami and *Sleeping with a Long Sword* (*Dakine no Nagadosu*) by Sadao Yamanaka, both period dramas being unique in that they contained no swordplay. The spirit of rebellion was not lost but only played down. Nihilism was replaced by an advocacy of freedom portrayed in the resistance of common people to feudal authority, and by mockery of Bushido, the moral system of the elite.

The leading liberal scriptwriter was Shintaro Mimura, who had worked on many of the period drama masterpieces of the 1930s and who was to create a new hero, nonconforming and free in spirit. During the Taisho period Mimura had participated in the *shingeki* movement for modern, realistic drama by joining Sojin Kamiyama's troupe of nonconformist actors and playwrights, and was heavily influenced by their free spirit. His main characters were *yakuza* (gangsters), who were usually small-time gamblers, masterless samurai (*ronin*), petty villains, and itinerant entertainers. These types had appeared before in nihilistic period dramas, standing up to the establishment and even attacking it, thereby assuming an important position in the vanguard of the proletariat. Mimura, however, returned them to their appropriate station of malcontents in an age of domestic tranquillity (set in the Edo period from 1630 to 1850 but actually reflecting the so-called Showa Restoration from 1933 to 1940), and gave free rein to their impertinence by letting them brag and gripe to their hearts' content.

Mimura did not admire *yakuza* and malcontents but saw in them the possibility of gaining freedom by casting aside the respectability attendant upon being a full-fledged member of society, and he used them as vehicles of his own free-thinking nonconformity. Before (and after) Mimura, *yakuza* heroes were not "free" souls, but bound by a sense of obligation toward their boss or "elder brother," and the complex emotional ties that are involved in the concept of *giri ninjo* (see p. 50). In fact their behavior was more restricted than the samurai's, and many masochists among them felt that the stronger the restrictions the better they liked it. Mimura's *yakuza* heroes, on the other hand, were free spirits who extricated themselves from such restrictions regardless of their impression on others. A good example of one such hero is Matahachi in *Journey of a Thousand and One Nights* (*Matatabi Sen-ichiya*, 1936).

This itinerant *yakuza* gambler, temporarily employed in the construction of a new residence for a feudal lord, makes the acquaintance of the lord's young son. In exchange for his ordinary lunch of rice and pickled plums he gets a chance to ride the boy's horse and thereupon gallops off. The search party sent after him, formed of Matahachi's coworkers and some masterless samurai, are led a merry chase by the reckless Matahachi, oblivious of his obligations to his construction gang boss and fellow workers.

Matahachi belongs to a long line of wandering gamblers whose adventures (*matatabi mono,* often based on the novels of Shin Hasegawa and Kan Shimozawa) formed a major subgenre in *yakuza* movies since the late 1920s. They were often on the run because of some good deed performed for the sake of the common people. Unlike Matahachi, who simply made sport of the authorities, they took up arms against them, thus revealing similarities to the nihilistic hero. However, they lacked audacity because they knew the ways of the world too well. They seem to be saying that as common men it is above their station to talk about how society should be. In contrast, Matahachi was neither humble nor sentimental and his audacity is revealed when he addresses the young lord as "leaky drawers" (*shobendare*).

Mimura's forte lies in the mood of good cheer that his dialogues convey. Although the bad guys in his films are made fools of, they do not get their just desserts, and in the end it is his heroes who are usually defeated. Still, even in defeat they continue to be in high spirits, and thus they achieve the victory implied in the old Japanese saying: To lose is to win (*makeru ga kachi*). They do not cry over spilt milk, and by accepting defeat gracefully and cheerfully, they have the advantage over their oppressors.

Mimura does not cloak his attitude in an antiestablishment

ideology but reveals it in the flavor of his dialogues, a flavor that combines the humanity of the common people with their sense of style and taste.

Although Mimura wrote for many directors, he had a greater affinity with Hiroshi Inagaki, the director of *Journey of a Thousand and One Nights*. They both preferred sabotage to open rebellion and protest, and this attitude is even evident in *Festival Across the Sea (Umi o Wataru Sairei*, 1941), a film they made when militaristic propaganda was predominant. At first the sole purpose of this film seemed to be to present the lighthearted joy and exhilaration of a village festival, the transient feeling of well-being of the common people. In the midst of the festival, however, the rough-necks who train the circus horses appear to harass the weaker en-tertainers. A masterless samurai currently doing a sword act in the troupe comes to their defense, but he does not go on a tragic rampage as a nihilistic hero would. The roughnecks challenge him, and he merely slips quietly off to engage them, never to return. The ending resembles the last scene in *Easy Rider,* where the heroes are shot down by bigots. From Mimura's combination of exhila-ration at the film's start and pathos at its ending, we might assume that had Mimura been a young man in the late 1960s, he would probably have been a leader of the hippy culture.

MUSASHI MIYAMOTO: *Festival Across the Sea* went against the trend of the times, for a new current began in 1940 with the release of Tomu Uchida's *History (Rekishi)*, which was called a historical movie rather than a period drama. Similar films ap-peared in 1941, such as Kinugasa's *The Battle at Kawanakajima (Kawanakajima Kassen)* and Mizoguchi's *The Loyal 47 Ronin of the Genroku Era (Genroku Chushingura)*. These historical movies did not directly endorse militarism and can be considered progressive because the directors adhered strictly to historical accuracy. How-ever, thematically they negated the antiestablishment and escap-ist tendencies of the nihilistic and liberal period dramas, stressing instead the idea of compliance with the times and the theme of the Japanese people as a fated, common body. They portrayed individual destinies as mere ripples on the great wave of history.

In spite of the historical movie's tendency to dilute heroism in period dramas, a new hero still arose in the person of Musashi

Miyamoto, popular since the early 1940s. Most of the movies about him are based on Eiji Yoshikawa's novel that was serialized in the *Asahi Shimbun* newspaper from 1935 to 1939. Yoshikawa's theme was simply that refinement in the art of swordfighting equaled spiritual development. As a simple man of the sword, Musashi appeared to be the antithesis of intellectualism, but Yoshikawa's portrayal of him had a great influence on the thinking of the Japanese people because it was able to guide them through uncertainty during the years when Japan embraced fascism.

Although Musashi never opposes the mores of society, he has no sense of social responsibility and is never moved to action for utilitarian purposes, or out of loyalty, like the old *tateyaku* type of samurai. He only acts through his keen, but egoistic, desire for self-development. Furthermore, his pursuit of perfection in swordfighting continually leads him to perform the most antisocial act of all, that of killing people. However, because of the supreme danger he faces each time he tests himself, this killing was seen as the most noble form of action, not an evil one, even though some of his victims were not villains.

In Musashi's world the root of all evil is weakness, and only the strong are noble in spirit and character. Ironically, his sweetheart, the physically frail Otsu, provided the model of behavior for the weak by performing everything to the utmost of her capability. She thus gave courage to all those Japanese who, in spite of their lack of strength, put on a bold face and went off to the Sino-Japanese and Pacific wars. In those dark days both the strong, who in reality were few in number, and the weak calmly acknowledged their combined weakness. It was believed that as long as there were those who, despite their weakness, were willing to submit their all to the highest good, it was possible for Japan to restore order to the world. This was a terrifying, savage way of thinking and the exact opposite of humanism. However, rooted in the darkest desires of people, it had the power to captivate them at a time when the outer veneer of civilization was being stripped away.

2. BUSHIDO

All Japanese movies were censored during the Occupation until

1949, and regulations concerning period drama were especially severe. Swordfighting scenes were prohibited because they ran counter to the aims of pacifism, and *Chushingura*, the perennial favorite, which would eventually be made into a movie about one hundred times, was banned because it not only affirmed feudalistic loyalty but also kindled a spirit of revenge through the victory of the loyal forty-seven retainers against the enemy of their dead lord. Even Kurosawa's *The Men Who Tread on the Tiger's Tail* (*Tora no O o Fumu Otokotachi*, 1945) was not released until 1952, perhaps because it was the story of a defeated general who escapes. The Occupation forces actively encouraged the production of films critical of feudal society, but as with the case of love stories, this was not entirely necessary since some directors had ventured in this direction during the prewar years in spite of censorship by the Japanese government.

The first noteworthy period drama of the immediate postwar era was Daisuke Ito's *The Paltry Ronin Forces His Way Through* (*Suronin Makaritoru*, 1947). The film is based on the famous story of the imposter Ten'ichibo, who tries to succeed to the shogunate by claiming to be the son of a woman in the shogun's past. In Ito's version, however, Ten'ichibo is depicted as a sympathetic young man who avidly desires to meet his real father at least once. Incensed by the feudalistic system which would not grant this natural wish, the hero, Iganosuke (Tsumasaburo Bando), comes to his aid, knowing that in so doing he seals his own doom.

Since a swordfight climax was ruled out, Ito employed his forte —the equivalent of the chase in American movies. Pursued by a throng of lantern-carrying policemen, Iganosuke leaps from rooftop to rooftop. Just before his inevitable arrest he suddenly stops running and, raising himself to his full height, a tragic figure against the night sky, he glares down at the insignificant policemen below, silencing them with his glance. The next instant, in a marvelous display of showmanship, he turns and jumps adroitly, landing in their midst.

The image of Bando in that single scene is far more important than the criticism of feudalism in the whole film. At that moment Bando becomes the epitome of a samurai, and his image is central to my own idea of Bushido. This character is a true follower of the way of the warrior because he gives no thought to personal gain and goes to his death for a just cause. This is strength, but not one based only on physical prowess; this character also possesses compassion and will never do anything disgraceful. These attributes alone constitute an exemplary samurai even though the classical element of loyalty (*chusei*) is not shown.

Another film, *The Yotsuya Ghost Story* (*Yotsuya Kaidan*, 1949), made by Keisuke Kinoshita and based on the famous Kabuki play, presents the other side of the coin and debunks the popular myth of the samurai. The main character, Iemon, a destitute samurai, reluctantly murders his wife, Oiwa, so he can marry a rich merchant's daughter, only to be haunted by his wife and driven to suicide. Kinoshita's Iemon is a much weaker character than the role in the original play, and this is poignantly conveyed in those memorable scenes where his repeated attempts to kill Oiwa are thwarted by her trusting looks. Through the faint-hearted Iemon we are shown that samurai can also be reduced to trembling wrecks in certain situations despite the airs they assume in positions of authority.

Masahiro Makino's *A Horde of Drunken Knights* (*Yoidore Hachiman Ki*, 1951), a remake of his prewar masterpiece *The Street of Masterless Samurai*, is also important because it demonstrates that even shiftless *ronin* can maintain a warrior's code of honor. For the sake of a woman and their own sense of pride the *ronin* engage the retainers of the shogun in a bloody battle that recalls the dark gloom of a prewar nihilistic film.

All these films are critical of feudalism, but their real emphasis lies not in presenting an age that has passed but in depicting characters who find themselves in adverse situations and have to cope, whether gallantly, ineptly, or desperately. Since this problem can exist in any society, feudal or modern, such films formed the core of postwar period drama and the main theme of many of the genre's masterpieces in the 1950s and early 1960s. This theme also appeared in prewar films, such as Hisatora Kumagai's *The Abe Clan* (*Abe Ichizoku*, 1938), based on Ogai Mori's short story, where its connection with Bushido is revealed much more clearly.

The head of the Abe clan wants to commit self-sacrifice (*junshi*) after the death of his lord because he had received favors from his master during his lifetime. As his new lord won't permit this, he abides by his wishes. However, his fellow samurai look down on him for being "unfaithful," and, feeling disgraced, he commits suicide. The new lord regards this as an act of willful disobedience and punishes the whole family for it. The Abe sons, in turn, affronted by this, rise up to rebel against the lord, and the whole clan, retainers included, are annihilated in the end.

In this film the absurdity of the feudal institution of self-immolation upon the death of one's lord is exposed, and the barbarity of samurai society is revealed in the ridiculing of a man who is denied martyrdom. However, Japanese audiences were more impressed by the awe-inspiring manner in which the entire clan maintained its pride despite its absurd predicament and by the way the Abe sons relied on their sense of honor as samurai to face their inevitable doom.

During World War II, when I was a boy, we were taught that central to Bushido is loyalty and devotion toward one's superiors. In *The Abe Clan,* which I saw after the war, it seemed that one's sense of honor takes priority and must be maintained even at the cost of abandoning this loyalty.

This sense of honor is not an attribute of the samurai class alone, as we shall see in Mizoguchi's *A Story from Chikamatsu* (*Chikamatsu Monogatari,* 1954). The young wife of a merchant and a clerk, shocked by their master's false accusation of adultery (an affront to their honor), run off together and bravely accept the fate of crucifixion (the feudal punishment for adultery), rather than renounce their love. Their love affair is not a "handsome man meets beautiful woman" encounter, however, for when they realize that the merchant is their common enemy, the desire to fight him kindles a comradely affection that later blossoms into love. Although they do not go through the exaggerated posturing of a warrior in the same situation, their pride and honor are maintained through their execution. The acceptance of public crucifixion is their act of revenge because the disgrace of it brings about the downfall of the merchant's house.

Nevertheless, it is usually easier to present the conflicts and pressures involved in maintaining pride and honor if the central character belongs to the samurai world. Furthermore, since pent-up indignation usually erupts dramatically in a bloody, action-packed swordfight, the audience can give vent to its own frustrations. In fact, this is the real reason Japanese audiences love the samurai in period drama—their appeal has nothing to do with admiration for the old ruling class.

Proof of this rests in the fact that lords, or daimyo, and chief retainers have seldom been portrayed as sympathetic characters. More film heroes come from the ranks of lower samurai, with the classless *ronin,* who have no official status since they serve no master, the most popular of all. With the exception of Lord Asano in *Chushingura,* daimyo are hardly ever placed in a situation where their honor is at stake. As for *ronin,* however, while they possess the pride of samurai, they are usually as destitute as poor commoners, and this disparity between their ideal and their reality places them in situations where their pride and honor are most subject to attack.

The most thoroughgoing treatment of this dilemma can be found in Masaki Kobayashi's *Harakiri* (*Seppuku,* 1962). The story is set in the Tokugawa period (1603–1868). A *ronin,* who calls himself Hanshiro Tsugumo, appears at the Edo residence of the lord of Hikone and requests the use of his courtyard to commit ritual disembowelment since he is tired of the disgrace of having to live in poverty. In those days this was a common ruse to obtain money since the *ronin* would be paid to go away, thus preventing gossip. The Hikone retainers, however, see the perfect opportunity to punish those not worthy of the samurai name and so they agree.

While preparations are being made for the ceremony in front of an audience of Hikone retainers, Tsugumo requests that one of their swordsmen be present to cut off his head after he has pierced his own belly and begun the painful cut to the side. The man is immediately sent for, but for some reason is unable to be present. Tsugumo names two other retainers who are also sent for but fail to appear. While everyone waits, Tsugumo relates the story of his family.

He had once been a senior councillor of a lord, but the fief went bankrupt through oppression from the shogunate. One of his fellow samurai took responsibility for the bankruptcy and committed *harakiri.* Tsugumo then assumed the care of his friend's son, later giving the boy his own daughter in marriage. As this young man is constantly in financial straits, he comes to the

Hikone residence one day and asks to be allowed to commit *harakiri* there, probably hoping for money. However, the Hikone retainers decide they really want him to carry this out because they like true demonstrations of Bushido.

When the young man hears this, he turns pale because he had already pawned his swords and wore only bamboo imitations. His request to leave to collect his swords falls on deaf ears and in the end he is forced to perform ritual disembowelment with the short bamboo sword, killing himself eventually by biting off his own tongue.

Tsugumo finishes his story by revealing why the swordsmen he had requested could not attend. Outraged by this inhuman treatment of his son-in-law, he had secretly challenged each of the three men directly responsible and succeeded in cutting off their topknots, a symbol of samurai status. Tsugumo then tosses the three topknots onto the white sand of the courtyard. As he has thus ridiculed all the Hikone retainers, there is no way for him to leave the place alive. They come at him in droves, and he cuts down several of them before his own death.

In this film we see the essence of samurai pride and honor, the most important theme in period drama. Tsugumo had felt deeply for his son-in-law, who had been placed in the predicament of trying to commit *harakiri* with a bamboo sword. Worse than this, however, was the fact that the Hikone retainers had not granted him his request to leave to get real swords. Even after he had given them his word as a samurai that he would return to carry out this ritual act, they had looked down on him as a blatant liar, a *ronin* completely devoid of the warrior spirit.

For Tsugumo, a samurai reduced to the status of *ronin* was still a samurai. Although his son-in-law had disgraced himself by making such a request, he could not bear the thought that he had been regarded as an outright fraud and beggar. He could not allow this humiliation to go unpunished. For Tsugumo, this was the essence of Bushido.

As a rule, Japanese audiences do not find the ideal samurai as appealing as the outcast, who is outside the confines of the ruling class. A real samurai is one who struggles to maintain his pride and honor, and thus real models from the samurai class are not necessarily needed. People who have this spiritual quality and find themselves in wretched straits are far more appealing, and this is one reason for the popularity of movies about feudal *yakuza,* or outlaws.

Yakuza originate from the classes of farmers and craftsmen. They become outlaws because they seek freedom from legal restraints, although they do conform to their own code of social order based on *ninkyodo,* a Robin Hood–type of chivalric code. In reality of course, feudal *yakuza* were merely gamblers, neither free men nor champions of *ninkyodo.* In films, however, chivalrous *yakuza* are imagined to rush to the defense of the common folk against samurai excesses.

Since self-denial and stoicism is emphasized in their code, it often appears to be a mere imitation of the Bushido code. However, it is at direct odds with Bushido because it replaces loyalty with obligation or duty (*giri*), which is, in turn, counterbalanced by humaneness (*ninjo*). In other words, human relations should not be regulated by duty alone, for duty without compassion is as rigid as the concept of loyalty. One must sympathize with the lamentable position of the weak, and in this respect *ninkyodo* is incompatible with Bushido, which advocates the sacrifice of one's own feelings for the cause of duty or justice. Furthermore, whereas the emphasis on honor in Bushido centers around the pride of the ruling class, its concern in *ninkyodo* is with the rebellious feelings of the oppressed commoners. Thus, *yakuza* movies convey the message of pride and honor better than films about samurai.

There were no special codes governing the conduct of townspeople and farmers, and it is difficult to imagine a charismatic figure emerging from these ranks. A commoner could only adopt the moral code of *ninkyodo* by becoming an outlaw. In fact, in period drama the samurai and the *yakuza* are the only heroes, while the common people are depicted as dullards with neither pride nor courage. This is a deep-seated prejudice that is even found in some of Kurosawa's finest films. A look at history is enough to reveal the inaccuracy of this inclination. Noble *yakuza* were rare, and the written accounts of Europeans and Americans often describe the samurai as a shifty lot who usually shirked their responsibilities. Just as there were probably many cowards among their numbers, the common folk, the ancestors of most Japanese, were not always stupid and timid.

This misinterpretation is due unfortunately to the Japanese education system, which, since the Meiji Restoration of 1868, was largely determined by descendants of the samurai. They fostered the illusion that all the spiritual qualities and virtues of the feudal period were monopolized by the samurai social class. Consequently, Japanese film-makers could not imagine a commoner as a splendid figure asserting his will to accomplish acts of justice. While this is a sad limitation, Japanese directors have managed to portray, with a haunting beauty, the behavior of model samurai and *yakuza,* who lived according to a strong sense of pride and honor.

In this respect period dramas differ greatly from American Westerns, with which they are often compared. Although both genres have fighting scenes as their forte, their differences are deeper than the type of weapon used. With the exception of the U.S. Cavalry, there is no distinction in the rank of characters that appear in Westerns. The sheriff, outlaw, cowboy, farmer, etc., are more or less on an equal social footing. In addition, there are no equivalents to Bushido and *ninkyodo* in the form of special codes for the sheriffs and poker players, and each group may have its heroes and villains, its strong and weak, its brave and cowardly. Their common feature is the pioneer spirit and pride, which is not exclusive to a single social class, such as the warriors.

3. MODERN *YAKUZA* FILMS

A new vogue for *yakuza* movies, this time set in the 1900s, began in 1963 and lasted for a decade, and its success is unparalleled in the history of Japanese film. This new *yakuza* movie completely usurped the position formerly held by the old period drama, despite the sameness of the storyline and the sentiments, which always lead to the tragic climax.

The story usually takes the following line. In Tokyo, or a large provincial capital, there is a certain *yakuza* gang that still adheres to the code of *ninkyodo,* a Robin Hood–type of chivalric behavior. Apart from the vice of gambling, it is careful not to cause trouble to ordinary citizens. The boss is usually a moral man, who is revered by the gang. However, in the same district, there is a rival gang, headed by a man who has no qualms about robbery, fraud, or even murder, and is deeply involved in shady business deals. (In films set in the 1930s this gang boss usually had some undercover connection with the military.) He maintains an office in a modern building and has close ties with one of the giant Japanese corporations.

This mean boss, bent on achieving his ends, persecutes the good boss's gang, whose members are eager to have a showdown but are restrained by the boss. Finally, the latter is murdered, and this provides the crowning provocation for the fight. The headquarters of the evil boss is attacked and geysers of blood spurt in a gory climax. After cutting down several dozen baddies, the hero slays the archvillain himself and then surrenders calmly to the police. The sequel will usually begin with the hero emerging from prison, only to discover that his old gang members have degenerated into modern gangsters seeking to profit from illicit business deals. They are now persecuting another *yakuza* gang, whose members still follow the *ninkyodo* code, and so the story goes on.

These modern *yakuza* movies successfully projected the feelings of a small group shunted aside by social change, and were thus extremely popular in the 1960s. During the previous decade the *yakuza* series with the biggest following had been *Jirocho of Shimizu* (*Shimizu Jirocho*), a dashing, cheerful tale of a large clan that makes it big in the underground world by gaining control of all the gambling dens along the main road from Edo to Kyoto in the latter part of the nineteenth century. As television began to invade the home in the 1960s and the majority of families abandoned the movie theater, motion pictures began to cater to the solitary bachelors in the big cities. Most of them, myself included, came to the city alone from the provinces and were without family connections. They empathized with the *yakuza* hero, an orphan in the universe, and longed for the desperate friendship of a *yakuza* gang. Thus the modern *yakuza* movie offered a kind of utopia for the lonely young men. The more unreal it was, the more beautiful the ideal became, which was none other than the dream of the lost home floating before the eyes of an audience of loners.

Alienated people, unlike those content with work and family, are constantly in search of a purpose in life. Some may participate in political or religious movements, but the vast majority roam the streets looking for something of their own. These people cherish the wish of belonging to a small tight group bound by friendship and loyalty—a group of individuals like themselves, seeking an unrestricted life-style. When they see the presentation of such a group in a modern *yakuza* movie, where violence is used as a counterattack on large, profit-oriented enterprises, they applaud heartily.

These sentiments are common to all of us and are not exclusive to modern *yakuza* movie fans. No matter how far society may progress, large enterprises or hierarchical organizations can never satisfy human needs completely. Most people would wish to belong to a group of individuals who are so close that there is no need for words to be spoken, a group bound by a trust that leaves no room for betrayal. This desire transcends all social distinctions, and if an age of control by computers does arrive, it will become all the more precious.

The hero of the old *yakuza* movie, in his clash with some big gang, is sentenced to certain death, or to an existence even lonelier than his previous one. The modern *yakuza* hero, however, does not perish in the showdown, thus alleviating the loneliness. With constant repetition of the theme, an element of insincerity was gradually introduced, but the message still rings clear: We have entered an era in which an assault on a big organization by a small group in the name of justice is no longer doomed to certain failure. The student demonstrations in the 1960s definitely had an effect on this change in attitude.

The new, invincible hero was not only a less tragic but also a less human figure, as manifested in the acting style of Noboru Ando, a real-life *yakuza* who turned film star in the late 1960s. Ando always wore a serious, deadpan expression, which became his trademark, as if to suggest that the life of a *yakuza* was devoid of fear, laughter, or sexual desire. This immobility of expression is by no means due to his lack of acting experience, for the accomplished actor Koji Tsuruta played *yakuza* roles with the same expression.

This expression of resignation seems to be a trait of men who have given up more sophisticated forms of communication, choosing to assume, instead, the stern, ostentatious pose of one who is prepared to die at any time. This death resolve adds a streak of beauty to the gory swordfight climax, with the fight becoming its ultimateexpression.

Swordfighting scenes have always characterized the climax of old *yakuza* films and period dramas. As mentioned earlier, the balletic Kabuki style was replaced by a faster, more violent one in the 1920s, although the pace of the swordplay was quickened intentionally to heighten the tragedy of the nihilistic hero, thereby sacrificing realism for beauty of form. With *Rashomon* and *Seven Samurai* (*Shichinin no Samurai*, 1954), Kurosawa waived beauty of form and had his actors assume gauche but realistic poses, or had them rushing about wildly, cleaving the air with their swords. This certainly added a vivid touch, but the slightly comical effect never quite convinces us of the cruelty involved in man killing man. I believe that the true period drama precursors of the climactic fights in modern *yakuza* movies are the postwar films made by Tomu Uchida (1898–1970): *A Bloody Spear at Mount Fuji* (*Chiyari Fuji*, 1955); *The Great Bodhisattva Pass* (*Daibosatsu Toge*, 1957); and *Beautiful Yoshiwara and the Murder of Hundreds* (*Hana no Yoshiwara Hyakunin Giri*, 1960).

The first film, consisting of a few tragicomic sketches of fellow travelers on their way to Edo, suddenly assumes tragic proportions with the killing of a young, weak-hearted samurai and the subsequent revenge of his old lance-bearer (Chiezo Kataoka), a man completely untrained in the martial arts. Yet, with his rage aroused to fever pitch, he is able to track down these professional swordsmen, charging at them with his spear slashing in all directions, and kill every single one of them.

The depiction of the murderous frenzy of a complete novice in martial arts is an obvious extension of the kind of realism Kurosawa innovated in *Rashomon*. However, the malice exhibited by the bearer, who is thoroughly intent upon killing his foes, marked a further cinematic step. Their deaths do not occur haphazardly, or comically; they are presented with the cold force of real death.

The shock of this climax in 1955 was stupendous. After the last killer is impaled on the spear, the camera gives us a bird's-eye view of the carnage. In the midst of the scattered corpses stands the hunched, paltry figure of the lance-bearer, looking dazed and utterly confused. The effect of this scene is like a nightmare suddenly exploding in the middle of a humdrum dream.

Perhaps it is worth mentioning by way of explanation for this show of utter violence that Uchida made this film after his return

54

to Japan from China, where he had been imprisoned nine years after the end of World War II. The nightmare he conjures up may have reflected his own war-time experiences, for nothing like it had been seen in his prewar masterpieces. *A Living Doll* (*Ikeru Ningyo,* 1929) and *The Revenge Champion* (*Adauchi Senshu,* 1931) were both leftist tendency films, while *Unending Advance* (*Kagirinaki Zenshin,* 1937) and *Earth* (*Tsuchi,* 1939) were films in the critical realism genre. His reputation and experiences in China led many to expect a leftist film after his return. However, *A Bloody Spear at Mount Fuji* was devoid of ideology, and the portrayal of humor and warmth makes it seem initially to be a yearning for prewar days. This is soon changed, however, with the momentary aberration of the lance-bearer. Perhaps it is safe to say that it was an evocation of the war in China, which had led to Uchida's making the film in the first place.

In Uchida's version of *The Great Bodhisattva Pass,* the shock effect of the lance-bearer's reckless attack is carried still further in the portrayal of Ryunosuke Tsukue, the archetype of the nihilistic hero. This mad swordsman (Chiezo Kataoka) has a compulsion to kill and each time he feels the demoniac rage rising within him, we see him standing on a revolving stage against a red or dark gray backdrop. With this abstract effect, Uchida reveals the lurid psyche of this homicidal intoxication.

In *Beautiful Yoshiwara and the Murder of Hundreds,* we can glimpse the intense romanticism with which Uchida imbues his depiction of the climactic fight, where cruelty is tinged with beauty. The heroine, arrested for prostitution in an Edo neighborhood where it is prohibited, is sent, by way of punishment, to a licensed brothel in Yoshiwara, where she is made to offer her services free of charge. She meets a rich, middle-aged bumpkin (Chiezo Kataoka), who falls desperately in love with her, which only makes her treat him more like a fool and wheedle more money out of him. When he realizes that he has been tricked he draws his sword. She runs outside, where the cherry blossoms of Yoshiwara are at their most beautiful, their petals fluttering through the air as she pushes through a procession of beautifully clad, high-class geisha. She continues to flee but is finally cut down.

Here Uchida transforms the main theme of leftist movies of the 1950s—the resentment of the underdog erupting against society—into a chain reaction, initiated by the resentment of the heroine at her harsh sentence and culminating with the indignant rage of her old lover. This rage is likened to a flower, a flower of madness and destruction, one that scatters to the winds as soon as it has bloomed.

1. *A Crazy Page* (*Kurutta Ippeiji*, 1926), directed by Teinosuke Kinugasa. Japan's first avant-garde movie depicts the life of inmates at an asylum (see Preface).

2. *Seisaku's Wife* (*Seisaku no Tsuma*, 1924), directed by Minoru Murata. The *onnagata* is replaced by one of the first screen actresses, Kumeko Urabe, in Japan's first movie with an antiwar theme (see Chapter 1).

3. Denjiro Okochi (1898–1962), one of the most representative actors of the noble *tateyaku* type, is cast as the judo master in Akira Kurosawa's *Sanshiro Sugata* (*Sugata Sanshiro*, 1943) (see Chapter 1).

4. Shin Saburi is another *tateyaku* actor, who, even in a modern role, still wears the stern countenance of his traditional model (see Chapter 1).

5. Keiji Sada (1926–64) was one of the most popular actors specializing in *nimaime* roles of pathetic, ill-fated men who could never give happiness to the women they loved (see Chapter 1).

6. *The Compassionate Buddha Tree* (*Aizen Katsura,* 1938), directed by Hiromasa Nomura. This sentimental love story, which set the prewar box-office record, depicted the thwarted romance between the weak *nimaime* hero (Ken Uehara) and the unfortunate heroine (Kinuyo Tanaka) (see Chapter 1).

7. *What Is Your Name?* (*Kimi no Na wa*, 1953), directed by Hideo Oba. This postwar box-office success once again demonstrates the popularity of sentimental love stories centering on the *nimaime* lead (Keiji Sada) and the sorrowful heroine (Keiko Kishi) (see Chapter 1).

8. *The Life of Matsu the Untamed* (*Muho Matsu no Issho,* 1943), directed by Hiroshi Inagaki. Period drama star Tsumasaburo Bando (1901–53), as the uneducated ricksha man, brought to contemporary drama the spirit and pride that was once reserved for samurai (see Chapter 1).

9. *The Human Condition* (*Ningen no Joken,* 1959–61), directed by Masaki Kobayashi. The postwar synthesis of the *tateyaku* and *nimaime* roles is best represented in this odyssey of a brave man (Tatsuya Nakadai) who loves a woman (Michiyo Aratama) (see Chapter 2).

10. *The Great Bodhisattva Pass* (*Daibosatsu Toge*, 1935), directed by Hiroshi Inagaki. Denjiro Okochi plays the archetype of the nihilistic hero, a samurai tormented by the ghosts of those he has killed (see Chapter 3).

11. *Journey of a Thousand and One Nights* (*Matatabi Sen-ichiya*, 1936), directed by Hiroshi Inagaki. The adventures of this carefree *yakuza* gambler (Kan'emon Nakamura, *left*) best manifest the new "free spirit" hero of the 1930s (see Chapter 3).

12. *Musashi Miyamoto* series (*Miyamoto Musashi*, 1961–65), directed by Tomu Uchida. This tale is of a swordsman (Kinnosuke Nakamura) who excelled at his profession and became the model hero in war-time Japan (see Chapter 3).

13. *Harakiri* (*Seppuku*, 1962), directed by Masaki Kobayashi. A poverty-stricken samurai (Tatsuya Nakadai) forfeits his life out of his warrior's sense of pride and honor (see Chapter 3).

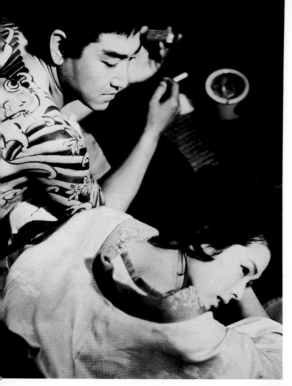

14. *Hishakaku* (*Hishakaku*, 1963), directed by Tadashi Sawashima. The movie that started the modern *yakuza* vogue, with Koji Tsuruta (*left*), its first star, and Yoshiko Sakuma (*right*) (see Chapter 3).

15. Junko Fuji was the most popular actress of women *yakuza* during the latter part of the modern *yakuza* movie vogue in the 1960s (see Chapter 3).

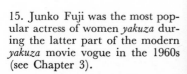

16. *A Bloody Spear at Mount Fuji* (*Chiyari Fuji,* 1955), directed by Tomu Uchida. The bloody climax of this film, in which the servant (Chiezo Kataoka) avenges his master's death, anticipated the violence in modern *yakuza* movies (see Chapter 3).

17. *Soshun Kochiyama* (*Kochiyama Soshun,* 1936), directed by Sadao Yamanaka. The prewar model of the unfortunate woman (Shizue Yamagishi), who dies for the man (Chojuro Kawarasaki) she loves (see Chapter 4).

18. *Taki no Shiraito* (*Taki no Shiraito*, 1933), directed by Kenji Mizoguchi. This famous shot of the heroine (Takako Irie) gazing down at the youth (Tokihiko Okada) she loves epitomizes Mizoguchi's worship of women (see Chapter 4).

19. *Osaka Elegy* (*Naniwa Ereji,* 1936), directed by Kenji Mizoguchi. By leaving home, this young woman (Isuzu Yamada) makes her protest against all the men in her family and her life (see Chapter 4).

20. *Intentions of Murder* (*Akai Satsui,* 1964), directed by Shohei Imamura. Through her rape, this woman (Masumi Harukawa) becomes stronger, thereby representing the tough, survival-type morality of the common people (see Chapter 4).

21. Fujiko Yamamoto, a top star of the 1950s, is considered by the Japanese to possess the most traditional type of beauty (see Chapter 4).

22. A top star from the late 1930s to the 1950s, Setsuko Hara had the image of a modern and intelligent woman, qualities that endeared her to Japanese audiences (see Chapter 4).

23. *Floating Clouds* (*Ukigumo*, 1955), directed by Mikio Naruse. The tenacity of this ill-fated woman (Hideko Takamine) is much admired despite her love for a worthless man (Masayuki Mori) (see Chapter 4).

24. *Eros Plus Massacre* (*Erosu Purasu Gyakusatsu,* 1970), directed by Yoshishige Yoshida. The life of the anarchist Sakae Osugi, who tried to advocate free love in Japan in the 1910s, is also the story of a woman's (Mariko Okada) pursuit of freedom (see Chapter 4).

25. *The Story of Tank Commander Nishizumi* (*Nishizumi Senshachoden,* 1940), directed by Kozaburo Yoshimura. Ken Uehara portrays the humanistic war hero who died during the Sino-Japanese War that began in 1937 (see Chapter 5).

26. *The War at Sea from Hawaii to Malaya* (*Hawaii-Marei Oki Kaisen*, 1942), directed by Kajiro Yamamoto. This film depicts in semidocumentary fashion the training of the pilots who attacked Pearl Harbor in 1941 (see Chapter 5).

27. *Mud and Soldiers* (*Tsuchi to Heitai*, 1939), directed by Tomotaka Tasaka. Training scenes were important in war films, and here the battlefield provided a training ground for the human spirit (see Chapter 5).

28. *Carmen's Pure Love* (*Karumen Junjosu*, 1952), directed by Keisuke Kinoshita. Uneducated women working as strippers (Toshiko Kobayashi, *left*; Hideko Takamine, *right*) protest against Japan's postwar rearmament (see Chapter 5).

29. *The Tower of Lilies* (*Himeyuri no To*, 1953), directed by Tadashi Imai. The antiwar theme of this successful film, which highlights the solidarity of the common people, centers around a group of high school girls (Kyoko Kagawa, *center*) who perish in the battle for Okinawa (see Chapter 5).

4
Film Heroines

1. THEIR OCCUPATIONS

Since the beginning of Japanese cinema the leading female role
was often either an entertainer, a geisha, or a prostitute, and several films with such heroines—such as some of Mizoguchi's works
—were masterpieces. Although such occupations are looked down
upon in society, paradoxically, respectable maids, factory hands,
and hardworking women in farming and merchant families have
seldom featured as film heroines. This was probably because the
choice of marriage partners rested with the parents and romance
between respectable men and women did not blossom of its own
accord. Japanese love stories in movies usually centered around
affairs with geisha or prostitutes that ended tragically because
society did not want these women to be happier than their respectable counterparts. Even these days, when romantic love

between respectable people is accepted, more men and women have marriages that are arranged by parents or company bosses.

One exception to the above rule was the nursing profession, the first modern woman's profession to be extolled in Japanese film. Since her job required her to help men, it was natural for gratitude to turn into love, and popular acceptance of this situation is evident from the success of *Messenger from the Moon* (*Tsuki yori no Shisha*, 1934), about the love between a poor nurse and a rich man, and of the 1938 *The Compassionate Buddha Tree*, which established a new box-office record.

Another profession where women could meet respectable men and even fall in love with them was that of teaching. This was the case in *Young People* (*Wakai Hito*, 1937), with its triangle theme involving the woman teacher, the man she loves, and one of their students, a rather eccentric girl. This film created quite a sensation, and, given the seriousness of the teaching profession, the feelings of all concerned had to be expressed delicately and indirectly, and there was no explicit love scene.

In 1942 *New Snow* (*Shinsetsu*), a film about two young primary school teachers who do their best to give their charges a good education, won the overwhelming approval of young movie fans. The depiction of their love was so subtle that it was even passed by the censors, who generally regarded all love stories as pornography that distracted concentration from the war effort.

After defeat in 1945, the love story between a man and woman as social equals became part of the process of democratization, and one of the biggest hits was *Blue Mountains* (*Aoi Sammyaku*, 1949). In it a woman teacher and her students try to convince the backward leaders of their provincial town that love is wonderful, healthy, and respectable.

Office girls have often appeared in Japanese films, but their initial portrayal was not favorable since, nurses, doctors, and teachers excepted, it was popularly thought that a woman only worked because she had to and the term "working woman" was tinged with contempt. This attitude is even reflected in Mizoguchi's *Osaka Elegy*, where the switchboard operator for a small company becomes the mistress of the boss to save her family from destitution. By 1939, however, this attitude changed, as seen in *A Brother and His Younger Sister* (*Ani to Sono Imoto*, 1939). The secretary (played by Michiko Kuwano, the most modern type of actress then) demonstrates her competence by typing a letter into English while her boss is dictating it in Japanese.

During World War II, Japanese women, like their counterparts elsewhere, entered many occupations new to them in order to fill the labor shortage. Although they subsequently returned to domesticity, it became customary for women to take a job after school and before marriage. Thus more women had the chance to seek their own sweethearts at their places of work, and the opportunities for romance increased.

2. THE UNFORTUNATE WOMAN

Tai Kato's *Flower Cards Match* (*Hanafuda Shobu*, 1969, from *The Red Peony Gambler* series, *Hibotan Bakuto*) was an impressive *yakuza* movie both for its colorful Kabuki-like beauty and its striking presentation of the unfortunate woman, a central motif in Japanese film. In it a middle-aged woman is traveling around the country with her blind daughter. By claiming to be the famous professional gambler O-Ryu of the Red Peony Tattoo, she gains employment in a gambling house until the real O-Ryu (Junko Fuji) appears and exposes her. At first the imposter is filled with spite toward her rival, but her attitude changes when she discovers that O-Ryu had once rescued her daughter from being crushed by an oncoming train. She then regards O-Ryu as her benefactor and feels a great sense of debt toward her.

Soon afterward the imposter is given an opportunity to repay her moral debt when she learns that her *yakuza* boss has kidnapped the son of O-Ryu's *yakuza* boss. She thereupon contrives to free the son and his sweetheart, but, just as they are making their escape, they are discovered by her boss's henchmen, who come in hot pursuit. As soon as the trio are out of the building, the woman orders the lovers to flee ahead, and, by pressing her body against the door, she keeps the pursuers inside. Finally one of the henchmen thrusts his sword through the door panel, piercing her throat, and a crimson geyser of blood spurts forth. She shrieks in pain, her face turns deathly pale, and she topples over, still trying to hold the door shut.

A similar moving, unforgettable scene is found in Sadao Yama-

75

naka's prewar masterpiece, *Soshun Kochiyama* (*Kochiyama Soshun,* 1936). While it is probably no coincidence that the director of *Flower Cards Match,* Tai Kato, was the nephew of Yamanaka, the liberal period drama film-maker, a more crucial influence is the persistent Japanese attachment toward images of unfortunate, self-sacrificing women.

Yamanaka's film was adapted from Mokuami's famous nineteenth-century play of the same name. Kochiyama, a brawling, outlaw samurai, roams about with his best friend, Ichinojo Kaneko, looking for trouble. Despite this, he is basically a decent fellow who dotes on a young brother and sister, Hiro and O-Nami, trying to save them from the Moritaya gang. One day, while Kochiyama, his wife O-Shizu, Ichinojo, and Hiro are all in a tavern, there is a knock on the door and O-Shizu opens it only to find the whole yard swarming with the Moritaya gang. Without hesitation, she slips outside, slams the door behind her, and confronts them by blocking their passage with her body. The rest of the Kochiyama party is now trapped inside the tavern. They draw their swords and prepare to cut their way out. Suddenly one of the gang outside yells, "If you don't come out, your old lady will breathe her last!" Ichinojo rushes to the door but Kochiyama restrains him.

"Ichi! This may seem beside the point, but she's *my* wife . . . Kochiyama's wife!" In effect, he is saying that he can count on her all the way and, as the line is delivered, there is a shot of O-Shizu smiling faintly as she is surrounded by the Moritaya gang.

It is interesting to note that because prewar censors forbade kissing or embracing scenes—not to mention bed scenes—there developed a subtle kind of love scene with no sensuality, which attained a high level of refinement. While a couple like Kochiyama and O-Shizu kept their distance, socially and physically, they came to count on each other, and the intimacy and fulfillment they achieved was a sublime negation of prewar restrictions.

This kind of love scene also suggests the extent that Japanese men are indulged by their women. The women, in turn, by having their men rely on them to the ultimate degree, take this dependence to be the most profound expression of love. It is a relationship that is closer to a mother-son relationship than to romantic or conjugal love. Men cause suffering to women by demanding from them all kinds of concessions and self-sacrifices, and then transform the women's suffering into a stimulus toward achievement on their part, while being plagued by guilt. Then, in the web of their guilt, the women finally trap their love. This psychological pattern is still evident and probably explains why suffering women are such a persistent theme in the Japanese cinema.

The above psychology has also acted as a thrust toward modernization. Ethnologist Kunio Yanagida was once asked what had inspired Meiji-period (1868–1912) scholars to their tremendous achievements in letters and science, which propelled Japan into the modern age. Yanagida answered that it was the image of their mothers back in the provinces. Trusting in their sons, they toiled away until the early hours of the morning, sacrificing themselves in order to put them through college in the city. This image, branded into these scholars' minds, spurred them on. The image became an archetype and Kochiyama's trusting, self-sacrificing wife is almost certainly an emanation of it. The fact that it was re-created in *Flower Cards Match* over thirty years later is a tribute to its sway over the imaginations of contemporary Japanese.

Although the woman in *Flower Cards Match* did not die for her man, like O-Shizu she also suffered on account of her husband. He was a wandering gambler who had deserted her and their blind daughter, and it was her fate to go from province to province in search of him. Since she met her death through the actions of her errant husband, both she and O-Shizu belong to the same type of unfortunate, suffering woman.

The image of the unfortunate woman engenders moral indignation against the man responsible and thus creates an undercurrent of loathing in the audience. In films the unfortunate woman almost never complains of the injustice done her and the misfortune she must endure. The image of a single woman's suffering in itself is a powerful enough indictment against oppression by the whole male sex.

Most movies depicting this theme tend to be low-brow, sentimental fare, so-called women's melodramas, and are scorned as reactionary by those who see them as attempts to instill resignation in the poor. Yet the whole genre cannot be so easily dismissed because its effect on us can transcend the shallow dimension of sympathy, or the relief in seeing those worse off than ourselves. The image of a woman suffering uncomplainingly can imbue us with admiration for a virtuous existence almost beyond our reach, rich in endurance and courage. One can idealize her rather than merely pity her, and this can lead to what I call the worship of womanhood, a special Japanese brand of feminism. This worship is rooted in the moral consciousness of the common people, and since the images of unfortunate women in films like *Soshun Kochiyama* and *Flower Cards Match* have the power to arouse it, they leave an indelible impression on Japanese audiences. While the worship of womanhood can be found in many Japanese movies, both before and after 1945, it was best expressed in the works of Kenji Mizoguchi, Kaneto Shindo, and Shohei Imamura.

Mizoguchi's oldest reasonably intact film is *Taki no Shiraito* (*Taki no Shiraito,* 1933), based on a popular Shimpa drama from a novel by Kyoka Izumi, about an itinerant female entertainer whose stage name is Taki no Shiraito. She falls in love with a youth she meets in a provincial town and, as he has his heart set on studying in Tokyo, she raises the money for his tuition. She borrows that sum from a moneylender at an exorbitant interest, and when she is unable to return the money on time, she is hounded by the loan shark, whom she eventually stabs to death. At her trial, the judge turns out to be none other than the young man she has helped. In spite of the fact that he owes his success to her, the law must be upheld and he condemns her to death. Afterward, filled with remorse, he takes his own life.

78

Although the plot is fraught with coincidence and the acting is melodramatic, this film has a marvelously redeeming quality in that it connects the image of the unfortunate woman with the tragic side of modernization. The sacrifice Taki no Shiraito made to send her young man to college reflects a dominant pattern in Japanese society, and also Mizoguchi's own situation since his sister had given him money to attend a fine arts school. Ever since the Meiji period average families have made enormous sacrifices to send one son, usually the eldest, to a university in Tokyo, thereby banking on his future success. His mother, sisters, and brothers would give up their own happiness and resign themselves to a life of drudgery. These women were seldom compensated for their sacrifices: if successful the sons would usually live in a different world, a tragic paradox of modernization. In addition, a college education seldom guaranteed success. A good job, especially during hard times, was difficult to find and an intellectual was often left with only two bleak prospects: to become a poor scholar or a revolutionary. Either way, everything amounted to a betrayal of the women left at home.

Taki no Shiraito was a masterly reproach for this betrayal, since the successful man not only fails to acknowledge the sacrifices of the heroine but also condemns her to death. The fact that he later commits suicide shows his atonement, as well as revealing the psychology behind Mizoguchi's own worship of women, evident in two scenes.

The first scene takes place late at night on a bridge in the outskirts of a town, when Taki no Shiraito and the youth reveal their love for each other. The youth is squatting near the bridge railing when she calls out to him. He looks up and there she is, standing slim and elegant, gazing down upon him, and the uncontrived composition of this shot conveys the director's reverent attitude toward women. The second scene occurs when she tells the usurer that she cannot return the money but refuses to give him her body. He reacts brutally by grabbing her hair and dragging her across the floor. This violent act is a marked change from Taki no Shiraito's earlier appearance on the bridge, and the horror evoked is not so much a reaction to the physical cruelty as a cry against the sacrilegious defilement of a woman of dignity.

Both scenes reveal how much Mizoguchi's worship of women 79 was based on his own compassion for unfortunate women. He idealized them by assuming that they had all originally been noble, and he saw their subsequent transformation into despicable wretches as a result of male, social, and even human sin.

Critics often point to Mizoguchi's *Osaka Elegy* and *Sisters of the Gion* (both 1936) as the turning point in his career, when he made an abrupt departure from the aesthetic, sentimental romanticism of such films as *Taki no Shiraito* toward stark, realistic treatment. Despite this transition, however, his reverent attitude toward women remained. The only difference was that in *Taki no Shiraito* he was content with showing only the beauty of a pathetic woman, while in *Osaka Elegy* and *Sisters of the Gion* he recognized that such women have a right to protest against men. His use of cinematic realism was clearly an attempt to make this protest more palatable and more convincing.

In *Osaka Elegy* a girl goes astray for the sake of her father and brother who, in turn, reject her for it. Thereafter, she pursues this wayward path in earnest. While at first it appears that Mizoguchi was merely relating her unfortunate circumstances, it is later evident that she is accusing the male-centered social system of crime, the male gender of sin.

The same is true of the younger geisha in *Sisters of the Gion*. Her elder sister, also a geisha, abides by the old-fashioned mores whereby one is obligated to take care of a former patron, even when he can no longer pay. The younger sister is the complete opposite, and makes a profession of wheedling money out of men. She continues to lead her men by the nose until one of them gets even by pushing her out of a moving automobile. The older sister, intending to give her a lecture in the hospital, is stopped cold when the young girl cries out, "The whole geisha profession stinks." In this scene all the men that the profession exists for are implicated.

As with the heroine of *Osaka Elegy,* the young geisha's behavior is not dictated by life's necessities, nor is it the result of an evil disposition. Both girls act with innocent glee, almost to the point of seeming naive. In contrast, the men they twist around their fingers and who turn on them in the end are all presented as comical philistines who only deserve contempt.

80 It was only with Mizoguchi's postwar masterpieces, where the romantic and the realistic approaches were combined harmoniously with the central theme of worship of womanhood, that he could be regarded as the creator of a unique world. The pathetic Taki no Shiraito and the accusing young girls were replaced by women like the wife in *Ugetsu* (*Ugetsu Monogatari,* 1953, script by Yoshikata Yoda) and the mother in *Sansho the Bailiff* (*Sansho Dayu,* 1954), women who shoulder alone the evil of men and cleanse it by their self-sacrifice. With these strong, almost divine heroines, Mizoguchi's films became hymns to womanhood, and he transformed a personal penchant into a universal, religious principle that transcended the simple, sensual aestheticism often associated with the worship of women.

Another director, Kaneto Shindo, who had studied script-writing under Mizoguchi, can be considered the inheritor of this theme. Perhaps it would be more accurate to say that Shindo's view of women blossomed under the master's encouragement, but once in bloom revealed itself to be of a different hue. Since he wrote scripts for many directors, he did not pursue this theme consistently but, with two or three exceptions, all the dramas he directed himself were centered around women, with his wife Nobuko Otowa almost invariably in the leading role.

Shindo's women, in contrast to Mizoguchi's heroines, are neither naively beautiful nor awe-inspiring. However, they are more outspoken and attack the male-oriented society with more fury. In earlier works like *Epitome* (*Shukuzu*, 1953) and *Only Women Know Sorrow* (*Kanashimi wa Onna dake ni*, 1958), Shindo differs from Mizoguchi by idealizing the intimidating capacity of Japanese women for sustained work, and contrasting them with shamefully lazy men. In the 1960s, however, the pattern of the lazy, haughty male lording it over the hard-working unfortunate female changed with Shindo's introduction of the theme of impotence in *Lost Sex* (*Honno*, 1966) and *The Origin of Sex* (*Sei no Kigen*, 1967). The only remedy for this seemed to be the love of a more maternal woman, although this was not enough in *The Origin of Sex*, where the impotent, aging male suddenly dropped dead despite the woman's ministrations.

Both Mizoguchi and Shindo, in his earlier films, had portrayed women as victims. By contrasting the comical weakness of the male with the unbridled strength of the female, Shindo seemed to be saying in the 1960s that women had wrought their revenge. This could have been a reflection of postwar society, since it is commonly said that in Japan women have become stronger because men have lost all confidence in their masculinity due to Japan's defeat. With the decrease of tyrannical husbands, this may indeed have occurred within the home, but not in society, where the status of women had not changed much. Also, according to Shohei Imamura, Japanese women had always been strong in the home and there was no need for any postwar change.

In order to understand Imamura's view of women, an examination of his attitude toward the masses is necessary. To Imamura ordinary women realistically mirrored the condition of the masses since they seldom rose to positions of leadership or became members of the ruling class. Imamura made his debut in 1958 with *Stolen Desire (Nusumareta Yokujo)*, about a literary youth who becomes involved with a troupe of vulgar, itinerant entertainers who initiate him into a lewd world. Far from being repelled by it, the hero believes that he loves these people for what they are and hopes to create a new art form based on the life of common people. In the end, however, it all turns out to be a pipe dream. He falls in love with one of the daughters of the *tateyaku*, a girl who has maintained her innocence despite her surroundings, and together they escape from the brawling, decadent world of the troupe.

The hero, a self-portrait, while admiring the raw energy of the common people, does not know how to convert it into "positive" values. After tortuous attempts, he eventually gives up. He decides that at best this milieu is a throbbing volcano of humanity, which, without a shred of idealism, favors a passive affirmation of the status quo. This indeterminate conclusion is reflected in the ending when the hero and his sweetheart slink off to the city lights and the world of organized labor, while the itinerant entertainers head in the opposite direction, chased by farmers whose chickens they have stolen.

Attraction-repulsion, love-hate, positive-negative: such is the ambivalence characterizing the young Imamura's attitude in his chosen milieu. The pattern is just as apparent in his first big success, *Pigs and Battleships (Buta to Gunkan,* 1961). Small-time gangsters begin to breed pigs, expecting to use the garbage from a neighboring American military base as feed. However, when their official permit turns out to be forged, hilarious squabbles arise within the gang.

The hero is a young gangster who dreams of becoming top dog in the gang, but his girlfriend, seeing the stupidity in this, minces no words when it comes to giving him sound advice. She herself, however, is no paragon of rationality. She gets drunk and is raped by a group of American sailors. Even then she does not seem to know when to leave well enough alone, for she tries to get even by stealing the sailors' wallets. Caught and thrown into jail, she is still clear-sighted enough to see the gangsters as nothing more than human trash. She has the inner capacity for sizing up the important things in life, and this particular ability is common to many of Imamura's subsequent heroines. When her boyfriend is killed, she decides she has had enough of this life. Like the hero in *Stolen Desire* who abandons the itinerant entertainers for organized labor, she goes off to get a decent job in a factory in Kawasaki, near Tokyo.

In both these films Imamura seemed to categorize elements in the common people as good or bad, progressive or reactionary, encouraging the good and criticizing the bad. Thereafter, however, he stopped trying to grasp the psychology of the lowest social classes by analyzing their "good" and "bad" sides, and set himself the task of apprehending their milieu as a single whole. He paid closer attention to common women, who were often the object of Mizoguchi's and Shindo's worship of womanhood. With a new coscriptwriter, Keiji Hasebe, he portrayed women as representatives of the vitality and toughness of the masses.

The first product of Imamura's collaboration with Hasebe was *The Insect Woman* (*Nippon Konchuki*, 1963), an account of a woman who leaves her mountain village in the northeast to become a prostitute in Tokyo. After several ordeals she becomes the unsuccessful boss of a call-girl ring. Since the life she leads is a completely natural one for her, she is presented without sadness. When frustrated she considers herself unfortunate, reveling in self-pity and using whatever cliches pop into her head. These expressions of grief are so hackneyed and mundane that the audience involuntarily breaks into laughter, and the film almost becomes a comedy. However, the laughter is not only a ridicule of her ignorance but also an expression of admiration for her tough vitality, since by this she rids herself of frustration and goes on living, no matter how immoral her existence may appear.

Through such heroines Imamura portrays common people as leading an existence transcending conventional morality. They do have a moral code, but what is not particularly useful is cast aside, while what is necessary is remembered and respected. In short, with this film Imamura began his investigation of the conception, suitability, and advocacy of morality.

Yet, judging from Imamura's relentless depiction of the sexual immorality, shamelessness, and ignorance of the heroine in *The Insect Woman*, one has the impression that he views lower-class women with contempt. Unlike Mizoguchi's and Shindo's early films, where the misfortunes of women were a general indictment of male oppression and the male-oriented social structure, which aroused guilt feelings in male audiences, there is nothing in *The Insect Woman* to make one feel that the heroine has been made unhappy on account of men. Nevertheless, Imamura can still be regarded as a "woman worshiper" because in later films, like *Intentions of Murder* (*Akai Satsui*, 1964), he presented women who not only exemplified the survival-type morality of the common people but also controlled the psyches of their men.

The heroine in *Intentions of Murder* is the wife of a librarian in a city in northeast Japan. She is ignorant, sluggish, and quite plain, yet she brims over with audacity and sex appeal. Her husband, the tyrant at home, is in reality more like a spoiled child, calling her "Mommy" in bed. This documentarylike film changes pace when the wife is attacked and raped by a burglar when she is alone at home. She stumbles into the kitchen, sobbing and muttering that she must die for the shame of it. When she finally comes to her senses she finds that she has been gobbling fistfuls of boiled rice. Although aware of the traditional Japanese code that calls for a wife to commit suicide after she has been raped, her spontaneous act of eating rice is actually a betrayal of this moral and shows us the abundance of her vitality. She is not without morals; however, she balances them with the necessities of life as the occasion demands.

Later she is raped again by the same young man, who, it turns out, is dying of tuberculosis. He far from dominates her, but rather, out of despair, seeks her love. This time she has feelings of guilt but dismisses them. When he suggests that they elope, she consents, but considers poisoning him when she has the chance. In the end, however, tuberculosis gets the better of him and he dies coughing blood over the snow. After watching his death throes intently she simply returns home.

The plot then turns upon the fact that her husband's girlfriend had snapped some pictures of her and the man during their elopement. When she is hospitalized as the result of an automobile accident, her husband comes to visit her and shows her one of the photographs.

"Here, this is you, isn't it?"

She looks at the picture intently and then asks, "Who took this?"

"It doesn't matter who. Look, this is a clear shot. There's no doubt it's you."

"No, it's not me."

"It *is* you. Those clothes are the same as yours. And there aren't many people around as fat as you."

"But it's not me."

"Well then, why did you go to the train station? That was rather strange, wasn't it? Why?"

"You're always so suspicious of me . . . so I thought of going someplace far away."

"By yourself?"

At this juncture the heroine assumes a defiant attitude, as if to say that even if she did run off with another man, she has done nothing wrong, and her husband suddenly becomes timid and confused, lending humor and irony to their confrontation.

Imamura's implied message is that getting through life safely is more important than insisting on principles. When life is lived by this standard, the heroine has a clear advantage because she knows the survival-type morality of the common people better than men. Moreover, she holds the key to domestic order. Her husband may brandish the principle of male authority, but in reality he cannot insist on it due to his mother complex, through which she controls him.

The hold Japanese women have over their men is not simply the result of the men's mother complex. In Imamura's *The Profound Desire of the Gods* or *Kuragejima: Tales from a Southern Island* (*Kamigami no Fukaki Yokubo*, 1968), women represent primitive society and thus control the most primal base of the spiritual consciousness of the Japanese. Moreover, like Mizoguchi's Taki no Shiraito, who gives her life for her man, women can also arouse feelings of guilt because this native society was sacrificed for modernization.

This film takes place on a small island, perhaps in the Okinawan archipelago, and is a strange story that combines fact and myth to such a degree that it is difficult to distinguish between them. The central figures are two sisters. The elder one is the mistress of the village headman and has an incestuous relationship with her broth-

85

er. The younger sister is retarded, born of the union between her mother and her mother's father. The conditions on this narrow stretch of land and its isolation conspire to weave a complex web of commingling family blood, with the incest in the family symbolizing the backwardness and stagnation of the island society.

This family has set aside some rice paddies for cultivating rice offerings to the island gods, eventually angering the rest of the community when they refuse to sell the plot to help build an airport. In addition, the younger sister seems to be sabotaging the modernization process by seducing the engineer from Tokyo, thereby distracting him from the job on hand. Therefore, on the pretext of their incestuous behavior and background, this family is eventually punished.

The last scenes of the movie are extremely moving. The elder sister, whose brother has already been brutally killed, is tied to the mast of a red-sailed boat that is set adrift on the ocean. Then, five years later, a planeload of tourists flies over the island to land on its airport. Beyond the plane, the boat, a red speck on the horizon floating with its ghastly cargo, is still visible. In a following scene the ghost of the younger sister is seen moving across the tracks of the island's first railroad.

The two sisters represent the cohesion that once existed in their communal society, which was destroyed by the islanders for the sake of modernization. The modern society built on the wreckage of the old cannot be very different from what Imamura delineated in *Intentions of Murder*, where the woman, symbolizing the old society, seemed to be in control.

86

In contrast to Mizoguchi's saintly, forgiving women, Shindo's heroines later revenged themselves on men, but for Imamura's later heroines revenge is no longer necessary. Japanese men had used women as stepping stones to build a new culture, but since its foundation rested on the old, they could only progress so far. By eventually binding their men hand and foot, Japanese women consummated their revenge.

The two sisters in *The Profound Desire of the Gods* are *miko,* women serving a Shinto shrine during childhood who often become occult mediums or shamans. Although not much significance is attached to this in the development of the plot, it is extremely important to Imamura's worship of womanhood. Imamura views women as the priestesses of the old, common social body, the disintegration of which only produced smaller units that had existed from the beginning, the small family. Imamura clearly indicates that in this small social unit women, as in the past, continue to function as *miko*, or priestesses.

Imamura's films show a keen yearning for the illusion of the priestesslike woman, who, at the same time terrifies him, and appears on the screen as a collective image of all those values crushed underfoot by the modernization of Japanese society.

3. BEAUTIFUL WOMEN

Some years ago an interesting experiment was undertaken for the Japanese television program called "All the Earth Is Our Family." The portraits of five Japanese actresses were shown on a university campus in New Guinea, in a native village in the African bush, in an Eskimo village in Greenland, to passersby in Paris and a city in Brazil, amongst other places, and the people there were polled as to which one they thought the most beautiful. The five actresses were: Fujiko Yamamoto, the then acknowledged representative of Japanese beauty, Kaoru Yumi, an attractive dancer, Akihiko Maruyama, a transvestite, Nijiko Kiyokawa, a middle-aged comedienne who plays a kindly female gangster boss, and Ruriko Asaoka, a sensitive modern type. Japanese audiences were surprised to find that the favorite was usually Ruriko Asaoka, not Fujiko Yamamoto, who only ranked top in the African and Eskimo villages, with Nijiko Kiyokawa, where Ruriko Asaoka fared poorly.

The reasons for the choices are both revealing and interesting. The criteria for beauty in the African village is a woman's healthiness, her capacity for hard work, a kindly disposition, and her capacity for bearing many children. Thus Ruriko Asaoka was not considered beautiful because she looked too frail. Although the popularity there of the maternal Nijiko Kiyokawa is understandable, that of Fujiko Yamamoto is something of a mystery. Ruriko Asaoka's appeal in cosmopolitan cities is not surprising because her popularity in Japan rested on her modernity. One Parisian youth reportedly quipped: "Eh? Is this really a Japanese actress? Isn't she a Parisian?" Evidently, her expression of *ennui* not only

87

appears beautiful but conveys sentiments common to all city-dwellers. One New Guinea college student was asked why he chose Akihiko Maruyama as the most beautiful. His reply was that she/he struck him as being "truly Japanese."

Another example of the gap between the Japanese concept of feminine beauty and that of other peoples occurred several years ago during a Franco-Japanese film production. The Japanese side recommended Fujiko Yamamoto for the female lead in the proposed film, but were forcefully countered by the French, who preferred Hitomi Nozoe, an actress most Japanese do not consider beautiful at all. The Japanese probably thought that Fujiko Yamamoto, who comes from a well-to-do family, would be popular among Europeans. However, since she was brought up by maids who waited on her hand and foot, her calm, gentle disposition is too different from the boisterous personalities that Europeans or Americans are used to. Fujiko Yamamoto rarely asserts herself, usually deferring to her male escort. This trait is probably only appreciated by Japanese and other Orientals.

Setsuko Hara, one of Japan's best-loved actresses and a woman who was always considered a true Japanese beauty, is another example. I know a young German who was so enraptured with Ozu's films that he learned Japanese in order to come to Japan and study them. He felt they were perfect except for one glaring flaw: Setsuko Hara. Even Donald Richie, the foremost American critic of Japanese films, once told me that he found her constant and often incongruous solemnity strange.

88 Reflecting upon such opinions, one is forced to admit that Setsuko Hara's performance was too solemn and stiff. Although this seemed unpalatable to Westerners, to the Japanese she embodied that spiritual tenacity which made it possible for Japan to attain the economic level of the West. She reminds us of the suffering of Japanese who had to bear much psychological strain during the modernization process. While such an aesthetic consciousness might appear forced and pretentious to the more advanced Westerner, to the Japanese such sincerity was the mark of true beauty in a woman. Perhaps this aesthetic sense is exclusively Japanese, for Setsuko Hara appeared most beautiful when she played a schoolteacher, the role most symbolic of modernization.

Fujiko Yamamoto is another actress who gives the impression

of sobering sincerity. Both women have faces that show little emotion, thus attesting to single-mindedness of purpose. These characteristics are said to be typical of the women of the old Japanese bourgeoisie, the upper- and upner-middle-class families, and the beauty of both women depends on the manner in which they embody this personality, not on the shape of their nose or their eyes.

In modern Japan, where success in university entrance examinations is the key to future success, a family's fortunes can decline after a generation or two if the men fail in this fierce competition. While the members of such a family may appear nonchalant on the surface, they are all keenly aware of the ever-present danger of downfall. Consequently, their women are not only expected to have the spiritual strength necessary to endure the insecurities of life but also the nobility and grace appropriate to their station. These characteristics are a part of the unconscious criteria of the Japanese in judging feminine charm, and when all these qualities are integrated in one personality, such a woman is called a "bourgeois beauty." Together with the common-woman type of beauty to be dealt with shortly, she reigned over the hearts of all Japanese men.

Besides Fujiko Yamamoto and Setsuko Hara, Keiko Kishi, Shiho Fujimura, Yoshiko Kuga, Kyoko Kagawa, and many other successful actresses have absorbed this air of bourgeois anguish, and consequently radiate an austere beauty—the result of unwavering endurance of misfortune. When, for instance, Yoshiko Kuga plays the wife in some mundane household, audiences assume she has suffered terribly because she has the image of a well-born girl, and her uniquely Japanese beauty is apparent in that subtle smile that transforms her anguish into tenaciousness. Mieko Takamine was perhaps the first actress to convey this beauty in such films as Kozaburo Yoshimura's *Warm Current* (*Danryu*, 1939) and Ozu's *The Brothers and Sisters of the Toda Family* (*Toda-ke no Kyodai*, 1941). She and others like her were favorites of young Japanese intellectuals from not very affluent homes. They were probably dreaming of rescuing such a brave, gallant girl from the inevitable downfall of her upper-class family.

In *Warm Current* a young man is torn between marrying a girl from a declining bourgeois family (Mieko Takamine) or a nurse

(Mitsuko Mito) from his own class. He finally picks the nurse. This was the romantic dilemma of the time; and Kurosawa's *No Regrets for Our Youth* was a postwar example of this kind of romance without the dilemma, for in it the daughter (Setsuko Hara) of a famous university professor decides to marry an anti-war leader from a farming family.

Since the social mobility in modern Japan allows lower- and lower-middle-class families to pursue the dream of rising socially, the women of such classes are expected to show fierce determination and pride. Among those actresses who radiate these qualities are Kinuyo Tanaka, Isuzu Yamada, Machiko Kyo, and Ayako Wakao. Without exception, all of them made their debut as sweet, virginal maidens. In time, however, as their acting ability developed, they all glowed with determination on the screen. With Kinuyo Tanaka this transformation is apparent in Mizoguchi's *The Woman of Osaka (Naniwa Onna,* 1940); for Isuzu Yamada in *Osaka Elegy;* for Machiko Kyo in Yoshimura's *Clothes of Deception (Itsuwareru Seiso,* 1951); and for Ayako Wakao in Yasuzo Masumura's *A Wife Confesses (Tsuma wa Kokuhaku Suru,* 1961). They may not have come from lower-class families themselves. Kinuyo Tanaka, for instance, was born into a wealthy provincial family that fell on hard times, and her success stems from her determination to restore the family name and recoup its losses. All that is required is for these actresses to project the stubborn vitality of the rising social classes.

The women portrayed by the above actresses are peculiarly Japanese. They complain bitterly of their hard lot as women, yet do not despair over the egoism of their men. Instead, they actually lead or goad them to make more money, or even to foment revolution. In prewar films this stubborn type was often a woman who struggled against becoming the servile wife in a feudal household. In postwar films, however, she took the negative form of a geisha or bar hostess who refuses to give in to overbearing men and actually makes a profession out of getting the better of them.

In Kon Ichikawa's *Bonchi (Bonchi,* 1960) and the television version of *Side Canal (Yokoborigawa,* 1966), there are startling portrayals of the vitality of merchant wives who are more influential in the family business than their husbands. This should come as no surprise, since even in feudal times only samurai husbands had absolute preeminence over their wives; a merchant husband and wife often had to work side by side. The difference between merchant and samurai family backgrounds is exemplified by Kurosawa and Keisuke Kinoshita. The former was the son of a military calisthenics instructor, and he created almost nothing but male-oriented films, whereas the latter was the son of a wholesale grocer, and specialized in films about women.

Since films nowadays are aimed at the young, the tradition of the proud, determined merchant wife is only allowed to flourish in family-oriented television drama. There, actresses like Junko Ikeuchi, Masako Kyozuka, and Haruko Sugimura exhibit the powerful position and prestige of middle-aged women in ordinary households, and the special charm they communicate is something that had not existed before in dramas about women.

In the postwar era the distinction between the bourgeois and commoner type of beauty was not always so clear. Still, the following films best display the spirit of the modern Japanese woman, be it the fierce determination of the commoner, the perseverance of the austere beauty, or both. Kinugasa's *Actress* (*Joyu*, 1947), Ozu's *Late Spring* (*Banshun*, 1949) and other films starring Setsuko Hara, Yoshimura's *Night River* (*Yoru no Kawa*, 1956), and Ichikawa's *Her Brother* (*Ototo*, 1960) are all films with heroines who are beautiful because they embody all the virtues that their men lack. This forms another kind of worship of womanhood, and its last expression is seen in Yoshishige Yoshida's *Akizu Hot Springs* (*Akizu Onsen*, 1962).

The hero of this film is a young intellectual who believes that Japan's defeat in World War II is actually a liberation, but he becomes a philistine and loses his ideals amid the turmoil and confusion of the immediate postwar era. In contrast, the heroine is a simple young girl who sincerely grieved over the defeat and now grieves over his loss of ideals. She continues to watch over him, until she loses all hope and commits suicide.

The denouement of this film is symbolic of a major change in postwar Japan. Up until the early 1960s such dispirited men in Japanese cinema were often contrasted with persevering heroines who had a rather drab kind of courage. However, ever since the Japanese realized that they had built an affluent society unparalleled by any in their past, this contrast ceased to appear. In fact, it seemed to vanish with the suicide of this heroine. Thereafter, the call for Japanese men to recover their self-confidence was increasingly heard in the mass media. However, this call for a rejuvenation of masculinity may simply be to cover up the fact that Japanese men, like the hero in *Akizu Hot Springs,* have lost their humble aspirations of the immediate postwar period.

4. WOMEN AND KARMA

When the karma, or inevitability, of a woman's life was depicted in Japanese film it was done with a combination of sympathy for her misfortune and admiration for her spiritual tenacity. This view of women reached its ultimate expression in the following films directed by Mikio Naruse: *Lightning* (*Inazuma,* 1952), *Older Brother, Younger Sister* (*Ani Imoto,* 1953), and *Floating Clouds* (*Ukigumo,* 1955).

The heroine of *Lightning* is a guide for a Tokyo tour bus company. She detests her mother, who had all her children by different men and, feeling that her wayward brothers and sisters are no better, she tries to leave her sordid family to live alone. Yet in the end she cannot sever the relationship with her mother, and one is even left with the impression that she will someday find contentment in a grumbling but persevering existence.

Older Brother, Younger Sister begins when a loose-living woman returns to her parental home on the outskirts of Tokyo along the Tama River. Her brother, a laborer, feels sorry for her but, nevertheless, maintains a gruff exterior, to the extent of even beating her up. Sulking over the beating, she comes to understand how much he loves her, and feels relief. This does not mean that she will mend her ways, however, for in the end one is certain that she will return to her former life-style. Only her intelligent younger sister really knows how unfortunate she is and feels sorry for her.

In the above films the loose mother and the fallen sister are representative of Naruse's women, who neither reform nor make any progress in life. Naruse did not believe in human development. For him life is simply a string of foolishnesses, and however hard one tries to avoid it, one cannot escape fate. Naruse did not despair of life, for he saw nothing wrong in the foolishnesses one commits through love of life. By rejecting progress and loving life, one can attain a fulfillment that cannot be mocked.

At the core of this view is tenacity, not fatalism, and this is best expressed in *Floating Clouds* through the heroine (Hideko Takamine). During World War II she has an affair in Vietnam with a married Japanese engineer sent there by the government. Their hopeless relationship continues after their return to Japan. The man fails in his attempt to start his own business and walks about with a constant gloomy expression, trying to pick up other women even though he cannot provide for them adequately. Although it is a mystery what the heroine sees in him, she sticks with him to the bitter end. When he is finally offered a position on some faraway, isolated island, she follows him there in spite of her illness, and soon after their arrival dies alone, without the benefit of medical care, in a government housing facility.

While there is no denying that this is a tale of an extremely foolish woman, one never feels that she should have sought another kind of life. Instead, the audience is moved by her love for a worthless, lackluster man, and by the fact that their relationship was formed solely through her totally uncalculating, irrational tenacity. In Naruse's films the relationship between a man and a woman is usually portrayed as a precarious one. However, it is held together by a kind of persistence, too tough for such a pretty label as love and much more precious than progress or intelligence. Thus, the apparently foolish woman in *Floating Clouds* is respected precisely because of her blind persistence. Japanese women are admired for this unglamorous emotion, and within it, unexpectedly, spiritual security can be achieved.

5. WOMEN AND FREEDOM

The central figure of the main plot in Yoshishige Yoshida's masterpiece, *Eros Plus Massacre* (*Erosu Purasu Gyakusatsu,* 1970), is the prewar Japanese revolutionary Sakae Osugi. An anarchist, Osugi was against private property, and since monogamy fell into the same category, he also advocated free love. During one period of his life he had a continuing relationship with three

93

different women: Yasuko Hori, Itsuko Masaoka, and Noe Ito, the latter of whom was assassinated with him by the military police amid the turmoil following the Great Kanto Earthquake of 1923.

Into this story of a historical figure, Yoshida interjects a drama concerning the empty pursuit of free sex among contemporary youth. The main character of this subplot is a college girl who is doing research on the Taisho era (1912–26) and is particularly interested in Osugi's practice of free love. At one point in the film she interviews a young woman who is supposed to be the child of the liaison between Osugi and Noe Ito, but who was obviously not born over fifty years ago. The surrealistic handling of this scene suggests that historical events may be filtered through the imagination of this college girl, and thus bear contemporary relevance.

Yoshida presents Osugi as a melancholy figure rendered politically inactive by the intense oppression of his time. However, Osugi does not merely consider revolution in terms of political reform, for him it is also the complete liberation of all human sensibilities. In a scene with Toshihiko Sakai, a revolutionary socialist, Osugi states: "I want to reach the pinnacle of life. In that instant we will seize the ecstasy of freedom. A labor strike is not necessary to seize that ecstasy. We need individual courage and the outbreak of a general strike based on passionate zeal. Then, indeed, will the workers be freed from their centuries-old slavery. Then they can become the creators of their own history and values."

94   Sakai replies banteringly (actually making a pun on the Japanese word *sei* which means both life and sex): "You can't be serious, my dear Osugi. What you're saying does not go beyond the realm of the sensual and the literary. You seem to be advocating a philosophy of life (*sei*), but someone has said that the *sei* you mean is sex."

In the following scene with Itsuko Masaoka, Osugi explains his ideas on free love.

"I should have told you this when I first fell in love with you. I have a wife named Yasuko. She's an old-fashioned, uneducated woman, but she has the proper disposition for the wife of a revolutionary. I've placed burdens on her. I also love her. I love you in the same way."

"You love Noe in the same way, too. It's all right with me. I am truly happy for you."

"Good, I think all four of us can get along well together. That is, as long as we maintain three conditions."

"What are they?"

"First, all of us should be financially independent. Second, we will all keep separate residences. Third, we will respect each other's freedom, which, of course, includes sexual freedom."

Itsuko makes no reply.

"I have a lot of friends," he continues, "but none of them ever complains that I favor one over another. since I relate to all of them equally. Our love, too, will live on the same basis of equality and freedom."

For the contemporary college girl, as for director Yoshida himself, Sakae Osugi's perilous course of life in Taisho society was the result of these ideas, for which he was even criticized by fellow revolutionaries like Toshihiko Sakai. Although his political thought is no longer valid, his ideas on free love are still relevant, as seen in the relationship of economic independence to women's liberation. Still, while Osugi thought that recognition of one another's right to an independent existence would lead to freedom, the women concerned did not accept this and the situation provoked intense jealousy. The rivalry between the women built up to the incident at the Hikage Chaya Inn, where Osugi was stabbed by Noe Ito. This forms the climax of the film and Yoshida handles it in a surrealistic manner, demonstrating his originality and raising an important issue.

95

While it is a historical fact that Itsuko Masaoka (not her real name) stabbed Sakae Osugi causing him serious injuries, in the film it is suggested that she only attacked her lover's view of revolution itself. In this regard, the supposition that Noe Ito stabbed him is reasonable, since she had been most influenced by his ideas. Furthermore, Itsuko indicates that Osugi was also aware of the significance of their actions, and it can even be assumed that with the help of the two women, he attempted suicide for the following reasons.

Revolution is the overthrow of established authority. However, those who seize power become like their predecessors, and no changes are effected. Accordingly, if a revolutionary attempts to pursue revolution all the way, in the end he must negate himself. The same holds for free love. By rejecting a monopoly of sex, one secures the freedom of sex. However, a situation then occurs where there is free competition for sex. Although Osugi said he would love all three women equally, he was not able to accomplish this. Even if he did, from the standpoint of his politics it would be tantamount to a rich person monopolizing many women while a poor person has trouble finding one. This insistence upon sexual freedom led to a desperate struggle in which Itsuko hurt Osugi's wife, Yasuko, and then Noe hurt them both. This struggle made them even more aware of the desire for private ownership, in the sense of monopolizing a love object, a desire they were supposed to have abandoned.

This was especially true for Noe Ito, who sought liberation more than the others. As Osugi himself said, she had won and had taken over the position of his wife, but that was what she detested most, for possession of another human being contradicts freedom. Still, while Noe reached the extreme of this desire for private ownership, she was also possessed by the vision of dying with Osugi as a means of negating it, since in the midst of the surrealistic climax she reminded everyone of the historical fact that she was the woman Osugi was actually killed with. Furthermore, in the scene where Noe kisses the fallen Osugi on the forehead she reveals that her possession of him was also his possession of her and that she had to kill him to be free of it.

For Noe, her freedom could only be obtained at the expense of Osugi's and herein lies the contradiction. If each person insists upon his or her absolute freedom, it will only result in a violent competition where the strong win and the weak lose. Then again, we never know when the weak will revenge themselves upon the strong. At this juncture enters the concept, "All men are equal," and the freedom of the strong is restricted in order to avoid another selfish struggle. The words "freedom" and "equality" are often uttered in the same breath, as though they are inseparable, yet, actually, they are contradictory concepts.

Osugi's theory of free love was put into practice on the pretext of equal love for a number of women. However, in reality, this soon became a free competition for love which brought about a chain of selfish disputes and vindictive acts, inevitably restricting all parties involved. In short, the desire for more freedom led to a condition that was exactly its opposite.

The desire to win, or at least not to be outdone by an opponent, probably even distorts the value of the object won in the ensuing competition. Noe Ito may have been wondering why she had to go to such lengths to win Osugi's love or why he was so important. In this way perhaps she *did* stab Osugi more out of a desire to be free of him than to monopolize his love. Nevertheless, her action is also probably a manifestation of the competitive vanity of a woman who wants to outdo her opponent, Itsuko, whose feelings toward Osugi were simply possessive.

When Yoshida examined the concept of freedom and found that at some time or other it would become transformed into an opposite concept, it did not stop the main characters in *Eros Plus Massacre* from their pursuit. When they realize that absolute freedom is at the same time absolute self-negation, however, their only recourse seems to be suicide, either alone or with someone, or similar self-destructive behavior.

The analysis of *Eros Plus Massacre* would end there were it not for the subplot concerning the free sex of some contemporary youths. This was a vain, empty act because once they attain a sexual relationship, they lose their dream of obtaining something else from their partner. For human beings the opposite sex is not a mere sensual object, but also an ideal of domestic order, a source of honor or glory, a sense of security in life, a psychological or spiritual support, and so on; and all these dreams or ideals are probably crystallized in the emotion of love. As such, free sex is connected with the loss of ideals in the opposite sex. This issue becomes more important than that of free competition for love, and is alluded to in the first half of the film by Jun Tsuji, a bohemian poet who was Noe Ito's former husband.

"Both modernization and women's liberation will probably be achieved someday. I don't know whether it will take fifty or seventy years. Even now in 1916 locomotives run as far as Kyushu. Yet I wonder where that intense beam of light comes from, that beam of light which is transforming the ego from the inside into an empty thing. When the day comes when women are liberated, I feel that the emptiness of this ego will expand in correspondence with the times. Even though fifty years from now

97

we will be more advanced, it will still come to that."

In *Eros Plus Massacre* a twofold, tragic doubt is raised concerning the concept of freedom. First, there is the contradiction that self-negation may lie at the other extremity of freedom. Second, when we lose the visions or ideals we should passionately seek, freedom itself will become a meaningless, empty thing.

Yoshida had dealt with these problems in his previous films, the two most widely acclaimed ones being *Akizu Hot Springs*, where the heroine commits suicide when she realizes that the man she loves would never recover his lost ideals, and *A Story Written on Water* (*Mizu de Kakareta Monogatari*, 1965), where the heroine lives an affluent life but, nevertheless, often feels it is meaningless. As the plot unfolds, she marries off her son to the daughter of the man she is having an affair with. When her son learns of this, he leaves his wife and returns to his mother's house and rapes her. The following morning the mother commits suicide. While guilt over the incest might have been a cause, the heroine had also exerted her freedom beyond the realm of common sense and in the end was seized with a feeling of emptiness.

The problem of doubt in ideals about the opposite sex was well depicted in two of Yoshida's rather unsuccessful films of 1967, *The Affair* (*Joen*) and *Impasse* (*Honoho to Onna*). In both, a supposedly contented, upper-middle-class housewife has an affair with a laborer for sexual satisfaction. Neither heroine believes she can find a dream in the opposite sex, and both are tormented by the thought that all such dreams and ideals are illusions. In order to test this, they have to sleep with a laborer they meet by chance, someone who, in their minds, is just the opposite of those ideals.

The grand compilation of the themes in Yoshida's previous works lies in *Eros Plus Massacre* because it poses the question: what remains after all the visions of freedom and idealized relations are negated? The answer is Eros, which drives human beings on toward dreams of more and more freedom and whose all-out pursuit must lead in the end to self-negation. In Yoshida's other films, he portrays women in crises, women who are frightened by the loss of these ideals. Then, he was showing us one side of the modern condition, for people *were* losing faith in each other as they became more individualistic and as human relations in the family and society were losing cohesion. Finally, in *Eros Plus*

Massacre, with the portrayal of Noe Ito, a woman driven by the passionate ideal of greater freedom, the visionless modern age stands out in bold relief, and Yoshida presents us with the terrifying question of what form future civilization will take when it has lost all ideals in human relations.

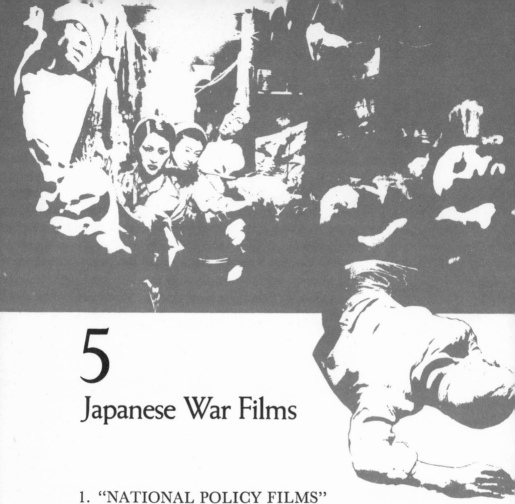

5
Japanese War Films

1. "NATIONAL POLICY FILMS"

From the outbreak of the Sino-Japanese War in 1937 until 1945, the Japanese film industry was thrust under the control of the Ministry of Home Affairs and the Media Section of the Imperial Army. The tough censorship of previous years increased in severity with the passing, in 1939, of the all-encompassing Motion Picture Law. Consequently, both the Home Ministry and the army, which had been heavily subsidizing the film industry, could force out of business any errant movie company; actors could also be fired and directors subjected to harassment. The authorities not only viewed every film made but also engaged in pre-production script censorship. Thus, film-makers were forced to operate within this ironclad framework. One director who broke the rules was Fumio Kamei, whose *Fighting Soldiers* (*Tatakau Hei-*

tai, 1940) depicted the tragic side of war. Kamei was stripped of his position as director and left idle until the end of the war. Another case concerned Yasujiro Ozu's 1939 script for *The Flavor of Green Tea over Rice* (*Ochazuke no Aji*), about a man who, on the eve of his induction into the army, sits down with his flustered wife to share this rather plain rice dish. The censors condemned the "purposely flippant" treatment of this scene, stating that the festive red-bean-and-rice dish would have been more appropriate. Ozu balked at this meddling and set his script aside until the war was over.

Censorship tightened even more in 1940, with the issuance by the Home Ministry of the following instructions concerning film-making.

1. The authorities hope that the citizens will be shown healthy entertainment films with positive themes.

2. While not restricted at present, screen appearances by comedians and satirists should not increase.

3. Films about the petty bourgeoisie and the wealthy, and those extolling private happiness are hereby prohibited, along with scenes of women smoking, cabaret life, frivolous behavior, and dialogues including many foreign words.

4. Films depicting the productive sectors of national life, especially agriculture, are to be encouraged.

5. Preproduction inspection of all scenarios shall be rigorously followed, and if violations are found, rewriting shall be ordered to correct them.

This new policy served to abolish the urban love story or melodrama, one of the most profitable film genres, and resulted in the almost exclusive production of "national policy films" (*kokusaku eiga*). The first of the three main characteristics that distinguish these films is the vagueness of the image of the enemy. Countries at war use the cinema as a tool for arousing hostility and hatred by depicting the enemy as cruel and inhuman, as in American propaganda war films where stereotyped Japanese soldiers were depicted as slant-eyed Orientals with hideous, barbaric grins. In national policy films, however, the enemy is usually shown at a great distance, such as Chinese soldiers shooting at Japanese pilots as they make a forced landing in Yutaka Abe's *Flaming Sky* (*Moyuru Ozora*, 1940). In Tomotaka Tasaka's *Five Scouts* (*Gonin no*

101

Sekkohei, 1938) the enemy is represented by a burst of machine-gun fire or a few scattered corpses. In Kajiro Yamamoto's series of air battle films, beginning with his famous *The War at Sea from Hawaii to Malaya* (*Hawaii-Marei Oki Kaisen*, 1942), the enemy is represented by planes and warships, and in Kozaburo Yoshimura's *The Story of Tank Commander Nishizumi* (*Nishizumi Senshacho-den*, 1940) the closest look at the enemy is the back of a dying Chinese soldier who shoots the hero as he measures the depth of a small stream. Such fleeting glimpses of the enemy could hardly incite emotional responses and, consequently, there is little suspense in these war movies. In only a few exceptions, such as Masato Koga's *The Tiger of Malaya* (*Marei no Tora*, 1943) and Masahiro Makino's *The Opium War* (*Ahen Senso*, 1943), were enemy soldiers seen torturing Japanese soldiers or civilians, but since Koga's film was an action thriller and Makino's a historical spectacle, they are somewhat outside the genre of national policy films.

A second characteristic of this genre, and one cause of its favorable postwar appraisal, is its concentration on the human side of Japanese soldiers, such as in the film mentioned above by Tasaka, who insisted on emphasizing the comradely bonds between them. In Akira Iwasaki's 1961 review of *The Story of Tank Commander Nishizumi* (from *Film History* [*Eiga-shi*], Toyo Keizai Company, 1961), the film-makers are praised for presenting the human side of Chinese soldiers and civilians, too.

"The film turns into a hymn to the warrior spirit, as the authorities intended it. However, Yoshimura and his scriptwriter, Kogo Noda, tried to follow their consciences as much as they could. They attempted to portray the human side of Nishizumi rather than to exaggerate his heroism. In scenes where Chinese farmers are fleeing the onslaught of war, we can glimpse their somewhat weak, but consistent feelings. Also, the shots taken from behind the Chinese soldiers who are desperately blasting away at a ferocious assault by Japanese tanks are unforgettable. While short, it achieved something previously unknown in Japanese war films in that it showed us the Japanese attack from the position of the Chinese, that is, the Japanese being viewed as the enemy. Yoshimura, although working on a project tailored to the purposes of the authorities, manages to maintain his artistic integrity."

102

It is evident that leading directors like Yoshimura did not want to make simplistic agit-prop films or try to arouse hatred, since the enemy was hardly ever shown. Still, their films served the war effort by taking up the problem of how to die bravely in battle. They created a uniquely Japanese form of cinematic propaganda by treating war as a kind of spiritual training, a third characteristic of national policy films.

Training scenes were an important part of many Japanese war films and *The War at Sea from Hawaii to Malaya* was no exception. As a sixth grader, I was so impressed by its semidocumentary treatment of pilot training that a few years later I enrolled in a similar Air Cadet Pre-Training School. However, my actual experience was entirely different, and each day was filled with brutal punishment. We were subjected to repeated slaps on the face and to the torture of endless calisthenics, and the NCOs constantly hit us with staves and ropes, often for personal gratification. This kind of torment caused a strange reaction among many of the boys. At first they would proudly mutter to themselves, "You bastards can't break me!" But later they turned into pure masochists, only thinking, "Watch this! I'm going to show you what real bravery is!" The film had not only ignored the brutality of such training but also its cruel method of eliciting submission.

The War at Sea from Hawaii to Malaya was revived in the mid-1960s and was a popular success, perhaps because audiences wanted to see Japan represented as a strong nation again. Then, too, while most modern Japanese are pacifists, there is the myth that their soldiers had fought with burning, patriotic zeal since few films conveyed the actual degeneration of people through war. Yet although young people may have admired the film's sense of purpose, they also felt the monotony of the training scenes, accustomed as they are to the strong stimuli of contemporary war movies.

This monotony was very much part and parcel of *Mud and Soldiers* (*Tsuchi to Heitai*, 1939), where the battlefield itself was the training ground for the human spirit. Director Tomotaka Tasaka had actually gone to observe the fighting at the China front, and discovered that "war is mostly walking." Consequently, most of this film consists of foot soldiers marching along mud roads. Battle scenes are captured in newsreel fashion, with long shots of shells

103

exploding in the distance. The monotonous activity of marching, seen as spiritual discipline, is what is valued most. In this film Tasaka hardly even touches upon the issue of the purpose of the war. His theme is simply that within the earnest repetition of a single activity, the spirit becomes subjugated, and at this juncture one discards one's ego and discovers a way of awakening to the love of one's fellow soldiers. This aesthetic is not only seen in *Mud and Soldiers*, but also in Tasaka's *Navy* (*Kaigun,* 1943), in Keisuke Kinoshita's *Army* (*Rikugun,* 1944), as well as in most Japanese war films.

2. THE POSTWAR "CONVERSION"

The majority of Japanese film-makers, who had cooperated with the war effort, complied once more with the wishes of the Occupation forces in 1945, which ordered films with democracy as their theme. Although these films were merely typical of the transition from war-time patriotism to postwar democracy, this "conversion" still warrants further consideration. Conversion was a grave, exacting issue for scholars and men of letters, but not for directors and scriptwriters, who were not hounded during the years of Occupation censorship since responsibility for war-time cooperation lay with film company executives, many of whom were purged from the business.

One reason why directors were not held responsible is because film was a saleable commodity, true even of leftist films made from 1929 to 1931. With the better organization of the industry in the 1930s, directors were often ordered by film companies to produce commercial successes regardless of whether they agreed with the contents or not. Thus, directors had the excuse that their national policy films were made in compliance with company orders.

A second reason directors escaped scrutiny was that since movie production is a group endeavor, it is difficult to pinpoint individual responsibilities. When a group as a whole starts to move in a certain direction, it is difficult for an individual to maintain an opposing position. Moreover, when an individual changes his ideological stand with the rest of his group, his capacity for self-criticism is comparatively weakened.

Considering these two factors, the about-face by some of Japan's leading directors in the space of a few years is probably not so startling. Consider Kurosawa, who in 1945 made *Sanshiro Sugata, Part II* (*Zoku Sugata Sanshiro*), in which he depicted the victory of a Japanese judo expert over a hairy, apelike Caucasian boxer. In 1946, one year later, he made *No Regrets for Our Youth*, about a heroic champion of the antiwar movement in prewar Japan. Tadashi Imai in 1942 made *The Suicide Troops of the Watchtower* (*Boro no Kesshitai*), a stirring portrayal of Japanese security troops giving Korean partisans their just desserts, and in 1946 he made *An Enemy of the People* (*Minshu no Teki*), involving impeachment of Japan's war-time leaders. In 1942 Satsuo Yamamoto's *A Triumph of Wings* (*Tsubasa no Gaika*) praised the bravery of the Falcon fighter pilots, and in 1947 his codirected (with Fumio Kamei) *War and Peace* (*Senso to Heiwa*) was the definitive antimilitarist film. In 1944 Keisuke Kinoshita made *Army*, which, despite its sentimental emphasis on the soldier's mother, was still fascist in content. In 1946 he made *A Morning with the Osone Family* (*Osone-ke no Asa*), a tale of the trials and tribulations of a liberal family during war-time Japan.

It is important to note that the postwar democratic films were born out of such ideological vaultings and were not the products of a new group of directors. Yet despite the apparent ease of these conversions, the men concerned suffered for them psychologically, as revealed in the way they handled their conflicts in later works. Two notable victims are Kinoshita and Imai.

Initially, it seemed that Kinoshita's postwar conversion was not accompanied by any grave, psychological problems. He always did portray basically good, well-meaning people becoming victims of adverse circumstances, and this was retained even in his war films. *Army* ended with a prolonged, tearful scene in which the frantic mother picks out her son from a troop of marching soldiers and watches him for as long as possible. Kinoshita had to succumb to his penchant, even though he probably knew that it would not be viewed favorably by the censors. In *A Morning with the Osone Family* he also sympathized with the sufferings of good people, as in his films thereafter.

In *Carmen's Pure Love* (*Karumen Junjosu*, 1952), however, Kinoshita gives full vent to his bitterness by rejecting pity for the victim and attacking instead the adverse circumstances themselves, thereby disavowing his war-time compliance. *Carmen's Pure Love* was made when the Korean War was coming to an end and rearmament became an urgent, political issue in Japan, with conservatives proposing a return to the "good old days." Especially memorable is the satirical scene where the widow of a naval officer, a militaristic mama with a noticeable mustache, ecstatically sings the Japanese national anthem, *Kimigayo*, while gazing reverently upon the little Imperial Navy flag in her Shinto family altar. Kinoshita's satire was neither indirect nor clouded by innuendoes. He deals with it forcefully by choosing a well-meaning but uneducated stripper as his spokesman to attack the philistines who persecute her. By placing himself in the position of the victim, instead of pitying her, Kinoshita achieved a genuinely artistic sublimation of his resentment. However, this was not long-lasting. In *Sun and Rose* (*Taiyo to Bara*, 1956), about juvenile delinquency, and in *The Eternal Rainbow* (*Kono Ten no Niji*, 1958), about the life of factory workers at the huge Yahata Iron Works, the righteous indignation of the victim was supplanted by pity; and from then on Kinoshita's films lost their moral tension.

Despite fluctuations between pity and indignation, a strikingly consistent feature of Kinoshita's films is his attitude toward his characters: he either loves or hates them. He spares no effort in painting beautiful portraits of those he loves—sad people with good intentions. However, when his artistic spirit was at its zenith, he not only thoroughly portrayed those he loved and the circumstances that caused them anguish but also those he despised. Furthermore, during their confrontation with the "enemy" he exposes their weak points as they are defeated in the struggle. In these instances Kinoshita transcends the simple formula of "the good guys suffering at the hands of the bad guys" to touch upon the sad core of the human condition. This was most perfectly expressed in *A Japanese Tragedy* (*Nihon no Higeki*, 1953) through the mother who commits suicide when abandoned by her cold-hearted, "postwar" children, and in *The Garden of Women* (*Onna no Sono*, 1954) through two young college girls, one who goes astray and one who commits suicide as a result of the oppressive nature of their education under reactionary teachers and administrators.

106

Tadashi Imai has, since the end of the war, consistently made democratic films from a humanistic standpoint, with his successful *Blue Mountains,* a story of democratically enlightened youth, and *Until the Day We Meet Again (Mata Au Hi Made,* 1950), a lyrical treatment of an antiwar theme. Imai had been a communist in his college days, before the movement was suppressed, rejoining it after the war, and it is debatable how much conversion he needed. Being a communist had its democratic side in that, not wishing to become the boss of a clique, Imai never formed his own team of assistant directors, technicians, etc. On the other hand, it also had its negative aspect in that he often made films not to his liking so he or his crew would not be out of a job. Moreover, on the pretext that he is simply placing his skills at the service of his company, he has even made films incompatible with his own ideas, which also occurred during the war.

Regardless of the above, Imai was true to his principles. He quit after the great labor dispute at Toho studios despite the fact that he was a top-paid director, preferring to act in concert with strikers who had been fired. As a victim of the red purge that soon followed, he was unable to work at the other big studios but managed to maintain his freedom of expression by becoming a pioneer in the independent production movement just starting then. Supporting himself as a junk collector, he joined forces with the Zenshinza theatrical troupe to make democratic films, the first being *And Yet We Live (Dokkoi Ikiteiru,* 1951), a story about Japan's day laborers.

Despite Imai's independent stance in the postwar era, his ill feelings about his own responsibility in the war resulted in his putting more weight on a humanistic and democratic message than on art or entertainment. The message can take the form of questioning the misery behind the lives of basically good people, or of sympathy for unfortunate human beings. In either case the audience is moved by his sincerity. In the following films, judged to be among his best, this message is especially clear: *Echo School (Yamabiko Gakko,* 1952), the story of a young teacher and his junior high school students who stick to their ideals by studying amid poverty in their mountain village; *Here Is a Spring (Koko ni Izumi Ari,* 1955), an idealization of the postwar "culture circle," showing how its members brought Western classical music to the common people; *Darkness at Noon* (*Mahiru no Ankoku*, 1956), a film which triggered criticism of the courts and the police; and *Kiku and Isamu* (*Kiku to Isamu*, 1959), the story of two children of mixed race raised by a loving grandmother.

Imai's strength in these films lies in the credibility of his scenario, prepared by scriptwriters like Yoko Mizuki, Yasutaro Yagi, and Shin Hashimoto, who researched the relevant subjects thoroughly. Imai's characters become lovable human beings, and his films are sketches of the daily lives of people whom the audience can easily feel affection for.

At the same time, however, Imai has great difficulty in establishing an objective distance between himself and his characters. Consequently, the gang of hoodlums in *Darkness at Noon* is simply portrayed as a group of pathetic good boys; the farmers in *Rice* (*Kome*, 1957) lack much character; and the juvenile delinquents in *A Story of Pure Love* (*Junai Monogatari*, 1957) become sentimental images of pure-hearted youths. This lack of objectivity, which he shares with Kinoshita, sometimes mars the reality of his best films.

Despite this lack, both Kinoshita, in his films that are critical of society like *Carmen's Pure Love,* and Imai, in his films with a democratic message, repudiated their participation in the war effort. They vindicated themselves by saying in effect that *then* they were working against their will and *now* they are making the films they really want to. Despite the change in ideology, however, their artistic spirit did not change, since they usually made good films even "against their will," and at the core of this artistic spirit was their belief in the solidarity of a common social body.

108

After the war this belief propelled Imai and Kinoshita to portray lovable people who stuck together. In their contemporary films the adversity of war was replaced by social ills, highlighted all the more by the suffering of these essentially good people who helped and heartened each other, and thus withstood the crisis. The theme of suffering together also appeared in their antiwar movies like *A Morning with the Osone Family* and *Until the Day We Meet.* In this respect there is not much difference between the postwar genre of antiwar films and the national policy films made during the war. Perhaps the only change was replacing scenes of victory with those of defeat, and this is evident in a comparison between Imai's *The Suicide Troops of the Watchtower* and *The Tower of Lilies* (*Himeyuri no To,* 1953). In both Imai glorified a group of sympathetic, yet tragic, Japanese (the security troops and their families in Korea; the schoolgirls in Okinawa), who were under attack (by Korean partisans; by American forces) and faced total annihilation. The only difference was that in the former the Japanese army comes to their rescue, turning defeat into victory, and in the latter the schoolgirls perish. This, however, is only a change in circumstance, not in theme.

The Tower of Lilies was a commercial success, as was *The War at Sea from Hawaii to Malaya,* probably because they both extolled a sentimental love for one's own people. In this regard Kinoshita's *Twenty-four Eyes* (*Nijushi no Hitomi,* 1954) ranks as the greatest Japanese antiwar film, being a bigger box-office hit than *The Tower of Lilies,* and has probably wrung more tears out of Japanese audiences than any other postwar film. In *Army* Kinoshita had expressed the sadness of a mother seeing her son off to war through one seemingly endless scene in which he employed a sympathetic camera on a dolly. In *Twenty-four Eyes* he replaced this mother with a woman teacher seeing her former pupils off to war, and since there were more than one, the sadness therein was multiplied. *Twenty-four Eyes* warrants a more detailed treatment because it is not only a chronological account of the daily lives of the common people in Japan from the rise of militarism until the immediate postwar period but also the ultimate expression of the theme of lovable and loving people suffering together in adverse circumstances.

On April 4, 1928, a young woman teacher named Hisako Oishi arrives at the primary school in a poor fishing and farming village on Shodoshima, an island in the Inland Sea. She is on a hard teaching assignment for one year, with only one other colleague, in an isolated branch of the island school on the edge of a promontory. Arriving in Western clothes and riding a bicycle, she shocks the inhabitants. In 1928 the dress for teachers and pupils was just beginning to change from the kimono to Western-style clothes. The Japanese viewer of that generation would certainly feel a tinge of nostalgia for those "innocent" bygone days, heightened by the adorable pupils—five boys and seven girls—the twenty-four eyes of the title, in their country kimono. Their school song comes on the soundtrack then, and when played thereafter recalls this nostalgic image.

The youth and cheerfulness of the teacher quickly charm the children, who give her the nickname Miss Koishi (*o* means "big" and *ko* means "small" in Japanese). One day the children decide to play a prank on her by digging and then concealing a hole into which she falls. It backfires, however, when she breaks her Achilles tendon and, since she has to use crutches as a result, she is no longer able to commute to the school. About half a month later the children, in secret, decide to visit her boarding-house, walking along a narrow, eight-kilometer-long road. They start off well enough, but soon tears are shed and sandals broken. Eventually they see her, however, and this incident further deepens the affection between them. It even made their parents, who had been worried about their disappearance, more congenial toward this teacher whose Western ways had drawn an unpleasant reaction from them at first. A commemorative photograph is taken of this class reunion, and this, along with the school song, would become important symbols throughout the film.

Miss Oishi is transferred to the main school on the island and is separated from her twelve charges. Four years later, when they became fifth graders, however, they begin to commute to the main school and are placed in her care once again. This occurs around the time of her marriage to a seaman, and the scenes of her simple country wedding and her fortuitous reunion with her pupils are both enveloped in the overpowering joy that comes with the arrival of spring on this small island.

These two scenes of dazzling beauty, the very pictures of peace and happiness, take place midway during the film. Thereafter, tragedy sets in, beginning with one of Miss Oishi's male colleagues who is taken to the police station on suspicion of being a communist. She is filled with righteous indignation at the cowardice of all the teachers from the principal down, when no one defends him. Then one of her twelve pupils, a girl from a poor family, has to leave school to work. On the graduation trip to one of the scenic spots on the island of Shikoku, she runs into this unfortunate girl at the noodle shop where she works. Then one day, when the cherry blossoms are in full bloom, two of the boys who have graduated visit her. One is wearing a junior high school cap, and the other that of a young apprentice at a merchant house, and she is struck by their unusually formal behavior when they leave.

The above scenes suggest the social conditions of Japan in the early 1930s: the persecution of suspected leftists; the poverty; and the graveness that came with the rise of militarism. Miss Oishi quits soon after her favorite twelve have left school, one reason being that the militaristic mood gradually invades the classroom. Many of her boy students talk about enlisting in the army, and when she disagrees with them they call her a "red" behind her back. The other reason was that she wants to devote herself to the duties of a wife and mother. The year she quit, 1934, was an important one in the history of Japanese education, for it was then that the government completely suppressed the education movement for being leftist as well as liberal.

The story then jumps to 1941. Some of the twelve are among the boys marching off to war, and the Patriotic Women's Association is assembled at the island's wharf to see them off. Miss Oishi is there, too, in her housewife's apron. The boys are boarding a transport ship. Suddenly, when the band strikes up a nostalgic melody, the boys burst into tears, as does Miss Oishi.

At this point in the film most Japanese of that generation in the audience, myself included, become utterly sentimental. Still, if one coolly reconsiders what has taken place, one cannot deny that perhaps director Kinoshita is guilty of taking the easier path by keeping his heroine cooped up at home from 1934 to the end of the war. Her reasons for quitting—her pacifist reaction against militarism and her motherly concern for her own child—are understandable; yet one wonders what would have happened if she had continued teaching. I can attempt to guess from my own experiences, since I myself entered primary school in 1937.

My recollections of my teachers are not too pleasant. One woman teacher dressed me down because I had fooled around during choral practice of the nationalistic song for Empire Day (February 11). I also remember the teacher who was in charge of our preparation classes for the secondary school entrance examination. She made us learn and recite in a grave voice something about "the august virtue of His Majesty the Emperor." In short, I can't remember any primary school teachers like Miss Oishi. Even if such people had really existed then, they would probably have been forced to resign. Or, if they had continued teaching during the war, they probably would have become like the unpleasant teachers I remember.

Miss Oishi is an idealization, and as such her appeal is strong throughout the film. However, as the main character she is weak because she drops out of the picture at the most important time, when she should be questioning the responsibility of teachers for indoctrinating their pupils with war-time ideology. Conversely, by reducing her responsibility to nil, the director is able to describe the war from the passive point of view of an innocent victim and to turn *Twenty-four Eyes* into a tear-jerker.

For Miss Oishi suffering does not end with the war. The adverse circumstances continue, for since she lost her husband to the war she is a hard-pressed widow with two children to support. However, the bonds of affection between her and those of the twelve still alive remain steadfast, and one of them, now a woman teacher at the main school, gets Miss Oishi a teaching job at the little schoolhouse on the promontory again. When she steps in front of her desk to greet the new students, she finds that many of them are nephews and nieces of her former twelve pupils. Whenever she begins to talk nostalgically about their aunts and uncles she bursts into tears and as a result she is nicknamed "Miss Crybaby."

In the last scene Miss Oishi has a class reunion with the surviving seven of her former pupils. Out comes the commemorative photograph taken after her accident. When it is shown to the youth who lost his sight on the battlefield, he tries to guess the name of each kimono-clad child as he runs his fingertips over the photograph. All of a sudden the school song is heard loud and clear. During this scene there is usually not a dry eye in a Japanese audience.

Twenty-four Eyes was based on a novel written by Sakae Tsuboi in 1952, when, despite Japan's abolition of the military as a result of its defeat, a defense force was being rebuilt in order to supplement the decreasing presence of the American army which was engaged in the Korean War. At that time Japanese pacifism, or the antiwar movement, took an urgent, concrete form of opposition to rearmament, not the sentimental one depicted in the film. This is inferred by the author's epilogue to the novel.

112

"I was halfway through this novel when one day, sitting in front of my desk, I happened to remember something which made me nervous and distressed. It was a newspaper account of the prime minister making a speech before the main division of the Security Force on Etchujima. The caption below his photograph, taken from his speech, read: 'You are the foundation of the national army!'"

Instead of lamenting the fate of "innocent victims" in the war, Sakae Tsuboi was more concerned about the likelihood of future generations becoming willing victims once again. In 1952 Kinoshita himself had vigorously criticized the reactionary trend of the times with *Carmen's Pure Love;* however, in 1954, with *Twenty-four Eyes,* Kinoshita merely contented himself with a sweet, simple swan song about how good, earnest people suffered on account of a bad, oppressive government, which was so far away that it was invisible.

This is not to say that Miss Oishi was not noble and conscientious when she quit an education system that was becoming reactionary, nor that her twelve pupils were to blame for the war. Yet it is unlikely that the five of them who became soldiers maintained their childlike innocence after they went to war. Miss Oishi remembers one who perished in the battlefield as an innocent, smiling schoolboy, a particularly moving image to a Japanese audience, as if the boy had been killed in all his purity. However, it does not take much imagination to suppose that these innocent schoolboys went to their deaths fighting. One wonders how many enemy soldiers they might have killed, whether they committed any atrocities or engaged in rape or pillage. Japan had started the war—it was not a matter of us Japanese suffering at the hands of some unseen power. Yet in *Twenty-four Eyes* we are only filled with the emotion that our peaceful lives were disrupted by the war and that we lost so many pure and sincere young men. The question of how much damage we did to the enemy is neglected entirely. We only feel that we, the Japanese people, were as innocent as those adorable children and that we suffered grievously. The essential point of World War II for us, however, may be that we were indeed as brutal as our reputation, and that even those innocent children from the Inland Sea area were perhaps also brutal in battle.

113

Perhaps Kinoshita was just going along with what has long been common knowledge in the commercial film world, that is, movies belong to the people. Since people do not like to look at ugly self-portraits, their cinematic image must remain untarnished, even in antiwar films. The people are most beautiful when united together, when Miss Oishi and the twelve have their class reunions, and when they stick together in a crisis. Kinoshita, Imai, and others probably thought that if this premise were rejected, it would be impossible to make films that had a democratic message and were a popular art form, and this became one base of the postwar antiwar film. Ironically enough, during the war these same directors had portrayed as beautiful the solidarity among Japanese soldiers and civilians, had eulogized it so much that it reached the stage of spiritual cultivation.

We should not forget two other powerful and unique films Kinoshita and Imai made in which they revealed their doubts about the beautiful solidarity of the people: *A Japanese Tragedy* and *Night Drum* (*Yoru no Tsuzumi*, 1958). In *A Japanese Tragedy* Kinoshita describes society as it is, making his one truly realistic film in a social sense. Against the backdrop of history between 1948 and 1953, shown through newsreel clips, he tells the story of a poor woman who works in bars, totally unaware of politics or the significance of postwar history. (In this respect, his film was a forerunner of Shohei Imamura's *The Insect Woman* and *History of Postwar Japan as Told by a Bar Hostess* [*Nippon Sengo Shi: Madamu Omboro no Seikatsu, 1970*].) Crawling out of the shell of defeat, with two children to support, this woman strives to make a living, but when she becomes a disreputable bar waitress, her children are ashamed of her and abandon her when they grow up. Eventually she kills herself by jumping in front of an oncoming train. Here Kinoshita questions the beautiful solidarity of the basic, common social body, the family, amid the adverse circumstances of postwar Japan.

In *Night Drum* Imai turned from beautiful portrayals of solidarity in contemporary drama to a period drama about the deep rupture that occurs between a husband and wife who truly love each other. Based on Monzaemon Chikamatsu's Kabuki tragedy, *The Drum of the Waves of Horikawa*, it is the story of a samurai wife who reluctantly gives herself to a professional drummer she had

114

been taking lessons from while her husband is in Edo in the service of his lord. When he returns home and finds out about it, he wants to forgive her, but as the affair has become public gossip, this loss of honor forces him to kill her. After this, however, he faces a desolate future.

Night Drum is an implicit criticism of feudal morals and customs, such as the samurai code of honor and the system whereby all the lords and their retainers had to reside in Edo every other year, thus causing tragic rifts between husbands and wives. Under such situations even the smallest unit of social cohesion, namely between husband and wife, is difficult to sustain. Imai leaves us with the sad possibility that human beings will not always remain good in adverse circumstances.

6
The Meaning of Life in Kurosawa's Films

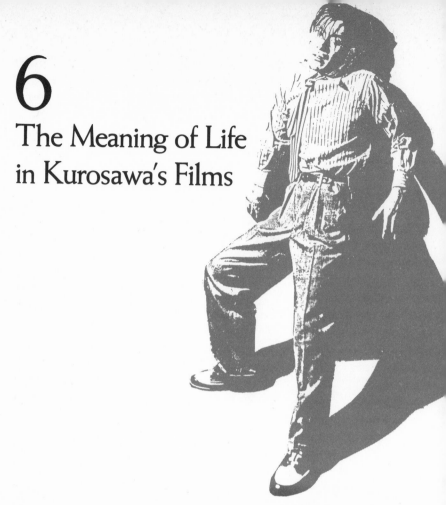

116 With defeat in World War II, many Japanese, who had made the objectives of the nation their objectives in life, were dumbfounded to find that the government had lied to them and was neither just nor dependable. During this uncertain time Akira Kurosawa, in a series of first-rate films, sustained the people by his consistent assertion that the meaning of life is not dictated by the nation but something each individual should discover for himself through suffering. *Ikiru* is the clearest expression of not only this assertion but also of the essence of Kurosawa because he used his whole range of cinematic techniques to imbue it with all the themes he felt deeply about.

Apart from the motif of suffering, which will be treated later, *Ikiru*'s four themes deal with how human beings should live in order to die contentedly, with bureaucracy's petty rivalries and its inefficiency and its irresponsibility—as well as with the obsequiousness of bureaucrats toward their superiors and their indifference to ordinary citizens—with the generation gap between parent and child, and with postwar hedonism. The film centers around the major theme—the meaning of life—while the three minor themes support its inherent tension and strengthen it by contradicting its idealism and suggesting that real life is different. However, Kurosawa gives each of the secondary themes equal attention and delineates them all with sharpness and acuity.

Take, for example, the theme concerning bureaucracy. Some housewives are shown coming to the municipal office with a petition that the sump in their neighborhood be filled and turned into a playground. They are sent from the Citizens Department to the Departments of Public Works, Parks, Antiepidemics, and so on, as one clerk after another refuses to take responsibility. Probably no other satire on public officials is as acid as this sequence, nor is any attack on bureaucracy as intense as the scenes of the wake for the main character. Here the pitiable baseness of minor officials is revealed by their self-justifications and their fawning on department heads. Still, it is not Kurosawa's intention to put down public officials or gloat over them. He is simply dealing with the meaning of life by forcefully relating how terrifyingly empty life becomes when work is performed merely out of habit.

The theme of the rupture between parent and child is treated just as powerfully in the film. An aging father, learning that he has cancer and does not have long to live wants to relate this to his son, whom he loves most, and thereby share his sorrow. His son, however, is only concerned about building a modern home on his father's retirement pension, and when the father overhears his son tell his daughter-in-law that they will live elsewhere if opposed, he realizes he cannot count on his son any longer. Without a word about his illness, the father goes to his room and recalls the childhood and youth of his son—the days when a silent but strong trust existed between them. This short sequence of flashbacks, an unabashed praise of the bonds between human beings and the inevitable sorrow therein, underlines the sudden, postwar collapse of paternal authority and the increase in households where the nuclear family is cherished above all else. Still,

Kurosawa is not simply making an emotional plea for the restoration of love between parent and child and condemning the egoism of the younger generation. Rather, he is demanding that his main character cease griping about such things and realize that he has no recourse but to rely on himself.

The treatment of the theme of frantic hedonism in *Ikiru* is no less spectacular. It is graphically and concentratedly illustrated in the sequence where the main character (played by Takashi Shimura), guided by a novelist he chanced to meet, makes the rounds of night spots to take his mind off his grief. In these successive scenes of an apparently cheap form of degeneracy, Kurosawa captures the very shape of that breathless, desperate pleasure-seeking that was an important aspect of the uncontrolled vitality of a Japan still in the process of recovery. Japanese of that generation felt that they should enjoy themselves to the utmost in order to compensate for their war-time experiences and were thus the forerunners of the so-called economic animals who challenged the world markets twenty years later.

The hedonistic sequence in *Ikiru* lasts only about ten minutes; yet it is as impressive and moving as Federico Fellini's treatment of the same motif in *La Dolce Vita*. Although Kurosawa had received liberal funds from the resurgent film industry, the number of extras at his disposal was still small compared with those in spectaculars. With extraordinary skill he created scenes with texture, conjuring up, amid packed dance halls and cabarets, the feverish atmosphere of the pursuit of pleasure. The cabaret scene where Toshiyuki Ichimura plays the piano and Takashi Shimura sings, is especially noteworthy. The rhythmic modulation of the cinematic images that accompany the music is so well done that it seems a pity Kurosawa never turned his hand to musicals.

In this sequence, however, Kurosawa is not simply depicting the mores of that era. As an expression of the main character's (and the director's) feverish attachment to life, this frenzied portrayal of the times is interwoven with the main theme of the film—the meaning of life. In this way the development of each secondary theme almost constitutes a separate and powerful film in its own right. Since these are then subordinated to the central theme concerning the problem of life and death, *Ikiru* has the overwhelming effect of a grand symphony composed of several movements. At the very start we are shown an X-ray of the main character's cancerous stomach, and the tragic nature of life is announced point-blank. In significance, this might be compared to the opening bars of Beethoven's Fifth Symphony.

In contrast to the consummate skill with which Kurosawa manages the secondary themes of *Ikiru*, his tone in expounding the film's central theme can be called somewhat paradigmatic, moralistic, even didactic. His conclusion is simply that those who sacrifice themselves and live wholeheartedly for other people and society can die content no matter how plagued by anguish. While true, it is rather embarrassing because it is so correct, and the viewer may feel like retaliating by bringing up problems in life that are not so easily settled. Kurosawa avoids such a reaction by his subtle treatment of this conclusion. From the words of a simple, vivacious girl, the main character gets an inkling that the purpose of life should be found in one's work. Thereafter, he becomes animated, like one born anew, and by completely devoting his services to the people who wanted a playground instead of a sump in their neighborhood, he lives a life above reproach during his final days and dies contented. These developments are not depicted objectively, however, but subtly, through the recollections of those who attend his wake.

If the presentation of this character, in all his acquired virtue, had been direct, the viewer might feel overawed by his nobility of purpose. However, as it is presented through the ordinary public officials who attend his wake, we can empathize with those who admit their own insignificance, wishing that they can share in his nobility. The fact that they are slightly comical because they have been drinking makes it easier for us to recognize ourselves in them, and we can hope to be like his assistant, Kimura, who vows to carry out his superior's final wishes. Consequently, *Ikiru* has a twofold conclusion: it is a powerful cry to us to emulate the virtuous life of the hero, and it is a whisper to encourage us to at least preserve a feeling of respect for the way he lived. In the breadth of this conclusion we can see Kurosawa's soft touch. He is by no means making a monotonous moral sermon; rather, the director himself is unable to make up his mind whether he is like the main character or like his assistant, Kimura, and many viewers, myself included, sympathize with his dilemma.

Both the themes and narrative style of *Ikiru* have continually recurred in his other films. The central theme of the purpose of life was taken up in, for example, *No Regrets for Our Youth*, *The Quiet Duel* (*Shizuka Naru Ketto*, 1949), *The Idiot* (*Hakuchi*, 1951), *Seven Samurai*, and *Red Beard* (*Akahige*, 1965). In my opinion its purest expression was in *No Regrets for Our Youth* and *The Idiot*, in spite of the simplicity of the former and the awkwardness of the latter.

The problem of bureaucracy appeared in *Red Beard*, where the main character, nicknamed Red Beard, is the head of a public hospital during the latter part of the nineteenth century. In the original story by Shugoro Yamamoto, Kurosawa seems to have been struck by the vision that if the main character in *Ikiru* had only lived with vigor from the start and earned a position of respect, he might have resembled that noble doctor. In *High and Low* (*Tengoku to Jigoku*, 1963) the bureaucracy shown is that of a private enterprise, not of the government. Its main character, an executive, single-handedly opposes his colleagues, who plan to make cheaper products, and stakes his own position on the policy of producing high-quality goods. He is very much the kind of character Kurosawa loves because he rejects conforming to the system and becoming impersonal. The police inspector in the film is the other side of the coin. As a man who has adapted completely to the systematized thinking of the modern police force, he becomes a terrifying, almost grotesque, bureaucrat. However, Kurosawa's most forceful criticism of bureaucracy appeared in *The Bad Sleep Well* (*Warui Yatsu Hodo Yoku Nemuru*, 1960), an impeachment of the corrupt ties between government and upper-echelon management.

120

The theme of rupture between parents and their children was shown at its most extreme in the masterpiece *Record of a Living Being* (*Ikimono no Kiroku*, 1955). Although this theme is secondary to the one of protest against annihilation in a nuclear holocaust, it managed to dominate and obscure the nuclear war theme, thereby leading many to regard the film as a failure. However, in the history of cinema, few, if any, films have presented the crisis in human relations as well as *Record of a Living Being*, and for this reason it should be given proper review and reevaluation.

Kurosawa's most vivid descriptions of the immediate postwar period were *Drunken Angel* (*Yoidore Tenshi*, 1948) and *Stray Dog*

(*Nora Inu,* 1949). The first evokes the anarchistic vitality of the black market district and the second the desolate cityscapes of occupied Tokyo. In both Kurosawa not only grasped the desolation of postwar Japan but also drew attention to the feeling of liberation from war-time oppression and frugality, thus outclassing the films of his contemporaries. As Japan recovered economically, it became difficult for Kurosawa to pursue the anarchistic and savagely vital aspect of reality in contemporary drama, and his preference for period drama deepened, particularly for those epochs when life was at its most brutal.

The dramatic narrative style of *Ikiru*—the story changing gears midway with the death of the main character and the theme pursued through the subjective views of people at his wake— had a powerful precedent in another masterpiece, *Rashomon.* Even the motif of sickness appears in many films: in *Drunken Angel* the young hoodlum has tuberculosis; in *The Quiet Duel* the young doctor inadvertently infects himself with syphilis while operating on a soldier in a combat zone; the inept lawyer in *Scandal (Sukyandaru,* 1950) is practically an alcoholic but reforms upon the death of his tubercular daughter; the main character in *The Idiot* is a schizophrenic; in *Record of a Living Being* the protagonist is a neurotic; in *High and Low* a horde of drug addicts appears; and even in a period drama like *Red Beard* doctors and patients dominate.

The sickness motif may be the result of Kurosawa's experiences during the immediate postwar era since both his first war-time films, *Sanshiro Sugata* and *The Most Beautiful,* portrayed a lively, innocent boy and girl, the epitome of health. As will become evident, this motif is closely related to his main theme concerning the meaning of life, and also has a bearing on Japan's recovery from defeat.

After World War II Japanese intellectuals, Kurosawa included, pondered the rise of militarism, and one heated topic of debate was whether militarism was the result of the weakness of the Japanese in asserting themselves as individuals and their tendency to go along with the crowd. It was agreed that individuals should build stronger egos and be more assertive, and Kurosawa, judging from the following quote concerning his intention in making *No Regrets for Our Youth* in 1946 (taken from *The Complete Works of Akira Kurosawa* [*Kurosawa Akira zensakuhinshu*], 1980), agreed. "I thought that for a new Japan to come into being, women had to have a strong ego, too, and that is why I made the main character a woman who had achieved the objectives she had set for herself." During the production of this film, however, it seems that Kurosawa's own attempt at self-assertion was hindered.

At the Toho studios he was affiliated with, the communist-led labor union had seized power and no movie could be made without their consent. Kurosawa cooperated with them, and since he himself, as many other intellectual youths around 1930, had participated in the Communist Party movement, it is not surprising that *No Regrets for Our Youth* touched upon the communist antiwar movement that lasted until 1945. In 1946, however, one of the union activists wanted to make a film based on similar material and union leaders put pressure on Kurosawa to stop working on *No Regrets for Our Youth*. Although Kurosawa opposed them and went on to make the film, he had to change the latter half of the story as a compromise.

As a result of this experience, it became clear to Kurosawa that not only militarists but powerful communists could also crush individual freedom of expression, and he was thereupon confronted with a dilemma. In Japanese society until the 1960s communists formed the nucleus of those forces that opposed mainstream society. Most films criticizing social evils were made by communists, or at least from that viewpoint, advocating that the evil of the establishment be destroyed through "the solidarity of the people." However, Kurosawa learned that free self-assertion, too, could be crushed in the process, and he began to make socially critical films that rejected "the solidarity of the people."

Since Kurosawa believed it was the individual's responsibility to criticize society, he was far from communist thought. Yet he never ceased speaking out on social problems like the terrorism of gangsters, bureaucracy, nuclear weapons, corruption in business and government, and so on. He picked a difficult road as we see in *The Bad Sleep Well*, for example, when the main character tries to fight alone against the evil of a bureaucratic structure, and thus degenerates into a shallow terrorist. In *High and Low*, too, when the police inspector tries to punish the kidnapper more out of an individual, rather than legal, sense of justice, he lapses into intolerable "heroism." In *Record of a Living Being* the plight of a man who tries to solve the nuclear weapons problem—one in which an individual solution is virtually unimaginable—proves its impossibility and leaves us with a strong, complex answer because he goes insane in the end.

If an individual tries to tackle social evils alone, he inevitably invites self-annihilation, but at the same time this has a certain beauty. This motif, appearing frequently in Kurosawa's films, is another way of saying that those who try to assert themselves forcefully should not fear their own destruction. A lack of fear of death and an acute awareness of annihilation can make one act even more effectively for justice. This is the most important requisite for a Kurosawa film hero, and it is best fulfilled by the main characters in *Ikiru* and *The Quiet Duel,* men who sought to live justly while combating grave illnesses. The sick people who appear in his other works are variations of these characters.

In Kurosawa's imagination the strength of an individual takes on the analogy of one who is fighting against grave illness. This may be eccentric and sentimental, but it reflects a necessary process through which the Japanese can recover from the shock of defeat and become independent individuals.

Kurosawa's heroes are often told by those around them that it is difficult for ordinary people to understand their special way of life, as in *No Regrets for Our Youth, Ikiru, Record of a Living Being, Red Beard,* and *Dersu Uzala.* These main characters do not try to "establish solidarity" with anyone. They decide for themselves how they should live and suffer alone from an illness that belongs only to them. They are human beings who discover the meaning of life by themselves, and who inevitably appear to others as either abnormal or sick. Herein lie Kurosawa's criticism of the Japanese tendency to toe the line and his suggestion that Japan's recovery from defeat did not have to be only an economic one.

7
The Family

1. KUROSAWA'S FATHERS

In 1942 the National Board of Information selected Kurosawa's script *All Is Quiet* (*Shizuka Nari*) as the winning entry for its annual award given to scenarios with nationalistic themes. While never made into a film, it is interesting to examine it since it reveals several characteristics of his later films, particularly, the close father-son relationship.

The hero, Keisuke Kikuchi, is a thirty-three-year-old chemist at a research institute working on processing soybean products. His father is a patriotic professor of Japanese architecture, who is especially interested in the connection between the aesthetics of the Nara temple of Horyuji and the spirit of the Japanese people. Both father and son are completely immersed in their respective pursuits.

On the day that Keisuke's conscription notice arrives, the whole family hides the tension behind a veil of calmness. The father comes home with a bottle of wine to celebrate the occasion. When Keisuke returns, father and son chat amiably as if nothing has happened. Because they are resigned to the inevitable both men remain composed, not showing the slightest surprise, for this, indeed, is the spirit of the Japanese people.

The only matter that disturbs Keisuke is not finding an appropriate replacement at the institute. For Keisuke, such a man should not only consider chemical research his duty but also his very life: "A man who is so impassioned with even such a mundane subject as soybeans that he is willing to sacrifice his life for it." He finally decides on Igarashi, a colleague who has published a treatise that embraced his own theory. The latter, however, as a result of idle gossip, is suspicious of Keisuke's motives and the two enter into a heated debate. Consequently, Keisuke spends his last night before entering the army arguing with Igarashi, after which they become close friends since they are able to confirm each other's fervor concerning the processing of soybean products.

Keisuke's love for his sister's friend, Reiko, may also have weighed on his mind, but during the war the following doctrine prevailed: Thou shalt not indulge in personal feelings. However, his mother and sister arrange a morning farewell meeting between them, cut short because of his late night with Igarashi. Reiko, therefore, resorts to playing the martial airs of Chopin's *Polonaise* to encourage him. In comment, the young Kurosawa wrote, "One can only wonder where such a brave spirit can have lain hidden in the heart of this shy, young lady."

Keisuke is seen off by his stoic mother, his tearful sister, Yoko, and Reiko, whose face is drained of color. He turns a street corner and does not look back. At around the same time, his father is giving a lecture at the university. "Those buildings idly placed here and there have no national character," he says. "They are not works of architecture, but ghostly apparitions. They are merely boxes to put people in." In contrast, the five-storied pagoda in Horyuji is an expression of the ideals of Prince Shotoku. "For more than 1,300 years, this pagoda has given silent testimony to the beauty inherent in the spirit of the Japanese people. It presents us with a classical example of the superior qualities of the Japanese. Due to its strength, it is silent to the bitter end." The students applaud.

Kurosawa, following the rules of the war-time government, managed to avoid a show of fanaticism and presented this family drama in a light, humorous vein. However, his insistence on his characters repressing all their fears about the conscription results in some unnaturalness, rendering the work superficial and mediocre. However, its portrait of the father and the love between him and his son is central to all the major works of Kurosawa.

Dr. Kikuchi, through excellence in his profession, has become a man of elevated character, always able to remain calm in a crisis. Accordingly, the son becomes devoted to his own profession and tries to be exactly like his father, aware that he is trying a little too hard.

This ideal father-son relationship of militaristic Japan appears in several other war-time films. The father in the home was a microcosm of the emperor in the nation: as the emperor was the embodiment of virtue, so each father should be a small model of virtue. This was hardly the case in reality, as often mediocre fathers took advantage of this heaven-sent authority to play the tyrant at home, alienating their children.

This ideal, thought to embody feudalistic thinking, changed swiftly after the war, when several films were made in response to the call to overthrow paternal authoritarianism. Yet Kurosawa continued to portray noble fathers, or father-substitutes, even after the war. In his first film *Sanshiro Sugata* (1943), the judo master Shogoro Yano (Denjiro Okochi) is even more unashamedly idealized than Dr. Kikuchi. By mastering the secrets of his martial art, he is able to face any crisis with tranquillity. His disciple Sanshiro lives with him in the hope of both mastering the art of judo and being morally influenced by him. Theirs is like an ideal father-son relationship where the young man is modeling himself after the old man. In Kurosawa's first film after the war, *No Regrets for Our Youth*, Denjiro Okochi plays a liberal college professor, who, on the basis of excellence in his profession, remains unperturbed in times of trouble. Although oppressed by an increasingly fascist government, he never wavers in his convictions and, after resigning his university post, lives his life in retirement. His daughter (Setsuko Hara) is so influenced by her father that she marries

126

a leader of the antiwar movement and is persecuted after his death. Kurosawa returns to the fictive father-son relationship, i.e., teacher-disciple, in *Drunken Angel*. At first it is hard to detect any higher goal in the relationship between the hard-drinking, middle-aged doctor (Takashi Shimura) and the young hoodlum (Toshiro Mifune) he is treating for tuberculosis. As a young man the doctor himself had "erred" and so he feels sorry for the young hoodlum and tries to take him under his wing in spite of resistance and threats of violence. Through his fear of death, the young man eventually succumbs to the good intentions of the doctor and begins to feel respect for him. Since they are both battling for his life, their relationship approaches that of a teacher and disciple. However, at this juncture the old gangleader returns to find that the young man has forsaken him, and in the ensuing fight the young man forfeits his life. The doctor and the young hoodlum fail in their effort to maintain a teacher-disciple relationship because while the doctor is an upright man with an honest occupation, the young man is not. Kurosawa's attitude is that human beings should refine their characters through their occupations before they can give or even receive moral training. If this process is accomplished in an orderly fashion, there is joy and happiness in Kurosawa's works. However, in the above case, Kurosawa's drama turns into tragedy.

In this respect, both *The Quiet Duel* and *Stray Dog* can be classified among Kurosawa's "joyful" dramas. In the former, the father is not given a very important role, but he and his son are both hard-working, dedicated doctors. In *Stray Dog* the fictive father-son relationship appears in the paternal affection the cool, calm veteran cop feels toward his impetuous, reckless charge. The training he gives him transcends simple guidance to include character-building. This is especially evident when the young cop finds out that the suspect he has been tracking is a former soldier like himself, and he becomes maudlin and sentimental, wondering if he would also have turned to crime in the same circumstances. The veteran invites him to his house for dinner and, over a few beers, reassures him that he and the suspect are so different in character that they are like two different species, thus renewing the rookie's determination to continue.

Ikiru, on the other hand, can be regarded as a tragedy

because the father is unable to tell his selfish son that he has cancer. Before *Ikiru,* Kurosawa portrayed people who were noble because of their devotion to their occupation. Excellence therein brought forth personal charisma, respect from their children, and/or the adoration of a worthy disciple. The main character in *Ikiru,* however, is only a mediocre official who had been rubber-stamping documents for years. No one respects him, and even his son only sees him as someone who will leave a retirement pension when he dies. For Kurosawa, this kind of man has to exert himself to the utmost in his occupation before he can really feel alive as a human being once again. A warm, touching relationship with his son is something that could have followed later if the son was not such a distasteful philistine, with whom strong ties were not necessary.

Ikiru is one of the high points in Kurosawa's career because he abandons one of his favorite conceptions—the beauty of trust between father and son, teacher and disciple—because it cannot survive in the face of bitter postwar realities and, as such, was able to create scores of incomparable images brimming with truth.

For Kurosawa the real culprit in society is none other than the dissolution of this trust as the younger generation becomes shallow and flippant. In *Ikiru,* however, he does not simply lament this condition and leave it, for what he detests most is not bringing the moral to its conclusion. In *Ikiru* his moral conclusion was that if modern youth rejects the beauty of the trust between father and son, one should cast them aside without regrets, with the consequence that work becomes the sole purpose of life.

Before cutting off his son, however, the father recalls how much he had loved him in a beautiful, emotion-packed sequence of flashbacks. He is with his grade-school son in the limousine following the hearse of his wife, and when it goes around a corner, his son cries out, "Mother has gone away!" Then he remembers turning down his brother's suggestion that he remarry, for fear of the effect on his son. There is also the time at the hospital when he bolsters his son's spirits at an impending appendectomy; and finally when he was in the stands rooting for him at a junior high school baseball game, his feelings rose and fell with his son's play.

In this sequence Kurosawa expresses the concept that a beautiful relationship between a parent and child is the most secure form of social order. Tragedy enters the picture when this is lost and a rupture occurs. The father's cancer is not *Ikiru*'s tragedy, only the trigger that forces him to realize that in reality there is no trust between his son and himself—a fact he has avoided facing previously.

When this trust is missing, human beings have to bind society with something that has a more universal meaning, e.g., work for the public welfare or common good. This is Kurosawa's tragic but profound theme. When something one loves above all else turns out to be an illusion, salvation is sought elsewhere, without rejecting this feeling of loss and in a high state of spiritual tension. At this juncture is born the nobility of tragedy.

After *Ikiru* Kurosawa made one more film on the same theme, *Record of a Living Being*. Toshiro Mifune plays the owner of a small factory who is terrified by the news of a hydrogen bomb test and starts planning to emigrate to South America. This would entail moving with his legal family and also his two mistresses and their children. His children and their families, alarmed by the possible change of life-style, refuse to go and even have him judged insane when he persists. Eventually the father really goes insane.

In comparison with *Ikiru*, a flawlessly executed film, *Record of a Living Being* is confusing and filled with inconsistencies. The primary reason for its failure lies in Kurosawa's attempt to explain the political problem of the hydrogen bomb in terms of the dissolution of the patriarchal family in Japan. Although the hydrogen bomb could be considered a family problem in the sense that the nation consists of a number of families, the wide gap between the two problems renders it difficult to treat together. The viewer begins to wonder if the father went insane because of his fear of the bomb or because he met with the opposition of all his sons when, hopelessly behind the times, he tries to brandish a paternal authority that is already lost. There is even doubt concerning the main theme: is it the bomb or the family?

It was Kurosawa's original intention to pose the question: Why don't people listen to all those warnings about the hydrogen bomb? However, his cinematic expression took the form of: Why is the powerful patriarch unable to convince his family of this terror? This merely confuses the audience, which has never

129

thought of patriarchal authority becoming an issue in such a situation.

This father-son relationship is not so obvious in the theme of *High and Low* until the last scene, when the head of a shoe company (Toshiro Mifune) meets the young kidnapper of his son for the first time in the visiting room of the prison. Mifune, through his single-minded devotion to his occupation, has become a man of high moral character. In the same face-to-face confrontations in other films, the older generation (here the company head) almost always overwhelms the younger generation (represented by the kidnapper) with his experience and personal charisma, evoking admiration. In *High and Low,* however, this does not happen, and the audience misses the refreshing feeling of similar scenes in *Sanshiro Sugata* and *Drunken Angel.*

After *High and Low* came *Red Beard* in 1965, and Toshiro Mifune, the immature confused youth in *Drunken Angel,* is cast in the role of the doctor, who is a teacher of life, and the confused youth role is taken over by Yuzo Kayama, who plays his young intern. The situation that existed in *Sanshiro Sugata* is repeated, only this time the arena is the world of medicine rather than that of judo. The doctor has the calm, composed air of days of old, seemingly saying to his intern: "Just be quiet and follow me." Youthful admiration for the teacher is restored, and the older generation ceases its fretting over the recalcitrance of youth.

All the vicissitudes in the relationship between father/teacher and son/disciple seem to converge in *Red Beard. Ikiru* represented the upswing, because the father was cornered into reviving the noble paternal image lost after the war. From *Record of a Living Being* to *Red Beard,* however, paternal authority is on the decline. It is as if the *Ikiru* father, now a noble individual, goes in search of the son who will admire him again, and when this does not happen he simply resorts to complaints, daydreaming of the past when it was possible, as in *Red Beard.*

The relationship between two persons always features importantly in Kurosawa's dramas because his main characters, usually men, need an observer of their behavior. A father behaves as a father should when his son is watching him, and vice versa. In the presence of such a son, the figure of a father acting as nobly as he can is surely one of Kurosawa's ideal images; alternatively,

130

a teacher being observed by his disciple will do just as well. This relationship is important because Kurosawa likes to portray virtuous human beings who exert moral influence, and for Kurosawa, the only way to do this is by upright conduct in the presence of another, a situation in which the entire personalities of both men are affected.

In the modern age, unfortunately, many fathers do not conduct themselves as they should at home since they are only there to relax. At work it may be different, but there it is difficult to effect the teacher-disciple relationship since social intercourse between older and younger colleagues is restricted to the job. One cannot act nobly and be concerned with the other's human development as though it were one's own. Consequently, Kurosawa came to prefer the teacher-disciple relationship in his premodern drama, where the older man was not only an intellectual mentor but also a moral one. In contemporary drama Kurosawa chose critical situations in which the father has to demonstrate the force of his personality. Ironically, however, although the modern father tries to exert the utmost influence on his son's character, it is already too late, and the best he can do is to try to live his own life beyond reproach. Kurosawa reaches this bitter conclusion in *Ikiru,* and in this film is reflected the true situation about the family and society in modern Japan.

2. OZU'S FATHERS

In contrast to Kurosawa, Yasujiro Ozu presents the dilemma of 131 a supposedly noble father who disgraces himself in front of his sons in his masterpiece *I Was Born But. . .* (*Umarete wa Mita Keredo,* 1932). Two young brothers, who have long believed their father to be faultless find out, through some home movies, that he acts like a clown at work in order to curry favor with his boss. They are indignant: "Father, you always tell us to grow up to be fine and noble, but you don't have any nobility at all, do you?" At first the father tries to calm them down, but as they are so persistent, he angrily slaps them. Later he is filled with contrition as his children have told him the truth.

In Ozu's 1933 masterpiece, *Passing Fancy,* the young son is teased at school because his widower father is flirting with a young girl and vents his anger on his father's precious *bonsai* plant. The father, after returning from the young girl's place, is enraged and sends the boy flying across the floor with a slap. The boy gets up, walks toward his seated father and, without a word, starts slapping his father across the face with all his might. The father is startled and simply stares at him in amazement. Suddenly he realizes the reason behind this and is utterly dismayed. The boy, still continuing to slap him, breaks into tears.

In his prewar films Ozu almost always portrayed this type of father, and *The Only Son* (*Hitori Musuko,* 1936) is no exception. Here the father is exposed by his own mother, rather than his children, and the comic relief present in Ozu's previous films is almost completely absent. The main character is a night school teacher in Tokyo who can barely support his wife and child. Although he had a university education, he lowers his standards during times of unemployment and becomes resigned to his lot. His mother, who had made great sacrifices to send him to college, comes to Tokyo to visit him. While outwardly acting pleased, deep down she is disappointed at her son's spinelessness. In the end she reprimands him while they are out on a walk together. The son tries to use the hard times as an excuse, but he eventually recognizes his own weakness, and his mother's bitter disappointment chills him like the cold wind blowing across the desolate area.

While Ozu's depiction of weak-willed men in these three films is poignantly real, his dethronement of the father figure casts some aspersions on the prewar patriarchal family system. According to official morality, a household called for a strict, authoritarian father and a kind, submissive mother. Although not universally upheld by all classes, nevertheless even ordinary families preferred the noble authoritative type of father. Patriarchal households were commonplace in feudal Japan, and to the extent that Japan remained feudalistic from 1868 until 1945, they were the rule then, too. However, they were seldom the theme of movies, even prewar ones.

Ozu's prewar fathers are not exactly an exception to the rule, since Japanese films seldom portrayed a strong patriarch, such as the aristocratic figure played by Burt Lancaster in *The Leopard,* or a noble type, like the Greek father in Elia Kazan's *America,*

America, who preserves the happiness of his family by his
carefully thought-out plan for all of them to gradually emigrate
to America.

Examples of patriarchal fathers appear only in period drama
or Meiji-period (1868–1912) films. In contemporary drama the
father is usually understanding and sagacious, entrusting all domestic responsibility to the mother. A lesser example of a contemporary patriarch can be found in Mikio Naruse's *Older Brother,
Younger Sister.* Although the father (Reizaburo Yamamoto) had
been a powerful construction contractor, he is now an old man
who spends most of his time fishing. Since the return of his wayward daughter he has been in a bad mood and stays away from
the house as often as possible. When he learns from his wife that
the man who got his daughter pregnant has come to visit them,
he hurries home to confront the young man in question, glaring
angrily as he presses him with questions about his responsibility
toward her. This seedy-looking old man suddenly assumes the
dignity of a boss who used to control several hundred laborers
and, as head of a fallen household, endeavors to protect the
family's honor at all costs.

Another lesser example of a contemporary patriarch is the father
in Tomu Uchida's *Theater of Life* (*Jinsei Gekijo,* 1936). The proud
household has fallen on bad times, and the only hope now is for
the son to achieve distinction in the future. In order to impress
this fact upon the son the father resorts to suicide, leaving behind
a flowery final testament.

Both these films are set in the early 1920s, and the patriarchs
are already fallen old men, not central characters. While the patriarchal family system is often referred to in Japanese movies, the
typical patriarch only appears as a nostalgic remnant of the past.
When cast in the leading role in postwar films like Miyoji Ieki's
Stepbrothers (*Ibo Kyodai,* 1957), as a tyrannical military officer, and
Keisuke Kinoshita's *Broken Drum* (*Yabure-daiko,* 1949), as a par-
venu father, he is already a shadow of his former self, a living
corpse. The typical father had already been established in Ozu's
realistic prewar films about average urban families. Robbed of
authority and deprived of firm trust and respect, his family still
prefers him to try to act like the model father.

Since reality differed so much from the model in the 1930s,

one begins to wonder what happened to the strong patriarch and even to doubt that he ever existed. Perhaps a brief examination of the sociohistorical origins of patriarchy will throw some light on this problem.

Patriarchy is a product of a feudalistic society where an individual's status and occupation depend on the household he is affiliated with. If the house fell, so did the individual. Consequently, each household member had to maintain the honor of the family name, and the ultimate responsibility for this had to rest with the head. A patriarch was also necessary because the household was regarded as a single political unit. If an individual conspired against the government, it was deemed a conspiracy by his or her entire household, and everyone was punished. Since the head or patriarch assumes most responsibility, he is given the authority to control this political unit.

In the above respects, the samurai households of feudal Japan were surely patriarchal, as were those of large landowners, upper-class merchants, and craftsmen with many apprentices. On the other hand, tenant farmers, lower-class merchants, and ordinary craftsmen did not guarantee their members any special social status or occupation. Their children were sent out to work and the best each individual could do was to make enough to live on. These people had no strong sense of family honor to be defended, and the idea that the father, as head, exhibit forceful leadership was not particularly necessary. If the mother had more fight in her, she could assume leadership, or if the father was ineffectual, the eldest son had to be aggressive. In short, everyone was happy if the whole family cooperated—an attitude similar in modern postwar families. Among ordinary people during the feudal period, it was not necessary to institutionalize a clear-cut chain of command or to observe formalities that prevented disturbances in the regulation of a household.

The new ruling class which came to power with the Meiji Restoration in 1868 and began to modernize Japan was aware that patriarchal households were securely institutionalized among former samurai, large landowners, and upper-class merchants. However, they had to admit that they had no idea what held ordinary families' households together. Therefore, they legalized the patriarchal family system (*kazoku seido*) and, through the new

134

universal education system, compelled each citizen to believe this was a virtue characteristic of Japan.

Although the Meiji rulers came from lower-ranking samurai families, they still belonged to the old elite and they were psychologically motivated to impose their morals on all social classes. They also had a political motive, since to organize all the people into tight units it was necessary to institutionalize a chain of command that extended all the way down to the ordinary household. Just as the emperor, head of the nation, compelled obedience from the citizens, so could the father as head of the household. By legally guaranteeing the patriarch some legal prerogatives, such as disowning a willful child, the Meiji leaders subjugated them and their families, instituting a chain of command from the emperor at the top to the father of common households as the lowest-ranking group leader.

This paradigm was graphically illustrated in *Stepbrothers,* when on New Year's Day the patriarch, an army officer, assembles the whole family in the yard to pay homage to the distant Imperial Palace.

Regardless of the patriarch's legal prerogatives, his authority could only be assured if it could be passed on. If his wealth or special status were not hereditary, his attendant authority lost substance. In this respect, the Meiji leaders undermined patriarchal authority, because, through their new education system, the success of youths was determined by their school entrance examinations. While parental wealth may be important to academic competition—as financial support during preparation periods, for example—its role eventually diminished rapidly.

The new education system also undermined the father's previous educational role. In the past, if the son was to inherit the father's status and occupation, his father had to give him the same training he had received. A leader, such as the boss of a group of workers in some trade, had to instill in his son the necessary bearing and ability to be a man among men. If he was too soft on his own son, he might send him to another such leader, perhaps a fictive brother he had served his own apprenticeship with, for under his friend's tutelage his son would undergo the necessary harsh training.

In contemporary times, however, regardless of the social status of the father, the son cannot become successful if he is not superior academically. Conversely, the son of a poor man can reach the top of the social ladder if he does well at school.

In this way, sons of ordinary families who went to school rarely entered their fathers' occupations, and many made academic progress precisely because they did not want to do so. It became meaningless for youths to merely obey their parents for the purpose of inheriting their status, and it became futile for fathers to raise their sons to follow in their footsteps.

The majority of modern Japanese fathers have realized this change and have begun to make friends with their children, rather than play the strict father role. Ozu's *I Was Born But. . .* can be considered the story of such a father, and Ozu was the first director to succeed in creating an artistic vehicle for this idea.

When the father in *I Was Born But. . .* loses his temper at his sons' criticism, he is already reduced to equal terms with the sons, and the father, aware of this, engages in self-deprecatory remarks. On the following morning the boys are still incensed at being slapped and decide to go on a hunger strike. The father and mother try to comfort them and get on their good side by offering them *nigiri,* rice balls, which they consent to eat. Afterward the father joins the boys as they walk to school. Soon the father's boss passes by in his car and offers him a ride to work. Now the father is placed on the horns of a dilemma, as his obsequiousness had led to the confrontation the previous night. The eldest boy surmises his difficulty and simply says, "Go ahead, father." Relieved, the father gets in the boss's car, and the boys, having learned a little about the complexity of life, continue on their way to school.

It is indisputably clear in this scene that father and sons are now equals. They are like friends who are careful not to hurt each other's feelings, quite different from the one-sided subordination found in the old patriarchal family system.

Ozu's brilliance lies in the portrayal of the gentle, mutual understanding reached between father and sons, and he is equalled only by Vittorio De Sica in *Bicycle Thieves.* However, Ozu's treatment differs from De Sica's in that his father is made to consider himself a failed parent. After the children are sound asleep the father, full of regrets over slapping them, says: "I don't want those kids to become a useless, no-good clerk like me." Here the

136

alienation of office workers may be implied, but the level of self-ridicule is too strong. Perhaps there is a psychological motivation, too, since the father is supposed to be noble, and when Ozu presumes to portray an ignoble one who has fallen to the level of his sons, he may have felt it necessary to insert the vindicating excuse that such a father considers himself to be a failure as an adult.

The change in official morality after the war can be seen in *Good Morning* (*Ohayo*, 1959), which almost appears to be a remake of *I Was Born But*. . . . Two young boys, in a protest against their father, resolve to keep silent both at home and school, instead of undertaking a hunger strike. Although in the earlier film their protest forced the adults to engage in serious self-reflection, the reason in *Good Morning* is a trivial one. Their father had upbraided them for watching too much television.

While there is a superficial resemblance to the confrontation in *I Was Born But*. . . , in reality there is no confrontation at all and peace reigns supreme. When the sons get the better of the father and he looks embarrassed, the audience feels he is secretly enjoying it, and the unique humor of *Good Morning* lies in this overlapping of the psychologies of adults and children. When the father in *I Was Born But*. . . realizes that he has lost his authority, he becomes disconcerted and disgusted with himself, and later tries hard to be at least friends with the children. In *Good Morning* the father and sons are friends and equals from the very start. The loss of paternal authority does not seem to bother this father at all, as if Ozu concluded that a father's authority is no longer necessary in a postwar home.

Before *Good Morning* Ozu had made a series of films where he depicts this breakdown of the home. In *The Munekata Sisters* (*Munekata Shimai*, 1950) the husband loses his earning power after the war but continues to put on arrogant airs. Jealous of his wife's secret infatuation with the memory of another man, he suddenly subjects her to a severe beating. He is no longer a figure of authority but a mere bully. In *Tokyo Story* (*Tokyo Monogatari*, 1953) the father loses control over his sons and daughters who live in far-away Tokyo, and although they bear him no malice, when he and his wife come to visit them, they treat him coldly. In *Early Spring* (*Soshun*, 1956) the husband loses the respect of his wife through his infidelity and the subsequent crisis. *Twilight in Tokyo* (*Tokyo*

Boshoku, 1957) is a gloomy portrayal of an aging father, whose wife runs away, and his bitter daughters.

Since Ozu had already depicted paternal authority as an illusion in the prewar masterpiece *I Was Born But. . . ,* it seems strange that he should want to do so again in his postwar films. Perhaps one reason is that Ozu gradually began to depict noble fathers and confident males after the Sino-Japanese War erupted in 1937. In making *I Was Born But. . . ,* he might have thought that paternal authority, however illusory, was still necessary. He resolves this contradiction during the war by siding with patriarchal social order in making *The Brothers and Sisters of the Toda Family* and *There Was a Father (Chichi Ariki,* 1942).

A complete denial of paternal authority can be equated with a negation of leadership or guidance. Although the fathers in *I Was Born But. . .* and *The Only Son* were made powerless by the bitter realities of society, they still functioned as heads of their families, by clinging to the ideal. Their sense of responsibility brings about pangs of conscience, and the young boys in *I Was Born But. . .* and the old mother in *The Only Son* are symbols of their guilt. The men in *The Brothers and Sisters of the Toda Family* and *There Was a Father,* however, are saved from this predicament by their devotion to the morals demanded by the state during the war, and after regaining their confidence, they lecture those in the family who do not measure up.

This factor is well illustrated in Ozu's war-time script of *The Flavor of Green Tea over Rice,* probably his most frivolous script, but instructive because it shows how nationalism can uphold some concepts of masculinity. The wife in the script is a lady of leisure with an absent-minded husband whom she considers dull and worthless. However, when his military conscription order arrives, the tables are turned. While she panics and is at a complete loss, he remains cool, calmly eating his rice dish. She then realizes how important her husband really is, and at dinner he proceeds to give her a lecture on the virtues of manhood.

As indicated in Ozu's films before 1937, when the Sino-Japanese War broke out, the fall of the Japanese patriarchal family system was not brought about by the new postwar constitution. It was rather the result of a new education system and Japan's rapid industrialization, which drew youths away from farming villages,

138

which had been the core of the old feudal society. These young
men set up households in the cities and worked diligently to give
their sons a higher education than they had received. It was the
best they could do for them because they had neither wealth nor
social status to pass on. However, despite the better education of
the generation of the 1930s, during the depression years most people
were neither able to live affluently nor support their parents in
their old age. This induced strong guilt feelings, making them
antipathetic toward filial love. This situation Ozu superbly reveals
in *The Only Son*.

The militaristic leaders of the late 1930s unconsciously replaced
the loss of paternal authority with the slogan that Japan could
become affluent by winning the war. (Men who did their duty
in war were allowed to discard their families, since respect for
the emperor was equal to respect for the father.) Thereupon, the
previous acrimonious estrangement between father and son was
replaced by a feeling of optimism, as in *The Brothers and Sisters of
the Toda Family*.

When this optimism disappeared with Japan's defeat, Ozu
plunged into a thorough investigation of the postwar family. The
members of his families seem to be asking themselves: "As we are
so estranged from each other, why do we have to be together?"
The answer Ozu gives is both simple and profound: "It's just too
sad and lonely for human beings to be alone." The pretense of
paternal authority is still maintained, however, in those films
where Setsuko Hara plays the daughter and Chishu Ryu, the
father. Listening to his lectures as though they were hard luck 139
stories, the daughter becomes more like a mother, and by giving
her this role Ozu attempts to cover up the emptiness incurred by
the father's loss of authority.

3. THE "HOME DRAMA" GENRE

The Japanese directors who were most representative of the "home
drama" (a drama genre centering around a family) were all
originally from Shochiku's old Kamata studios, for example, Ozu,
Yasujiro Shimazu, Heinosuke Gosho, and Mikio Naruse. In their
best prewar films they presented the family in a tense confrontation
with society, and this tradition continued until 1939, in Naruse's

The Whole Family Works (Hataraku Ikka) and Shimazu's *A Brother and His Younger Sister.*

The Whole Family Works concerns a poor family which can barely cope financially despite three sons who are all working to help the father, a printer. When the eldest son announces his desire to quit the factory and attend a technical school, a crisis arises. The idea of the home as a fortress to be defended in hard times eventually leads the eldest son to renounce his own wish for advancement and continue to work for the benefit of all.

In this film Naruse uses the family to comment on society, realistically depicting the tough confrontation between home and society. Although *The Whole Family Works* was based on a novel written by the proletarian author, Sunao Tokunaga, in 1939, two years after the Sino-Japanese War began, it was impossible to take up social problems like job layoffs and low wages directly, and these could only be hinted in the home drama genre, in which Naruse excelled.

In Shimazu's *A Brother and His Younger Sister,* society is represented by the rivalries in the brother's office, where a dog-eat-dog atmosphere and survival of the fittest pervade the business world. In contrast, the home is sanctified as a place of warmth and generosity, feelings that were rapidly vanishing in society. The support men receive at home is represented by the hero's young sister, who turns down a marriage proposal for fear of inciting jealousy at his office. In this dialogue between them we can feel the tension between the home and society.

140

SISTER: I'm sorry if my fears are groundless. I was just afraid that since he's the boss's nephew, they would think that the marriage concerns more people than me alone.

BROTHER: You mean your marriage would look like a ploy on my part to maintain my position at the office.

SISTER: I don't want it to be considered a ploy. Then they would look down on you at the office. That's what I was afraid of.

Just as in *The Whole Family Works,* the home is a fortress, and defending it is the duty of father and brothers, and it is up to the mothers, wives, and sisters to lend support to their sense of honor.

As Japan approached the Pacific War, however, the "sense of honor" was demanded by the state, and mothers, wives, sisters, and sweethearts smiled while they waved flags as their men went off to war. Then in 1941, with Ozu's *The Brothers and Sisters of the Toda Family*, the home, a place that fosters generous, humane sentiments, was turned into an arena for ugly, egoistic rivalry. After the death of the father, the mother and youngest daughter are placed in the care of the older sons, who have set up their own households, and the married daughters. However, as mother and sister are both regarded as financial burdens, they eventually have to seek a place of their own. At the climax of the film, the youngest son, who returns from Manchuria to attend a memorial service for his father, severely rebukes his older brothers and sisters for their selfishness.

In *I Was Born But. . .* and *The Only Son*, dramatic tension was combined with bitterness and pathos because of the men's helplessness in society and the strong moral admonishment they receive from their children or mother. Home to them was the source of the traditional sense of justice, and the worse society became, the sounder the family was. In *The Brothers and Sisters of the Toda Family*, however, Ozu does a complete turnabout, for the youngest son, who has breathed the air of the new, "sound" social order, comes home to attack the perverted, stagnant situation there.

This change in Ozu can also be seen in *There Was a Father*. The only son, after a long separation from his father, finally tells him that he wishes to live in the same area, only to be rebuked: "You shouldn't even think of such a thing; one's job or occupation should not be thought of in terms of individual feelings. Believe that your occupation has been divinely appointed and apply yourself diligently." Here it is plain that society is now above criticism. If one is dissatisfied, it should be attributed to one's own avarice and should be corrected by oneself or within one's family.

On this Ozu was joined by Tomotaka Tasaka, who directed *Mother-and-Child Grass* (*Hahako-gusa*) in the same year, 1942. The story is of a mother who, with a smiling face, welcomes her blinded son home from the war. At that time the home drama genre advocated no confrontation between home and society, with the family completely subordinate to the state, typified by the slogan: "One Hundred Million People, One Heart" (*ichioku isshin*).

After the defeat, the idea of society's demands taking priority over the home was suddenly discarded. Kinoshita, with *A Morning*

141

with the Osone Family, and Ozu, with *A Hen in the Wind* (*Kaze no Naka no Mendori,* 1948), tried to revive social criticism from the standpoint of the family, but their films did not become the mainstream of postwar home dramas. When the authority of the state crumbled, people saw its replica in the family system and so the home, too, was rejected. Neither the nation nor the household could dictate morality any more.

The next major development in the home drama genre occurred in 1949, when Ozu made *Late Spring* (*Banshun*), a sketch of the daily life of a father and daughter who reside in a small house in quiet North Kamakura. This initiated a series of Ozu films with the theme: there is no society, only the home. While family members had their own places of activity—office, school, family business—there was no tension between the outside world and the home. As a consequence, the home itself lost its source of moral strength. Ozu almost dispensed with problems at work entirely and turned to the joys and sorrows of a father over his daughter's marriage proposal, a wife's distress over her husband's infidelity, and so forth.

Thus Ozu's postwar films about happy homes tend to lack social relevance because his affluent households were isolated from the disturbing currents occurring outside it. Yet Ozu's home dramas came to occupy the mainstream of the genre and can be considered perfect expressions of "my home-ism," whereby one's family is cherished to the exclusion of everything else.

With his death in 1963, my home-ism became more a part of television home dramas than of films, and the principal audience became the housewife. With few exceptions, the majority of these dramas in the 1960s followed the same formula. The family is quite large; the father (usually played by Hisaya Morishige or So Yamamura) is understanding, while the mother is not too bright but good-natured and usually in a dither worrying about the family. The sons and daughters are slightly flippant, but as they tell their parents everything, they are never the cause of any worry. Arguments are always settled amicably, since the family has both understanding and a sense of purpose.

This kind of home drama was quite illusory on several counts:

1. The size of a Japanese family dwindled rapidly in the postwar era. Whereas in 1950 a household averaged about five mem-

bers, in 1970 it had three. Therefore, the big television families of nine or ten are almost entirely fictitious, as is the television housewife, full of vim and vigor and forever doing things for the appreciative members of her large household. In reality, the average housewife of a nuclear family living in a small apartment does not even have much housework to do. As her husband rarely comes straight home from work—he may be playing mahjong or drinking with colleagues—all she has to cling to is their child, and by being overly solicitous about its education, she has drawn the critical appellation of "education mama" (*kyoiku mama*). Perhaps these television home dramas were well received because they so totally ignored the lonely, dreary lives of modern housewives and allowed them to live momentarily in an imaginary home.

2. The number of inadequate housing areas has increased due to urban sprawl and a government housing policy that lacks overall planning and objectives. In 1970 most Japanese families lived in one 6-*tatami*-mat room (8 ft. by 12 ft.) in a wooden building. In contrast, most television families live in spacious residences conducive to an active, free and easy life-style, with plenty of guests visiting them. These families also never quarrel—for example, over which television program to watch—and if something unpleasant occurs outside the home, the afflicted family member can beat a fast retreat to his room and sulk. Meanwhile, the rest of the family can hold a meeting in another room to determine how to console their unfortunate member. Such spacious accommodation did not exist, of course, in the one-room flats of most urban families in 1970.

3. Poor housing conditions and further urbanization has led to greater mobility. Students in universities in large cities often do not return to their home towns after graduation and tend to move frequently from one tenement flat to another. In 1970 most Japanese were not settling down and building a home, and close neighborly relations were declining fast. The majority of television families, however, almost always have close relations with a family nearby, and, since both of them own their homes, they can visit each other and chat for hours. When a family squabble occurs, the other home becomes a "demilitarized zone," and children do not have to run away too far.

4. Since 1968, partly due to the influence of the one-hundredth anniversary of the Meiji Restoration, many television home dramas have become retrospectives of past generations in one family, and the genre began to glorify the past in addition to misrepresenting the present. In these "historical" home dramas all the bitter struggles between the young wife and the mother-in-law are forgotten. The young wife usually loses because, according to the old custom of marrying into her husband's household as a newcomer and stranger, she has to bear the brunt of the old patriarchal family system. Regardless of her predicament, however, television invariably transforms her into a cheerful, magnanimous person.

Despite the gloomy aspects of the old Japanese home, the wife then did have many functions to perform since, in general, there was a much closer relation between her husband's occupation and home life than there is nowadays. A wife's counsel was influential in her husband's social intercourse and general community affairs, and there were many more opportunities to invite guests to the house. It was also important for her to look after his subordinates and younger colleagues. Such a housewife, leading an active life, rich in diverse human relations, would probably have a cheerful, magnanimous personality, for her social world was much larger than the relatively small circle of relations the wife in contemporary home dramas has. Unfortunately, this positive side of the past is seldom portrayed well, and historical home dramas usually degenerate into escapism.

144

30. *Twenty-four Eyes* (*Nijushi no Hitomi*, 1954), directed by Keisuke Kinoshita. A youth (Takahiro Tamura), blinded in the war, meets his former grade school teacher (Hideko Takamine) in the most successful sentimental antiwar film; it surveys the life of the common people from the rise of militarism to the immediate postwar years (see Chapter 5).

31. *Night Drum* (*Yoru no Tsuzumi*, 1958), directed by Tadashi Imai. The adultery of this samurai wife (Ineko Arima) and its tragic consequences question the solidarity of society (see Chapter 5).

32. *Ikiru* (*Ikiru*, 1952), directed by Akira Kurosawa. A bureaucrat (Takashi Shimura) in a municipal office is dying of cancer, which leads him to search for and discover the meaning of life (see Chapter 6).

33. *No Regrets for Our Youth* (*Waga Seishun ni Kui Nashi*, 1946), directed by Akira Kurosawa. The wife (Setsuko Hara) of a prewar antimilitarist leader (Susumu Fujita) perseveres with a life of hardship after his death despite being ostracized by the villagers (see Chapter 6).

34. *Drunken Angel* (*Yoidore Tenshi*, 1948), directed by Akira Kurosawa. Freed from war-time restrictions, people live life to the fullest despite the poverty and turmoil in postwar Tokyo (see Chapter 6).

35. *Rashomon* (*Rashomon*, 1950), directed by Akira Kurosawa. This film, the first to accord sex serious treatment, presents the ambiguity of life through the subjective views of its characters (Toshiro Mifune, *left*; Machiko Kyo, *right*) (see Chapter 6).

36. *Seven Samurai* (*Shichinin no Samurai*, 1954), directed by Akira Kurosawa. In this brilliant portrayal of life in feudal Japan, samurai (Toshiro Mifune, *left*; Seiji Miyaguchi, *right*) help farmers drive away bandits; the surviving samurai are left wondering about their purpose in life (see Chapter 6).

37. *Stepbrothers* (*Ibo Kyodai*, 1957), directed by Miyoji Ieki. This officer father (Rentaro Mikuni) takes advantage of the prewar patriarchal family system to act the tyrant at home (see Chapter 7).

38. *I Was Born But. . .* (*Umarete wa Mita Keredo*, 1932), directed by Yasujiro Ozu. When two boys inadvertently witness their father's (Tatsuo Saito) obsequiousness toward his boss, the noble father image is shattered, but the father is able to make friends with them (see Chapter 7).

39. *The Only Son* (*Hitori Musuko*, 1936), directed by Yasujiro Ozu. The young father (Shin'ichi Himori), realizing his own weakness of character after a visit from his mother, talks to his wife (Yoshiko Tsubouchi) about his failure (see Chapter 7).

40. *The Proud Challenge* (*Hokori Takaki Chosen*, 1962), directed by Kinji Fuka-saku. U.S. Army Intelligence officers assume the role of the villain in this foreign policy intrigue (see Chapter 8).

41. *Death by Hanging* (*Koshikei*, 1968), directed by Nagisa Oshima. The sister (Akiko Koyama) of the Korean prisoner facing execution and a police officer (Fumio Watanabe) reenact the crime in this film, where the villain is portrayed as society itself (see Chapter 8).

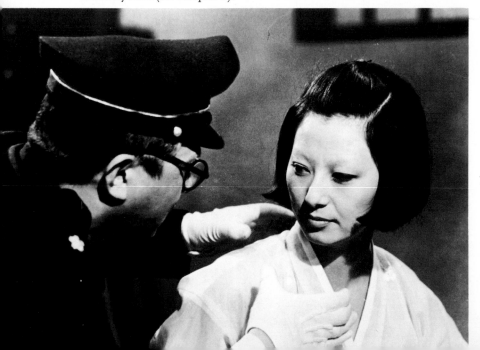

42. *The Eternal Rainbow* (*Kono Ten no Niji*, 1958), directed by Keisuke Kinoshita. The daily life of factory workers (Teiji Takahashi, *left*; Yusuke Kawazu, *right*) at a giant enterprise reveals the political apathy of Japanese workers during the postwar recovery period (see Chapter 8).

43. *The Song of the Cart* (*Niguruma no Uta*, 1959), directed by Satsuo Yamamoto. The funeral procession for the wife of the country drayman (Rentaro Mikuni, with Sachiko Hidari as the daughter) who in this film symbolizes the evil in us all (see Chapter 8).

44. *The Life of Oharu* (*Saikaku Ichidai Onna*, 1952), directed by Kenji Mizoguchi. In his use of original cinematic techniques to depict the vicissitudes in a court lady's (Kinuyo Tanaka) life, Mizoguchi achieved international renown (see Chapter 9).

45. *Tokyo Story* (*Tokyo Monogatari*, 1953), directed by Yasujiro Ozu. This scene of the elderly parents (Chishu Ryu, *left*; Chieko Higashiyama, *right*) at a hot spring resort reveals Ozu's preference for having characters in the same pose and facing the same direction (see Chapter 9).

46, 47. *Right*: Mother (*Okasan*, 1952) (Kyoko Kagawa, *left*; Eiji Okada, *right*), *below*: Lightning (*Inazuma*, 1952) (Mitsuko Miura, *left*; Hideko Takamine, *right*), both directed by Mikio Naruse. In these films the inner conflicts of the characters are glimpsed by eye movement, such as the absence of prolonged eye contact or glances filled with disgust (see Chapter 9).

48. *Children of the Atom Bomb (Genbaku no Ko,* 1952), directed by Kaneto Shindo. This story of a schoolteacher (Nobuko Otowa) returning to Hiroshima focuses on the endurance of the survivors of the A-bomb attack (see Chapter 10).

49. *Children of the Atom Bomb.* The suffering of the victims (Osamu Takizawa) of the A-bomb attack is further augmented by the prejudice they face in society (see Chapter 10).

50. *Record of a Living Being (Ikimono no Kiroku,* 1955), directed by Akira Kurosawa. Terrified by the news of a hydrogen bomb test, an old man (Toshiro Mifune) goes insane in this film depicting the bomb as a destructive psychological force (see Chapter 10).

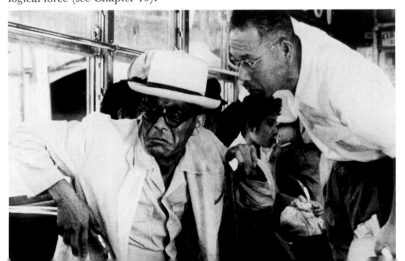

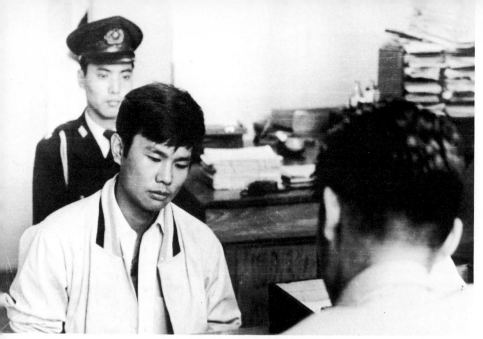

51. *Bad Boys (Furyo Shonen,* 1961), directed by Susumu Hani. This portrayal of juvenile delinquents, filmed entirely on location with an all-amateur cast, exemplified the new documentary approach to film-making (see Chapter 11).

52. *A Town of Love and Hope (Ai to Kibo no Machi,* 1959), directed by Nagisa Oshima. The bourgeois brother (Fumio Watanabe) shoots down the dove, symbol of sentimental humanism of films of the past, while his sister (Yuki Tominaga) looks on—heralding the new wave in Japanese film (see Chapter 11).

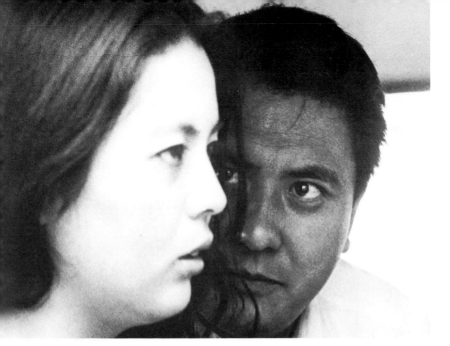

53. *Violence at Noon* (*Hakuchu no Torima*, 1966), directed by Nagisa Oshima. A rape victim (Sae Kawaguchi) and a police officer (Fumio Watanabe) pursue a rapist-murderer, who represents the sickness in society (see Chapter 11).

54. *The Insect Woman* (*Nippon Konchuki*, 1963), directed by Shohei Imamura. Out of love a daughter (Sachiko Hidari) suckles her mentally retarded father in this film where sex is associated with a childlike desire to return to the womb (see Chapter 11).

55. *Violence Elegy* (*Kenka Ereji*, 1966), directed by Seijun Suzuki. The sexually repressive 1930s propelled some youths (Yusuke Kawazu, *left*; Hideki Takahashi, *right*) to rush headlong into war and to a pathetic end (see Chapter 11).

56. *The Red Angel* (*Akai Tenshi*, 1966), directed by Yasuzo Masumura. The expression of sex as a lust for life is shown through the nurse (Ayako Wakao), who gives herself to soldiers on the battlefield (see Chapter 11).

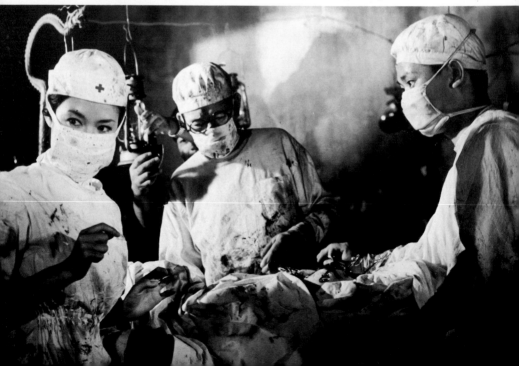

57. *It's Tough To Be a Man* (*Otoko wa Tsurai yo*, 1969), directed by Yoji Yamada. This comedy, depicting the warmth of the common people (Kiyoshi Atsumi, *left*; Sachiko Mitsumoto, *right*) living in the idealized "old" neighborhood, is the only series to remain successful in the 1970s (see Chapter 12).

58. The hero (Kiyoshi Atsumi) of this comedy series is a *tekiya*, or itinerant vendor, who sells his wares outside temples and shrines at festivals.

59. *The Call of Distant Mountains* (*Harukanaru Yama no Yobigoe*, 1980), directed by Yoji Yamada. Even in 1980 a *tateyaku*-type hero (Ken Takakura) can only confess his love for a woman indirectly, by showing affection for her son.

60. *The Four-and-a-Half-Mat Room in Back—Soft, Secret Skin* (*Yojohan Fusuma no Urabari—Shinobi Hada*, 1974), directed by Tatsumi Kumashiro. In this excellent soft-core porno, the tradition of the *nimaime*, who believe that love is the greatest joy in life, is affirmed (see Chapter 12).

61. *The Realm of the Senses* (*Ai no Korida*, 1976), directed by Nagisa Oshima. In this hard-core porno masterpiece, the tradition of the *nimaime* is maintained by presenting the hero's (Tatsuya Fuji) willingness to be killed in order to gratify the woman he loves (Eiko Matsuda) (see Chapter 12).

62. *Zigeunerweisen* (*Tsuigoineruwaizen*, 1980), directed by Seijun Suzuki. The world of the dead and the world of the living intermingle (Michiyo Okusu, *left*; Yoshio Harada, *right*), revealing the identity problems of the present generation (see Chapter 12).

63. *Kagemusha* (*Kagemusha*, 1980), directed by Akira Kurosawa. This film, in which a common man impersonates a great hero, reflects the current identity crisis of the Japanese people, which might lead eventually to positive developments (see Chapter 12).

8
The Villain

1. THE CHANGE IN HIS IMAGE

In Japanese film history there is a long tradition of films of social protest based on the vital premise that the villains are self-evident. In leftist tendency films of the late 1920s and early 1930s, evil capitalists fitted the bill, as in Yasujiro Shimazu's *The Belle* (*Reijin*, 1930). The heroine, a high school girl, is seduced by her bourgeois classmate's fiancé, who later abandons her because his fiancée's father is paying for his tuition. Pregnant, the heroine leaves school and home, and places her child in the care of her brother who lives in the country. To support herself she works in a bourgeois nightclub, where she meets her former seducer and becomes his mistress. He is now president of a company that is building golf courses, and one of his projects is to buy up land in her brother's village cheaply. The angry farmers protest, and after a riot ensues, it is disclosed that the man had paid bribe money to his father-in-law's political party. The two men are then arrested; the farmers get their land back; the heroine gives up the cabaret world of the city to raise her child in the country; and everyone lives happily ever after.

In this film the capitalists, the root of all evil, are portrayed as despicable, mean people, juxtaposed against good, honest common folk, whose anger is justified. This was a common pattern in urban melodrama then, whereas in period drama the capitalist was replaced by an evil magistrate or retainer.

When leftist films were suppressed in the 1930s, social protest films continued to be made, merely focusing on the misery of pathetic folk. Classic examples are Mizoguchi's *Osaka Elegy,* Hisatora Kumagai's *Many People* (*Sobo,* 1937), and Tomu Uchida's *Earth.* All of them are marked by the absence of a single, powerful villain. In *Osaka Elegy,* for example, several factors lead to the downfall and corruption of the heroine—her good-for-nothing father who embezzles company funds, her boss who makes her his mistress in exchange for covering up the embezzlement, the hysterical wife of the boss, her timid, irresolute boyfriend who always lets her down at the crucial moment, and her unfeeling brother whom she sees through college but who abuses her for disgracing the family. In the final analysis, there is no one who is upright and dependable in her immediate environment, and from this we infer that evil is inherent in society itself. Although this film appeared at the height of critical realism in the 1930s, it, like others of its kind, was somewhat disappointing simply because everyone was so bad that there was no point in hating anyone in particular.

162

After 1945, the villain began to make a comeback in the following films of social protest: Satsuo Yamamoto's *Street of Violence* (*Boryoku no Machi,* 1950), about mobsters who interfere in a local election and obstruct newspaper reportage; Imai's *Darkness at Noon,* concerning police officers who give suspects third-degrees in order to force confessions; and Kinoshita's *The Garden of Women,* about a women's college where the principal and dormitory head tyrannize the students. These villains are infinitely memorable because they exist in everyday life, as do their victims, and here cinema comes to the support of those who stand up against evil single-handedly. In the above films the identity of the villain is obvious, and the standard by which he is judged is more or less agreed upon. The mobsters, police officers, and school heads are all evil because they are enemies of democracy, and only by overthrowing them can democracy be saved.

This theme is echoed in films of the late 1950s and the 1960s. In Satsuo Yamamoto's *The Matsukawa Derailment Incident* (*Matsukawa Jiken,* 1961) and *The Witness Seat* (*Shonin no Isu,* 1965), and Shiro Moritani's *Head* (*Kubi,* 1968), police officers and prosecuting attorneys once again obtain false confessions through mental and physical torture. In Yamamoto's *The Human Wall* (*Ningen no Kabe,* 1959), a conscientious teacher is harassed by superiors and parents, and in his *The Great White Tower* (*Shiroi Kyoto,* 1966), the antidemocratic, feudalistic nature of a university medical department is graphically illustrated through the bribery of its doctors.

In these films the enemies of democracy are mainly within power structures like the police department, the prosecuting attorney's office, and the academic world. This attack on power structures marks an advance over prewar films, which only permitted attacks on individual capitalists. One reason why postwar directors of films of social protest did not attack individual capitalists was probably because the postwar dissolution of large cartels (*zaibatsu*) had eliminated most of them. When *Third-Class Executive* (*Santo Juyaku*) appeared in 1952, the film image of the Japanese capitalist had already changed. The term "third-class executives" is a reference to employees of large companies who took over the forcibly vacated posts of their presidents and top executives on orders from the Occupation forces. They were thus managers in name only, without any stock in the company. *Third-Class Executive* took the form of a comedy about the hardships of such a puppet company president who gets into trouble not only at his office but also in private life. So successful was it that it resulted in the famous *Company President* series (*Shacho shirizu*), some thirty films made from 1956, which were at the height of their popularity during Japan's period of rapid economic growth.

In contrast to tyrannical company presidents of pre-1945 movies, the *Company President* series' boss was a funny, likable fellow, "the old man" loved by all his employees. This trait is a reflection of actual postwar working conditions, where familial solidarity and cooperation between management and staff characterize Japanese enterprises, and are even cited as reasons for Japanese economic success. These characteristics are often explained as a tradition carried over from the past. However, from the depiction of company presidents in Japanese film, friendly management and staff relations developed through the Occupation forces, which swept away tyrannical executives of old in its effort toward democratization. The unique Japanese custom of the company president eating in the same cafeteria as the workers is, in fact, a postwar phenomenon.

Without any capitalists left to attack, film-makers turned to power structures as the enemies of democracy. In the 1960s, however, America joined the rank of villain as evidenced by an intense anti-American stance in a few films that purportedly exposed plots by the U.S. government. Kinji Fukasaku's *The Proud Challenge* (*Hokori Takaki Chosen,* 1962) dealt with CIA-type machinations, which included a deal with a Japanese enterprise to supply weapons to antirevolutionary forces in Southeast Asia. The hero, a reporter (Koji Tsuruta), is dismissed by a large newspaper during the red purge in 1950 and now leads a bohemian existence. When he gets wind of this sinister deal, however, his accumulated resentment of the establishment and of America suddenly erupts and he plunges into the investigation. However, all his witnesses are killed in front of his very eyes. In the final scene he stands alone in front of the National Diet Building, which has the sun shining in back of it. All of a sudden he takes off the sunglasses he has worn throughout and glares angrily at this symbol of the establishment. His protest is no longer that of a drop-out, it has evolved into that of a man who faces his nemesis head on.

164

Although the distinction between the good guys and the bad guys is too clear-cut, this becomes a merit rather than a shortcoming of the film. The root of all evil is American foreign policy in Asia, and the too-cooperative Japanese government. The hero is disappointed at the Japanese mass media for not taking up the struggle and, by going against this evil alone and by being ultimately defeated, he captures the audience's sympathy. Although the plot smacks of a cheap detective novel, this is not considered a flaw because of the mystery surrounding American foreign policy. Since we are all victims of the fear that our fate is being manipulated by a dark, sinister power, we can vent all our hatred on it.

Fukasaku later developed variations on this theme in *League of Gangsters* (*Gyangu Domei*, 1963) and *Wolves, Pigs and People* (*Okami to Buta to Ningen*, 1964). Here American spies are replaced by a modern gang, and a former gangster defies it either alone or with a teenage gang. However, compared with America, a modern gang as a sinister power symbol is absurdly unsuited as an object of hatred.

In Fukasaku's *yakuza* movies, the traditional gangs are just as ridiculous as the modern ones. An organized gang is usually oppressing the common people and a loner pits himself against it. The only saving grace of these films is the lone hero, who still abides by the lost virtues of chivalry and loyalty. When the hero (Koji Tsuruta) strikes a defiant pose and glares at his foe, audiences are more moved through sympathy with him than hatred for the villains.

Kei Kumai's exposé of America in *The Japanese Archipelago* (*Nihon Retto*, 1965), based on the director's own investigation of the subject, has more truth in it than *The Proud Challenge*. Kumai suggests that some murder cases during the Occupation remain unsolved because they were connected with U.S. Army Intelligence. The latter may resemble the evil capitalist of prewar leftist films but had little postwar appeal because of the friendly feelings the Japanese had for Americans after the Occupation. It is only when America shows signs of increasing military tension that the Japanese are put on their guard.

165

2. TRANSFIGURATIONS OF EVIL

Keisuke Kinoshita's *The Eternal Rainbow* reveals the everyday problems of the Japanese working people and their social consciousness, or lack of it. It is a thought-provoking movie about the life of the employees at Yahata Iron Works, one of the largest enterprises in Japan. Unlike war-time movies such as *Hot Wind* (*Neppu*, 1943, also filmed at Yahata), where increased production was urged, here the relative contentment of the employees is stressed. It does not focus on the solidarity among workers, as in postwar leftist productions, because the workers here are more conscious of the size of their company and the hierarchy of large enterprises and exploited small and medium-sized ones. In other words *The Eternal Rainbow* is a paean to big business and indirectly exposes the "double structure" of the Japanese economy—a postwar transfiguration of villainy—and also explains the political apathy and conservatism of the Japanese worker in 1958.

Like an advertisement, *The Eternal Rainbow* begins with a brief montage introducing the entire operation of the factory. The main characters then appear, in their respective places of work, and more than documenting the nature and function of their jobs, the scale of the enterprise is revealed, creating the impression that it is just like one big, happy family, or an autonomous fief.

This impression deepens when everyone returns after work to their well-furnished company housing units. Although young romance spices the plot, the majority of the characters lead uneventful lives. Everyone buys things at the company shop, eats in the company cafeteria, and listens to the company orchestra in a meeting hall. If workers get injured, they go for treatment at the company hospital. On some nights the company provides special entertainment, such as the water ballet performed by artists invited from Tokyo. Boys and girls date on such occasions and can even rendezvous at the company's House on the Hill, which resembles an artificial park. In short, all the necessities of life, and some luxuries, are provided in this little kingdom, and there is practically no reason for workers to be concerned about anything outside the company.

166 The most fortunate, apparently happy, couple to appear in this movie are an engineer and his girlfriend, a clerk in the administration building. Although they cannot complain about their jobs, they are not particularly absorbed in them either. Still, they make full use of the company's amenities and enjoy a relatively untroubled youth. Now they are talking about his future, since the company is sending him overseas. He seems to be thinking: "I could probably marry a better girl than the one I'm dating now, but then, when all is said and done, someone whose disposition you know is probably best."

All the older workers have docile expressions that seem to say: We're not really happy, but then, if you complain all the time, you'll be punished. They are not aware of any world outside

Yahata Iron Works, and they'll all work here until they retire, continuing to live in their company housing units. Things may not be perfect, but they are satisfied.

All is not bliss, of course. A new factory worker, a country boy fresh out of high school, senses that there is a barrier between the likes of him and the technicians and office personnel. His friend and mentor once proposed to, and was rejected by, an office girl. While there was not the slightest trace of ill-will or scorn, he feels that his friend's rejection was a question of social class. Although his friend was furious over the event, the boy feels that in the end he will swallow it and adapt.

There are those more discontented than the country boy and his friend, though, like the son of the foreman he is boarding with, who, as a result of illness, fails the job entrance examination to Yahata Iron Works. He wanders from job to job in small or medium-sized enterprises, but despairs when he realizes he is not getting on. Thereafter, he loafs on the job, sponges on his friends, and worries his parents. He picks a quarrel every chance he gets, not only with his parents but with the country boy. He actually envies the country boy, just because he has a job at Yahata Iron Works, and measures his own misfortune by not being able to enter its gates.

Eventually, the foreman's son goes to Tokyo and gets a job as an unskilled worker in a subcontracting company for Yahata Iron Works. While it is still a small enterprise, both he and his parents are happy because it is connected with Yahata.

It is unfortunate that *The Eternal Rainbow* makes no attempt to present an accurate picture of a large company such as Yahata Iron Works. The labor union, for instance, does not make an appearance, and the issue of the large number of temporary workers, who are paid much less, and their relationship with the union is largely ignored. In addition, the considerable increase in accidents and deaths due to poor working conditions is only dealt with superficially. However, the film should not be overlooked because it does provide us with an idea of the everyday problems of the Japanese worker of 1958 and his social consciousness.

First, it shows the tremendous gap between large enterprises, government offices, and public corporations on the one hand, and the small and medium-sized enterprises on the other. Although wages in the former are not especially high, unlike the latter there is a social security system that includes retirement pensions, housing, health care, and recreation facilities.

Second, it shows how difficult it is to move from one big enterprise to another, even if one has the necessary job qualifications. Large enterprises usually give job entrance examinations to young people, who work there until their retirement, and lifetime employment is provided for a fixed number of necessary employees. Economic fluctuations are regulated by the large number of temporary workers who can be laid off easily. Their status is actually similar to that of an employee of a small or medium-sized company since they have no company benefits.

Given the above factors, if an employee at a large enterprise, a government office, or a public corporation loses his job, he also forfeits his lifelong security; and if a young person is unable to land a job with a good company, he is more or less placed in the status of a small or medium-sized company employee, like the foreman's unfortunate son.

The above is largely a generalization and does not take into account various more complex factors, but it is sufficient to reveal an important psychological factor in the contemporary Japanese, one brought about by the large versus small enterprise, what is called the double structure of the Japanese economy.

This double structure originated with the collapse of the old bourgeoisie after the war, when bureaucratic and management posts were open to the masses. At the same time, the status of the worker and farmer was elevated, and former differences in income and education all but disappeared. This, in effect, meant that there was no longer a social class that compared with the old bourgeoisie, nor was there a class as low as the old proletariat, making the so-called middle class swell greatly.

At first glance this bears some resemblance to American society, where class consciousness and the inherent revolutionary spirit both waned. The Marxist vision of the working class becoming poorer and the bourgeoisie becoming more proletarian failed to materialize, and the white-collar class, poised between the old bourgeoisie and the proletariat, became the main social class. Advocates of a populist society correctly described this phenomenon as "mass society," or "the age of middle-class culture."

168

As in America, Japan, too, turned more conservative and lost the will to reform society through the rise in living standards, and more Japanese joined the ranks of the middle class. However, the chief reason for the waning of the revolutionary spirit among Japanese workers lies in the unique structural dichotomy of large versus small enterprises.

Immediately after the war Japanese workers, including those in large enterprises, made revolutionary demands that were respected politically. However, during the period of relative stability after the Korean War of 1950–53, it became difficult to organize workers for any reforms other than the antidismissal one. There were demonstrations against military bases and against a new act giving more power to the police force, but these represented a struggle to maintain the status quo, not to reform society. As inferred from the antidismissal fight, workers were loyal to an organized labor union that protected their jobs, not one with social reform in mind.

Eventually, Japanese workers also became loyal to the company which guaranteed their jobs. Just as job mobility between large enterprises without a salary loss was rare, conversely, these large enterprises and government offices, as a matter of policy, assured even incompetent employees a livelihood. In these circumstances it was difficult to nurture in such employees a sense of solidarity transcending the boundaries of their company, and thus the company became more important to them than their social class.

Even if workers in large enterprises get low wages, they still believe they are better off than people who work for smaller enterprises, and therefore have no wish to unite with them on common issues. This is the basis of their conservative attitude. On the other hand, it is difficult to organize workers of smaller enterprises into a powerful body because they are so scattered. They tend to be politically apathetic, too, since they are aware of the weak financial structure of their company and often will not strike for fear of bankrupting it.

As Japanese workers are so fragmented within their respective companies, they lack a unified social consciousness, with the result that there is not much of a labor movement on a national scale. This lamentable condition of the Japanese worker in 1958 was well presented in *The Eternal Rainbow*. Although some of the characters were dissatisfied, they could do nothing about it. Moreover, the basis of their dissatisfaction was more the result of occupational discrimination, that is, the prejudice against factory workers, than low wages.

The problem of occupational discrimination also appears in Kei Kumai's *Sun over the Kurobe Gorge* (*Kurobe no Taiyo*, 1968), although the strength of this film lies in its presentation of the exploitation of workers of smaller enterprises, thus revealing the villainy inherent in the "double structure" of the postwar Japanese economy.

The subject of the movie, the fourth Kurobe dam, was one of the cornerstones of Japan's rapid economic growth in the 1960s and major construction companies joined forces to build it. Through vivid flashbacks we are also shown the construction of the nearby third Kurobe dam. This was undertaken during the war, when Koreans were forced to work on the project like slaves. Now the responsibility for the most difficult task, the digging of the front line, is borne by the workers from a small subcontracting company. Even with the democratic, postwar reforms in labor conditions, their job is little different from what the Koreans had been forced to do, and even resembles the suicidal missions given to *kamikaze* pilots. At the end of the movie the names of the large number of workers who perished on the project are shown inscribed on a monument in front of the completed dam.

Kumai depicts this incident in such a way as to expose both the exploitation of smaller enterprises by large ones and the spirit of the economic animal, consistent with the double structure that results in a number of sacrifices from the ranks of small subcontractors. However, as the producer, and one of the stars, was Yujiro Ishihara, the younger brother of the novelist Shintaro Ishihara—now a politician in the ruling Liberal Democratic Party, which was committed to large-scale economic development—the project leaders, managers, and technicians are presented as heroes.

There is one scene showing the manager and the head technician deciding upon the undertaking while taking a bath together, which is not unusual in Japan. Here Kumai may have been satirizing the private way of decision-making by members of the elite. However, throughout the rest of the film he makes these two men appear as noble human beings.

170

Since the boldness of the project leaders is praised and they are not held accountable for the men who died, the sacrifices themselves inevitably become the result of a fanatical desire for economic development pursued "militaristically," and the upholding of the double structure of the Japanese economy. While it would be naive to present individual managers and technicians as amoral villains, their portrayals as sincere, upright men of principle also leaves something to be desired.

Yet, when director Kumai puts the finger of blame on the double structure of the economy rather than on the managers and technicians, he was merely pursuing the widespread belief that evil is inherent in the system. Even when those who live according to the system realize the intrusion of evil in their work and in their private lives, they defend themselves by claiming that this evil exists in their position vis-à-vis the system, e.g., as a manager in a large enterprise. Thus it became increasingly more difficult to portray evil in individuals, and this is probably why film-makers turned to those parts of the system where villainy was exposed, such as CIA-type conspiracies and police brutality, or else contented themselves with the imaginary *yakuza* world. There were even directors who stopped portraying villains altogether; one example is Tadashi Imai.

After Imai's success at depicting classical villains—brutal police officers in *Darkness at Noon*—he turned to movies with the underlying philosophy that it is not the individual who is evil but the social system, as in the following: *Rice,* about the hardships of poor farmers; *A Story of Pure Love,* concerning a victim of atomic radiation disease; *Pan Chopali (Are ga Minato no Hi Da,* 1961), dealing with the problems of Korean residents in Japan; and *The Old Women of Japan (Nippon no Obachan,* 1962), about the hardships of the elderly. Evil is discovered in the inadequacy of Japan's agricultural policy, the governments of America, South Korea, and Japan, and the social welfare system.

Imai did not attack such evils head on—perhaps to avoid being too ideological—but simply sympathized with the people who suffered from an evil beyond their control. These films may be sincere statements, but they sometimes border on masochism because Imai only magnifies suffering without showing how people can strike back. Even under the oppressive, anti-intellectual atmosphere of prewar Japan, Mizoguchi's heroine in *Osaka Elegy* rebels against her suffering by her criminal behavior.

Not all of Imai's films show the common people to be such helpless, self-effacing beings. In *Bushido—Samurai Saga* (*Bushido Zankoku Monogatari,* 1963), *A Story from Echigo* (*Echigo Tsutsuishi Oya Shirazu,* 1964), and *River without a Bridge* (*Hashi no Nai Kawa,* 1969), Imai shows people who are the very incarnation of evil and how the good people rebel against them. Since these films are set in the feudal and prewar periods, however, they lack contemporary relevance. Imai's masochistic images of the sad unfortunate are usually stronger than his depictions of evil incarnate or righteous rebellion, and even when his characters fight back, one is still left with the touching impression that they are frail, helpless beings, or pathetic victims.

This view of evil inherent in the system led to a form of resignation because the people who administered the system were shown as sincere, upright individuals (e.g., Kumai's managers and technicians in *Sun over the Kurobe Gorge*) or as pathetic victims themselves (e.g., Imai's characters). Since no one is to blame, one can only heave a sad sigh. Then, in the late 1960s, radical Japanese students abandoned this indeterminate attitude toward evil, charging that if the system was evil, so were its administrators. They refused to overlook injustices in the system called the "university," despite the administrators' claim that these injustices had existed with the founding of the universities and could not be reformed overnight. The students stuck to their logic that if the system was evil, the persons in that system should take responsibility and reform it.

172

Once these students took their stand, they were intractable. Consequently, law-abiding college professors began to look like villains, as if they themselves had evolved the evils in the universities. The tolerant, humanistic attitude of "They are not to blame because they are victims of the system themselves," was replaced by one which said, "Those who have lived comfortably in the shade of the system have to take responsibility for the evil in it."

A good cinematic expression of this attitude is Nagisa Oshima's *Death by Hanging* (*Koshikei,* 1968), a surrealistic drama about a prison execution. At first none of the people connected with the execution—the prosecutor, security officer, doctor, chaplain—appear to be villains. On the contrary, with the exception of a few undisguised authoritarian figures, their sympathies lie with the prisoner. Later, however, the prisoner does not die, even though all the steps of the execution are carried out, and the situation calls for him to be killed, although it is now evident that the real murderer is the state itself. All of a sudden, good people like the doctor and chaplain—people who have judged themselves and others solely on the basis of loyalty to the system—are put to the test concerning their responsibility for the evil therein. As a result, they disgrace themselves by panicking and becoming incoherent or by identifying with the system completely.

Death by Hanging was a new kind of social protest film that resembled the dialectical cross-examination by students of their professors on responsibility. Oshima had already touched on this in his very first film, *A Town of Love and Hope (Ai to Kibo no Machi,* 1959), in which a woman schoolteacher tries to help one of her less fortunate students to find a job in a large factory. She has made the acquaintance of the son of the entrepreneur and arranges for her student to take the entrance examination. The boy does not get the job, however, when his juvenile delinquent past is revealed. The teacher tries to explain to the entrepreneur's son, with whom she is in love, that the boy's past behavior was inevitable because of his family's poverty. He agrees but says that company rules, in other words, the system, will not permit such an excuse. At this point the teacher concludes that it is the system that has alienated her student, and those inside such a system must also be considered her enemies. She then leaves her lover for good. 173

Oshima, from the very start, did not view the system and people as two separate entities. He was not the first Japanese director to present this, however. As far back as 1952, in *Ikiru* and *The Moderns (Gendaijin)* Kurosawa and Minoru Shibuya, respectively, had stated that "The evil in the system is none other than the evil in human beings." The main character in *Ikiru* worked for over twenty years as a civil servant, and, just as the municipality, or the system, becomes unwieldy through the increase in red tape and the avoidance of responsibility, this man also becomes morally debilitated. The main character in *The Moderns,* also a civil servant, accepted bribes, and the system which inevitably encouraged graft could not help but bring about the downfall of his humanity. Still, neither Kurosawa nor Shibuya were as dialectical in their approach as Oshima.

Soon after *Death by Hanging* the evil in society and the evil in people were treated as a single, indivisible entity in Kumai's powerful *The Swarming Earth* (*Chi no Mure,* 1970), about prejudice against and among three of Japan's minority groups: resident Koreans; the victims of radiation diseases after Hiroshima and Nagasaki; and the *mikaiho buraku,* outcasts, who are now discriminated against because they come from a specific geographical area, but whose ancestors had been outcasts because their profession as leather tanners made them slaughter animals, a violation of Buddhist precepts. The main plot concerns the complications and animosities that develop when a boy from the ghetto for the radiation diseased is suspected of raping an outcast girl, and there is a subplot revolving around the guilt feelings of the doctor, possibly of outcast origins, who had made a Korean girl pregnant and abandoned her, thereby triggering her suicide. In the beginning of the film the characters from the mainstream of society seem so good and upright that one is convinced that prejudice only exists among the minority groups. However, later on, when their position as members of the majority—and the implicit double standard vis-à-vis minorities—is persistently questioned, they cannot but reveal their underlying prejudices; and these scenes form the significant crises of the drama.

In both *Death by Hanging* and *The Swarming Earth,* evil is revealed in apparently good people who break down when their position is questioned, and thus it is no longer the attribute of some archvillain who exists outside ourselves.

Compared with Oshima's and Kumai's view of villainy, that of Satsuo Yamamoto—perhaps the most representative director of the so-called socialist school—almost seems like a regression to prewar days because Yamamoto excels in the realistic portrayals of archvillains. His brilliant attack on the amoral entrepreneur in *A Public Benefactor* (*Kizudarake no Sanga,* 1964), probably the best depiction of an archvillain in postwar social protest films, adds flesh and bones to the old evil-capitalist stereotype.

In Yamamoto's first film after the war, *War and Peace* (codirected by Fumio Kamei), he depicts a gang of strike breakers, but it was censored by the Occupation authorities. He followed this

174

with other films of villains: the gangsters in *Street of Violence;* the corrupt officers of the Imperial Army Home Corps in *Vacuum Zone (Shinku Chitai,* 1952); the ruthless managers who try to break a prewar labor strike in *The Sunless Street (Taiyo no Nai Machi,* 1954); and in *Uproar over a Typhoon (Taifu Sodoki,* 1956), the local politicians who try to increase their disaster relief compensation by tearing down the school—a caricaturization resembling Gogol's *The Inspector General.* Yamamoto's list of villains includes the CIA, brutal policemen, Nobunaga Oda (a powerful sixteenth-century ruler), college professors—in short, anyone who flaunts his power, becomes a pet of the powerful, or is connected with power. In his films anyone who oppresses the people is branded a villain, presented in his most despicable aspect, and soundly beaten.

It is rare for any Japanese director to marshal such a colorful assortment of villains and to continue to portray them as interestingly, skillfully, or consistently as Yamamoto. An important characteristic of Yamamoto's films is that his villain frequently becomes a charismatic figure, for instance, the capitalist in *A Public Benefactor,* the professors who control the university medical department in *The Great White Tower,* Nobunaga Oda in *A Band of Assassins, II (Zoku Shinobi no Mono,* 1963). All of them show how captivating a force power is to human beings, and an aura of intoxication permeates their portrayal. The average leftist filmmaker tries to conceal this fact, preferring to believe that his heroes lead a revolutionary movement because of their wish to liberate the people. However, by concealing this thirst for power their films have a veneer of hypocrisy, which is why they are never as realistic as Yamamoto's films.

Yamamoto's villains are tough, energetic, and intelligent. They are men who also possess overwhelming personalities and are not to be taken lightly. This point is illustrated in *The Sunless Street* when the young female factory worker—a resolute fighter in the struggle—suddenly decides to sell herself to a brothel because she can no longer fight fair and square. The struggle is no place for niceties and the workers are not angels. If the enemy is a monster, you have to become one, too.

Yamamoto demonstrates the relationship between people and power most originally in *The Song of the Cart (Niguruma no Uta,* 1959), a chronicle of the lives of a couple in a mountain village in central Japan from about 1890 to 1945. The husband, a country drayman (Rentaro Mikuni), has worked hard since his youth, and his wife had to make a great many sacrifices. However, late in life when he gets his hands on a substantial amount of money, he takes a lazy woman in her fifties for his mistress and forces the humiliation of another woman in the same house upon his wife. The husband's vision of the good life turns out to be only this parody of happiness.

After the war Yamamoto seized every opportunity to curse and revile power and all those connected with it. However, in *The Song of the Cart,* he detaches himself from this social problem to observe the true face of the people, and comes up with this grotesque image. For Yamamoto, the people and those in power are not really two different species of human beings. The indignant attitude of the husband, when criticized by his family ("What's wrong in taking a mistress?"), is not so different from that of the entrepreneur when criticized for causing the people suffering ("What did I do wrong?"). They both have the power to do as they please.

Yamamoto's realistic portrayals of people do not imply that a "human revolution" should precede a social one, and this accounts for the appeal of his grasp of the human condition. No matter how foolish, the people must be supported; no matter how much charisma the powers that be have, they must be overthrown. The energy to denounce the powerful as villains surely comes from Yamamoto's definition of them as exploiters and oppressors.

Yet considering the transformation of the villain from the leftist films of the 1930s, Yamamoto's films seem to lack something. His villains, despite their vitality, still bear traces of the old capitalist stereotype and are thus removed from modern realities. Nowadays the responsibility for evil is borne by ambiguous figures who do not appear to be villains at first glance. In this age of the detective story, audiences need to see proof of the villains' guilt, which cannot be seen through Yamamoto's devices.

Despite the appeal of Yamamoto's films it is Nagisa Oshima who makes more representative films on the modern concept of the complexity of evil. In the beginning of Oshima's career he subscribed to the theory that delinquency is expressive behavior,

176

and he added a new dimension to Japanese crime movies because all his criminals commit such acts to express some need or drive. The college students in *Night and Fog in Japan* (*Nihon no Yoru to Kiri*, 1960) and the *ronin* and farmers who participate in a peasant uprising in *Shiro Tokisada from Amakusa* (*Amakusa Shiro Tokisada*, 1962) openly rebel against authority to fulfill certain needs, thus transforming their behavior from criminal to revolutionary. In *The Town of Love and Hope*, once the boy's behavior is labeled delinquent, he secretly decides to become a rebel. In these films Oshima regards crime as a stepping stone to revolution, and at the end of *Cruel Story of Youth* (*Seishun Zankoku Monogatari*, 1960) and *The Sun's Burial* (*Taiyo no Hakaba*, 1960), he darkly suggests that only by revolution can people realize their hopes and desires.

Pleasures of the Flesh (*Etsuraku*, 1965) is the last film in which Oshima still depicts the problem of dissatisfaction with a wretched, hopeless existence in terms that anticipate a revolution. With *Violence at Noon* (*Hakuchu no Torima*, 1966), he abandons such a simple formula, for the sex crimes of its main character transcend the bounds of social solutions and seem to be rooted in more fundamental, even diabolic, human needs.

In Oshima's later films—*A Treatise on Japanese Bawdy Song* (*Nihon Shunka-ko*, 1967), *Japanese Summer: Double Suicide* (*Muri Shinju Nihon no Natsu*, 1967), *Death by Hanging*, *Three Resurrected Drunkards* (*Kaette Kita Yopparai*, 1968), and *Diary of a Shinjuku Thief* (*Shinjuku Dorobo Nikki*, 1969)—he seems to be experimenting with the idea of a human craving for freedom that cannot be satisfied through social revolution, and he almost always repeats the despairing view that if people seek freedom, they can only become criminals. The corollary of this, however, is the hope that people ultimately cannot be domesticated, and if this is so, human beings have the potential to become anything at all.

9
Cinematic Techniques

1. MIZOGUCHI

Kenji Mizoguchi, considered a first-rate film-maker in the silent movie era, was ranked with Yasujiro Ozu and Tomu Uchida as one of the most important directors in Japan in the late 1930s and early 1940s. However, despite the acclaim, his films were also subjected to critically severe attacks, which increased in number after the war, until *The Life of Oharu* (*Saikaku Ichidai Onna*, 1952) achieved success in France.

One critic, Matsuo Kishi, dismissed Mizoguchi's Meiji-period films, in subject matter and techniques, as "hopelessly old-fashioned" (*Nihon eiga yoshiki-ko*, 1937).

"No matter where we turn we see the freedom of artistic expression being taken away from us. Mizoguchi's response to this phenomenon seems to be a return to the beauty of 'the old days.'

Since an interest in curiosities is all right, we may engross ourselves in contemplation of quaint lamps, antique porcelains, and old handwoven fabrics. Whoever visits Mizoguchi nowadays finds him absorbed in these antiquarian pleasures, and this strange devotion to meaningless trivia is so surprising that we can only say, 'Well, Mr. Mizoguchi, you do seem engrossed in old things.'

"Both *Taki no Shiraito* and *The Jimpu Group* (*Jimpuren*, 1934) [about the samurai rebellions from 1874 to 1878]. . . are admirable for their historical accuracy, but there is nothing of interest in *The Downfall of Osen* (*Orizuru Osen*, 1934) and *Oyuki the Madonna* (*Maria no Oyuki*, 1935). In these, historical authenticity is only an attempt to cover up a conspicuous lack of characterization. . . . They are uninteresting because the director has forgotten to depict the relationship between human beings and the era. The two-horse carriages trotting back and forth. . . and the paper money tossed on the *tatami* mat may be authentic, but they are not sufficient by themselves. Mizoguchi has gone too far in his addiction to . . . details."

Similarly, another critic, Tadashi Iijima, made an oblique assault on Mizoguchi's old-style cinematography in an essay on the latter's *geido mono*, films dealing with traditional Japanese arts (taken from *Gekkan bunsho*, May, 1941).

"It is already standard procedure for Mizoguchi to employ long shots in his films. Other Japanese directors do this, too, and in fact, compared with European and American movies, Japanese movies tend to consist mostly of long shots. There is even a school of thought that considers this a particular expression of the Japanese temperament, although it is by no means limited to Japan. As a rather rudimentary technique, it is common in countries producing second- and third-rate films, and the expressive power of these shots is debatable. Indeed there are many Japanese films where the use of the long shot does not differ from that in second-rate films. This cannot be said for Mizoguchi's movies, however, for in his austere depiction of the narrow world of traditional Japanese performing arts, his long shot actually serves an extremely important function, and the amount of time he spends in visual contemplation is amply justified by the nature of his subject. Yet if his artistic world is to expand, he will certainly have to shake himself loose from such old modes."

Despite these harsh words, both Kishi and Iijima regarded Mizoguchi's works highly. One critic, however, did not, and subjected Mizoguchi to a much more severe judgment. In *Film and the Modern Spirit* (*Eiga to kindai seishin*, 1947), Tadao Uryu dismisses Mizoguchi's Kabuki-like subject matter as old fashioned and his views of humanity and aesthetics as "premodern," and condemns his penchant for depicting servile geisha. According to Uryu, Mizoguchi makes no attempt to break free from feudal, anachronistic values to penetrate the essence of humanity, resting content with superficial social relations.

"As a man without a foothold in the present age, Mizoguchi immerses himself in material unrelated to the modern spirit. Furthermore, despite his choice of an intrinsically modern medium, he ultimately proves himself incapable of using it and inevitably resorts to his highly touted specialty—the long cut with the long or full shot as its center.

"By emphasizing human relations he neglects to examine Man himself, as well as evading his responsibility to analyze and criticize; this results in an inevitable plunge into the realm of emotion. When film is properly used the director designs a dynamic human structure by dissecting and then reconstituting Man. In creating such cinematic reality, he must be prepared to make bold cuts at the cost of continuity in time and place. Whether or not enough elements have been incorporated into any one scene is a false concern that should be avoided altogether."

The target of Uryu's attack was mainly Mizoguchi's war-time films on traditional performing arts, and his outspoken, critical rejection, unparalleled even today, never gained wide currency even then. Moreover, since it was written before Mizoguchi advocated women's liberation in *Women of the Night* (*Yoru no Onnatachi,* 1948) and *My Love Burns,* Uryu may have since relented.

At that time, however, it was the general feeling that while Mizoguchi's technique was a refinement of the highest order, his films were not progressive, harking back to the old, formalized aesthetics found in Kabuki and Bunraku puppet theater. Consequently, Mizoguchi's slow tempo was mistaken for an inexplicable addiction to old-fashioned sentiments and atmospherics, qualities that contemporary Japanese regard with ambivalence.

The oft-heard remark that contemporary Japanese first learned of the virtues of their cultural heritage from Westerners is totally fatuous. However, ever since the Meiji Restoration in 1868 most Japanese have felt the call to embrace "progress" and "modernism." As a result, old artistic traditions came to be seen as spiritual fetters that have to be cut off and destroyed. Although Mizoguchi's genius brought traditional aesthetic consciousness to its highest cinematic expression, he was often made a victim of this ambivalence. Revered in Japan long before his greatness was recognized in France, his apparent conservatism still irritated the Japanese film community.

After his European success with *The Life of Oharu, Ugetsu, Sansho the Bailiff,* and so on, and the recognition of the tremendous impact of Mizoguchi's film techniques on French *nouvelle vague* films, audiences in Japan abandoned the notion that he was old-fashioned. I, for one, was one of his many fans in the postwar generation, and I never missed any of his films and was deeply disappointed when *My Love Burns* did not make the top ten list. When *The Life of Oharu* premiered in Japan, I was sure that this was Mizoguchi at his best, and I saw the film over and over again. At that time the thought never occurred to me that his style was old-fashioned.

The close relationship between Mizoguchi's style and the old performing arts is apparent, and only in this limited sense can his works be called premodern. His characteristic "one scene equals one cut" technique, for example, is like the musical accompaniment in traditional dance, in Bunraku puppet theater, in Noh, and in *naniwa bushi,* popular storytelling accompanied by the samisen. Unlike the dynamic, rhythmic movements of European dance and ballet, Japanese dance emphasizes the beauty of shape, for the dancer momentarily holds a certain pose or gesture. These moments are called *kimaru* ("form resolution"), and in moving from one to the next, the body changes its balance in a smooth, flowing manner. Similarly, Mizoguchi's one scene, one cut technique is sequential motion; motion changing from one exquisite shape to another. Short cuts cannot possibly capture this subtle, relentless flow, which can only be caught by complex camera movements like panning and craning. Thus, far from being static, Mizoguchi's long one cut is filled with visual restlessness, interspersed with interludes of breathless anticipation for, even as we watch, the structure of any single scene is always in the process of dynamic transformation.

Doubtlessly, the aesthetics of Japanese dance are deeply related to the Buddhist notion of society and human life being in constant flux. Reality can never be grasped firmly, it changes from moment to moment.

The dramatic structure of *Osaka Elegy*, *The Story of the Last Chrysanthemums* (*Zangiku Monogatari*, 1939), and *The Life of Oharu* lies in this tense apprehension of reality as a constant flow. Other Japanese directors have used the same dramatic structure, but Mizoguchi is different in as much as he knew how to distill its essence —its tenaciously spiritual core—through the one scene, one cut technique. I once wrote the following about it.

"His pans and camera movements not only show the subject in the best possible light or express his point of view, but they participate in the drama by moving in such a way as to entrance the viewer. The following scene in *The Life of Oharu* is a good example. A low-ranking court attendant and bodyguard (Toshiro Mifune) is about to be beheaded for his liaison with Oharu, then lady-in-waiting (Kinuyo Tanaka). . . . There is an over-all shot of the place of execution, enclosed within a bamboo fence. Then the camera lingers on the full-length figures of Mifune, bound and kneeling, and his executioner, squatting in the background. After Mifune shouts his last words ('May there come a world where love is not a crime!'), the camera leaves his face to pan up to the executioner's sword, held aloft with water dripping off it. A tilt-up pan of the sword follows and then the camera freezes. This movement is comparable to a stroke in calligraphy, when pressure is applied at the point where the moving brush stops. It is similar to exhaling, and the camera freeze elicits this sensation. In the next instant the sword flashes down without a sound, but the camera remains immobile, staring out into space.

"Unwaveringly, the *kimaru* moment has been resolved. Later the sword moves back into the empty frame. The executioner, having finished, now holds it aloft in his left hand. The sword lingers there a moment, as if the executioner is stilling his own breathing, agitated by the execution. Then, as he slowly begins to lower it, the camera follows in a downward pan, which is the end of this long shot. In the final pan down, the camera seems to be hanging its head in profound sadness. In this manner, Mizoguchi's camera moves, stops, then moves again, thereby evoking moods as subtle and various as those produced by a Japanese dancer as she moves her arms, legs, or neck.

"A following scene features Oharu and her family, who have all been banished from the capital. It is dusk and, standing on the embankment of a river, they have just taken leave of well-wishers who have accompanied them this far, carrying lanterns. Oharu's party then begins crossing a nearby bridge and the camera, on the dry river-bed below, takes in this view at a slightly elevated angle. After they have reached the far embankment and have become tiny figures, the camera moves forward, all the way under the bridge, and begins peering up at them between the pillars.

"Until then the camera was so still that the viewer had no idea it was mounted on a rail, and its forward movement, while understated, fits the mood of this scene to perfection. . . .

"By staying motionless the camera seems to be viewing the subjects from a distance, as if to say, 'Abandon hope and depart, you unfortunate ones.' Then, appearing to relent, it stealthily creeps forward to take one last look at the exiles trudging out of sight. Although the director appeared to be cold and aloof, this single movement reveals that he has also been viewing the scene with compassion. His camera almost seems to be extending a helping hand from under the bridge, sympathizing with the fate of those human dots disappearing into the distance. The gloomy despair captured by the camera from this angle could never have been conveyed had the director used cut-backs or a following movement."

While there are advantages to this method, there is also the obvious danger of structuring a film according to a sequence of beautiful resolutions (*kimaru*), an overinvolvement with a static, superficial beauty. This was especially true in *A Picture of Madame Yuki* (*Yuki Fujin Ezu*, 1950), *Miss Oyu* (*Oyu sama*, 1951), and *Lady Musashino* (*Musashino Fujin*, 1951), where the pattern of relationships in bourgeois society are depicted as "things of fleeting beauty." The enchanting, almost precious quality of these films contrasts sharply with the merciless, grotesque realism of *Osaka Elegy*, *Women of the Night*, *My Love Burns*, and *Street of Shame* (*Akasen Chitai*, 1956), and sometimes it is hard to believe they were made by the same

183

director. Still, both types share a common theme of women suffering in a crisis, and even though they differ in content, Mizoguchi remains true to his technique of multiple pans within the framework of one scene, one cut.

The critic Tadao Uryu may have rejected this technique because it only evokes mood and emotion without treating its subject analytically. However, when Mizoguchi comes to grips with raw, contemporary realities as in *Osaka Elegy* and *Street of Shame,* it is obvious that atmospherics and emotional build-ups were not the sole objective of his technique. Although he was little concerned with beautiful shapes in these films, he still adhered to his one scene, one cut principle, with transitions using pans from one completed composition to another, a feature entirely consistent with his other works.

Even when there are movements in a single composition, as when a character enters or leaves a room, the unique length of his shot prevents jumps in time and space. This, coupled with a subject—usually a woman—in a difficult predicament, strengthens the feeling of suffocation in a hermetically sealed environment. The suffocating impression he evokes is akin to the suppressed sound of the musical accompaniment to traditional Japanese storytelling. In it lies the so-called strong beat of stoic endurance, and a good example of it can be found in the following scene from *The Story of the Last Chrysanthemums.*

The mistress has called the maid, Otoku, into the parlor to reprimand her for having designs on Kikunosuke, the adopted son of this famous family of Kabuki actors. Otoku argues that when she was seen alone with the young master, they had only been talking about his performance that night. She had been slightly critical but he had taken it well, and even seemed pleased with her honesty. Otoku insists on her innocence, but her protests only serve to increase her mistress's anger.

Mizoguchi films this long scene with a single shot in which he makes use of a number of pans. The camera, first concentrating on Otoku and the mistress, suddenly does a turnabout, taking in the adjacent room through open sliding doors, where several maids are eavesdropping. It was they who told the mistress about Otoku and the young master, and their expressions show that they are censuring her. The camera then does another turnabout, and

184

our attention is again riveted on Otoku and the mistress.

The unbroken flow of Mizoguchi's one shot method—active even within the narrow confines of the two rooms—conveys the hostility between Otoku and the other maids, and their positions—she has her back to them—shows us their psychological relationship. Thus Mizoguchi is able to show us *all* the characters involved.

As Otoku defends herself to the mistress, she is, at the same time, vindicating herself to the maids in the background. Since she cannot see their faces, however, she cannot react to them but only clarifies her own thoughts as she speaks. Thus, the camera concentrates on Otoku and seldom cuts back and forth between her and the other maids. Any slight change of attitude is sufficiently revealed in Otoku's facial expression, or in a positional shift in her relation to the others, and their reaction is also shown thereby.

Mizoguchi constantly changes the positions of his characters, having them move around in the frame of his single long shot. He keeps constant track of his heroine's subjective development, since any positional change reflects a change in her attitude or behavior. While the positions are in constant flux, the oppression in the feudalistic household remains the same, without a letup.

Mizoguchi's art is an expression of endurance and continuing protest against relentless oppression. In this he has much in common with traditional Japanese storytelling like Noh and *naniwa bushi*, in which heavy oppression and suffering were formalized into art. However, these formulas could not express the vitality of individuals, a vitality that Mizoguchi manages to convey by portraying people who assert themselves in the face of oppression, be it social or sexual. Mizoguchi's art lies in transforming heavy (oppressive) external conditions into heavy (strong) internal spirit. He was one artist who, through his assertion of the individual's will, was able to modernize this tradition from the inside.

185

2. OZU

Of all Japanese directors, Yasujiro Ozu has been considered the most Japanese, to the extent that his films were not even entered in international film festivals until near the end of his career. His forte was a detailed, sensitive portrayal of the daily lives of average or poor people—what the American film critic Donald Richie calls *shomin geki* ("dramas about common people") and considers a unique Japanese film genre. As mentioned in Chapter Two, however, the American films about average people made in the 1910s and 1920s had a strong influence on Ozu. When these richly emotional portrayals of simple folk in American cinema gave way to more glamorous productions in the 1930s, Ozu stuck to the content and forms he learned from America and refined them. By then he was able to imbue them with truly Japanese sentiments, and his formal beauty of style managed to transcend national boundaries.

Ozu almost always used the contemporary Japanese home as his theme: the love between parent and child, the reconciliation between husband and wife, or the mischief of children. On the surface he presents a modern Japanese life-style, which to those unfamiliar with it could be boring. Since swordfighting movies are both more appealing and more entertaining to foreign audiences, it is only natural that the first Japanese films to be internationally recognized were Kurosawa's period dramas.

Yet an Ozu film, with its brilliant use of cinematography, is never a simple, haphazard presentation of Japanese customs. It is through Ozu's superb cinematic technique that the humor and sense of order and tension inherent in the skillfully conceived forms can be understood cross-culturally. It is the distinctiveness of Ozu's style that makes it rare even outside Japan, a style that was polished in the course of his long career. Perhaps it is best to list here the features that make up his style.

186

The Low Angle Shot. Ozu positions his camera just above the floor or ground—at most two feet or so in height—and shoots his scenes from a slightly elevated angle hardly noticeable if one is sitting on *tatami* mats in a Japanese room. His camera never looks down on people, except for certain shots of a road from a window. Early in his career he used to shoot a bird's-eye view of things placed on *tatami* mats, but he gradually came to avoid such shots.

Ozu never explained the reason for this penchant. Perhaps he thought human beings were more dignified when viewed from a slightly elevated angle, or perhaps this showed the interiors of Japanese houses at their most calm and beautiful. Once he settled on this camera angle for the underlying tone of his shot compositions, shots from above probably would have been disturbing, and he improvised with props in order to maintain this uniformity.

The Stationary Camera. Ozu hardly ever resorts to a crane to move his camera up and down, or a dolly. The few times he does this he is careful to avoid any changes within the composition. For example, he has the actors walk at a steady pace in front of a fixed background like a moat or a wall, and he has the dolly pushed in a straight line at exactly the same speed, thus maintaining his shot composition. In the scene in *Early Summer* where the two actresses are walking down a sand dune, he used a rare crane shot in order not to lose them.

The Arrangement of Characters. When two or more characters appear in the same shot, they are often facing the same direction and assuming the same pose. When sitting on *tatami* mats, they may even lean forward at almost precisely the same angle. If two people are fishing along a river bank, everything from the angle of their fishing rods to the raising and lowering of the rods is the same. They have become analogous figures within the same shot. Even in situations which presuppose a face-to-face arrangement, such as a conversation, Ozu prefers to have the characters facing the same direction, lined along office desks, or sitting side by side in front of a Japanese garden.

The following is an example from *The Only Son.* The son, depressed that his mother came all the way to Tokyo to see him in his shabby state, talks things over with his wife, who is gazing at him tenderly. Considering the gravity of their conversation, the actors could not face the same direction and nod in unison. The husband is sitting in the left foreground facing right, and the wife is in the right background, facing the camera. Despite this unanalogous set up, when the wife is deep in thought during their conversation, she inclines her head to the right, and thus her figure becomes analogous with that of her husband, who is crouched slightly to the right. Ozu used to direct his actors' movements to the centimeter, so it is certain that during this scene he must have indicated the exact angle the wife had to incline her head.

Ozu's arrangement of characters as analogous figures might be

187

motivated by the rejection of confrontation and the creation of a harmonious world where two or more people share such similar feelings they are almost like one body.

The Avoidance of Movement. Ozu avoided violent action in his scenes, and the only exceptions are the husband knocking his wife down the staircase in *A Hen in the Wind* and the husband beating his wife in *The Munekata Sisters.* Not only did Ozu prohibit his players from aggressive behavior but he also restricted their movement. They hardly ever walk across a shot, and if they do, it is only in the distance. He prefers shots from a stationary camera in the middle of a long corridor where the figure is only seen in the center one-third, flanked on either side by a wall. Moreover, when characters enter the frame, he never has them come in suddenly from the side, but usually straight toward the viewer from the opposite end of a corridor. When leaving they often go behind the sliding door panels (*fusuma*) of the next room.

In the daily life of the Japanese, there are many occasions when people just sit on the *tatami*-matted floor and hardly move at all. In order to present such immobility appealingly, one has to detail slight changes in facial expression and hand movements. This concern may have led Ozu to restrict insignificant movements that will only distract the viewer's attention.

The Full-Face Shot of the Speaker. Ozu's aversion to having his characters walk across the foreground of a frame may also be
188 related to a desire to minimize profile shots as much as possible. He likes to have his players seated together looking in one direction, in profile or three-quarters profile, but when a character delivers a line, Ozu brings the camera around so he or she faces it almost head on (the actor gazes just to the side of the lens). Thus, profile shots of a character delivering a line are exceedingly rare in an Ozu film. In a conversation between two people facing each other, Ozu changes his camera position each time the speaker changes. Ozu did not use the usual method of inserting shots from the side at appropriate intervals, preferring not to emphasize confrontation.

In conversations where the two people are not face to face, Ozu often has them paired off vertically in the foreground and background of the frame—the speaker looking at the camera, the other to the side. When they are sitting together facing the same direction, the one about to speak has to turn and face the other each time, and the camera moves around for a full-face shot. Thus when people talk they are habitually filmed from the position of someone listening attentively to them, and hardly ever from the side or back. This, together with the low camera angle that never looks down on its subject, is Ozu's trademark, not simply a matter of form but of courteous respect for human beings.

In order to take these alternating full-face shots of two people conversing face to face, however, the camera has to be turned to the opposite direction each time the speaker changes. In the terminology of Japanese film studios this is called *donden*, meaning "a sudden reverse," and most directors are hesitant about using it because it can confuse the viewer. They would shoot one party from the front at a left oblique angle and the other at a right oblique angle, linking the shots by alternating the position of the camera so that the camera eye intersects a hypothetical cross. Although Ozu was told by studio personnel that the *donden* technique confused the directions of the gaze of the two actors, Ozu remained indifferent.

The Stability of the Size of Camera Shots. Even at the risk of going against professional theory, Ozu was always more concerned with making each shot a beautiful composition than with continuity, a factor reflected in his determination of the size of shots. With the exception of some extremely early films, Ozu never took close-ups, probably because they are unsettling no matter how well done, and, apparently for the same reason, he never used telescopic and wide-angle lenses. The basic sizes of his camera shots are: distant view, full standing figure from the waist up, full seated figure, and head and shoulders (the closest his camera ever moved in). If there were as many as five characters in an intended shot, he would move his camera back to include all five.

The above rules may seem simple, but it is exceedingly difficult to adhere to them, especially when filming people sitting on *tatami* mats in a Japanese room. If they are shot full figure and one of them stands up, he or she would probably be partially out of the frame. To avoid this ungainly image, Ozu would pull his camera back to include the standing person in the frame. No other director was as rigorous as Ozu in this, not only because of the tediousness of the operation but also because if the seated person is the lead, it is considered a mistake to reduce the frame size to accommodate the movement of a less important role. The following is an example from a scene in *Early Spring*.

At a dinner party an office girl is criticized by her friends for flirting with one of them who is a married man. Indignant, she suddenly rises, and the camera quickly withdraws to take in her standing figure. When a player becomes agitated, it is more common to move the camera in on her; however, Ozu's camera movement is just the reverse since he dislikes fragmenting the frame size and/or showing violent movements in the foreground.

Linking by Means of Cutting Alone. With the exception of *The Life of an Office Worker* (*Kaisha-in Seikatsu,* 1929), Ozu never used a dissolve to link shots in his films, probably because of the resulting disruption, even for a few seconds, to his carefully worked out composition. He eventually even abandoned fade-ins and fade-outs, which he had used in his early talkies. Ozu was thus well ahead of his time; for although they are now considered old fashioned, there used to be an established, worldwide rule to use them between sequences even through the 1950s.

Curtain Shots. This term was probably first used by the prewar film critic Keinosuke Nanbu. In place of fade-ins and fade-outs between sequences, Ozu always inserts a number of shots of scenery, which Nanbu compared to the curtain in Western theater. These shots both present the environment of the next sequence and stimulate the viewer's anticipation—be it the big red paper lantern of a neighborhood bar or the curved line of a small hill near a residential area. When Ozu's films are shown on Japanese television, these curtain shots are usually cut, a pity since they are indispensable for regulating the overall tone of an Ozu film.

190

Tempo. The sets for an Ozu film are always carefully constructed to match the tempo of the performance. Tomo Shimogawara, the set designer for *The End of Summer* (*Kohayagawa-ke no Aki,* 1961), relates the following in *Yasujiro Ozu: The Man and His Work* (*Ozu*

Yasujiro—Hito to Shigoto, by Jun Satomi, Tomo Shimogawara, Shizuo Yamauchi, et al., Tokyo: Banyusha, 1972).

"The size of the rooms was dictated by the time lapses between the actor's movements. If one party gets up to walk somewhere, there has to be the right number of *tatami* mats to last while shots of the other party are inserted. Thus. . . Ozu would give me instructions on the exact length of the corridor. He explained that it was part and parcel of the tempo of his film, and this flow of tempo Ozu envisioned at the time the script was being written. When the set was being constructed he would go through the floor plan in great detail, thereby creating precise pictorial continuity.

"If two people are in conversation and one goes to call someone from the second floor, the other left in the room is allotted that much time. Since Ozu never used wipes or dissolves, and for the sake of dramatic tempo as well, he would measure the number of seconds it took someone to walk upstairs and so the set had to be constructed accordingly."

Since a movie consists of fragmentary shots, if the interval between them is shortened, the speed of the performance is increased so that it is faster than actual human behavior, which does not disturb the viewer. When an actor gets up to leave a room, the walk down the corridor can even be omitted with the following shot showing him already in, say, the hall. This is said to actually produce a faster tempo.

Ozu, on the other hand, dislikes this speeding up process in consecutive scenes, perhaps because he wants to reproduce the pace of daily life without recourse to editing techniques. Of course, his tempo is an aesthetically contrived one, with no trivial distractions and a splendid rhythm added. In contrast to so-called cinematic tempo, it is a creation in which time is beautifully apprehended in conformity with the physiology of daily occurrences.

191

Choreographic Acting Directions. In contrast, say, to a Mizoguchi or Kurosawa film with impassioned performances, Ozu's characters are usually calm, taking their time and delivering their lines with a slight smile. They not only move at the same pace but also speak at the same measured rate. When Hisaya Morishige, an actor with fast movements and a rapid delivery, appeared in *The End of Summer,* Ozu was reputedly irritated because the actor did not follow his tempo, and after filming each scene, Ozu would say ironically: "Yes, well done, well done. Now please give Mr. Morishige *our* script."

Ozu made all his actors and actresses follow his tempo, and they were given explicit directions, such as "walk over there for three seconds and stop." For one scene in *A Mother Should Be Loved* (*Haha o Kowazu-ya*, 1934) it seems Ozu instructed actress Mitsuko Yoshikawa to stir her tea with a spoon two and a half times and then turn her head to the left. It eventually took about twenty-four hours of shooting time, and when she asked what was wrong, Ozu answered that her glance had to coincide with the turn, and that it was no good if either was ahead of the other.

Ozu manipulated his players like puppets but he created scenes of incomparable, formal beauty, though they lacked in vitality. Shohei Imamura, Ozu's assistant, criticized him for robbing his actresses and actors of their liveliness and naturalness, and resigned. Another director, Kozaburo Yoshimura, once said to me that I had not included in my book on Ozu his remark that the characters in Ozu's films were like vegetables. Ozu himself used to say, "I'm not a dynamic director like Akira Kurosawa."

Considering the overall purpose of Ozu's cinematic style it can be said that he wanted to make perfect still-life paintings on film. Ozu shot each scene in its most settled mood, within the most stable frame, charged with internal tension but linked on the surface by the most tranquil of sentiments. Film is said to be an art of motion, however, and although all large movements and dynamic sequences are suppressed in Ozu's films, they are never a collection of still photographs or cold geometric figures. Rather, as a consequence of this extreme suppression, or in spite of it, viewers concentrate more on what movement there is.

This is no mean feat because generally films lacking in action bore people, even if they are beautiful to look at. Ozu, however, captivated Japanese audiences for more than thirty years through his original style, where slight movements were packed with considerable beauty, and the beauty in turn was steeped in meaning.

The drama centering around the home is probably the genre best suited to Ozu, who worked in it throughout his career. His style is easily distinguished by the similarity of situation, sets, and scenery, and even the actresses and actors featured. Serious dissension in an Ozu family, where good sense prevails, does not lead to violent action, strong language, or agitated facial expressions, but is managed "inwardly" in delicate conversations. Since family relations are so close that everyone can understand each other without saying much, a slight change in facial expression or tone of voice carries profound meaning.

Although Ozu experimented in various genres in his younger days—tragic love melodrama, one period drama, suspense films—occasionally with interesting results, none of them succeed as much as his home drama masterpieces, probably because the contents gave full range to his talent for offering profound meaning in slight actions. Since it is thought that content dictates form, it follows that Ozu's penchant for home drama subjects led him to these unipue forms. However, in my opinion, it was his deep attachment to a tightly knit composition exuding quiet tension that came before the contents. As form and content are inseparable in that all works of art are a whole, it is meaningless to ask which came first; however, Ozu's preoccupation with form is so thorough that it deserves priority.

A good illustration of this is *Tokyo Story*, generally considered Ozu's greatest work. It concerns one family, whose members are neither noble nor base but are truly ordinary in character and behavior. The parents visit their sons and daughters in Tokyo, later the mother dies—ordinary, everyday incidents that occur in all families. Yet the viewer comes away profoundly moved for, while relating these happenings in the most tranquil way, Ozu raises the deep, eternal problem of the eventual severance between parent and child. In doing so, Ozu transcends national mores and boundaries to leave a profound impression on people who understand the essence of his cinematic presentation. Ozu tries to pin down the transience of life inside a very rigid framework, which is ultimately defeating given life's elusiveness. However, the will to try to pin it down highlights life's fleetingness even more and deepens our appreciation of it.

3. EYE BEHAVIOR IN THE FILMS OF OZU AND NARUSE

In the previous section we saw how Ozu avoided face-to-face shots in his films, preferring his characters to look in the same direction. This was probably the result of both his liking for analogous figures in a stable composition and his desire for people to avoid looking directly into each other's eyes. While two people may occasionally turn to look in each other's direction, the times their eyes meet is limited.

In Japan it is considered both uncomfortable to look at length into someone's eyes during a conversation and cold not to do so at all, so a proper balance has to be maintained. Most Japanese are unaware of this process and are shocked to find that in some countries conversation is carried on *while* looking into the eyes of the other person.

To Ozu this peculiar Japanese trait was important. His use of interiors of traditional Japanese houses is probably because they are ingeniously designed to limit eye contact, apart from their visual beauty. Besides the veranda (*engawa*) and garden, Ozu also made adept use of the alcove (*tokonoma*), usually decorated with a wall scroll and flower arrangement; the tea room hearth, shaped so the host and guests may sit at right angles to each other; and the farmhouse hearth where it is easier to sit and talk at right angles. Floor cushions (*zabuton*) can also be placed so that host and guest do not have to look into each other's eyes. Unlike the fixed arrangement of table and chairs, whereby people are continually facing each other, one's gaze is allowed to wander from the alcove, the garden, or the person sitting next to one.

194 Another director who felt the same discomfort in direct eye contact was Mikio Naruse, who, like Ozu, excelled at portraying the subtle, psychological interweaving of family relations. However, since his style was not considered as rigorous as Ozu's and his dramas not as profound, he was regarded as a "poor man's Ozu" for a long time. Nevertheless, the originality of his style is recognized today, and we see that it evolved largely from his own shy personality.

Naruse was extremely mild-mannered and quiet, and it was impossible for him to raise his voice or shout. Consequently, he was poor at filming on location where loud instructions had to be given to many people, and would limit such shooting to early morning or late evening—when no one else would be there besides his extras. As a reflection of his shyness, his films, too, were light sketches of daily life in which violent scenes rarely surfaced. Their subtle, interiorized complications, rising from the tautness engendered by the characters' emotional cross-purposes, made them almost as tense as suspense movies. This tension is not expressed through heated verbal exchanges or energetic gestures but through eye behavior. Naruse fills his scenes with glances of affection or revulsion, scorn and malice, forgiveness and resignation; his characters look away unexpectedly, eyes seem to make contact and then look away.

In order to emphasize this eye behavior, Naruse simplified other dramaturgical elements. He did not like intricate scripts and would cut superfluous lines. He disdained elaborate sets, "a nuisance," and his camera work was kept very simple, without pans or ostentatious frame size changes. His direction avoided any theatrical, flamboyant, or extravagant performances.

Naruse probably felt the above elements distracting because he wanted his audience calm and settled so they could catch glimpses of internal disturbance through slight eye movements. This cinematic mode was evident in *Mother* (*Okasan,* 1952). The older daughter grieves over neighborhood rumors concerning the relationship between her mother, a widow, and a man who helps her at her dry-cleaning shop. The man understands this simply by the way she averts her gaze in his presence and, carrying on as though nothing is amiss, he parts from them with a slight smile. The father in *The Whole Family Works* is looking for an opportunity to talk to his son about the financial problems involved in sending him to school. His son avoids him, however, and their silent discord is revealed when the father glimpses him holding a confidential talk with his brothers at the neighborhood coffee shop. The youngest daughter in *Lightning* wants to lead a virtuous life despite the bad influence of her brothers and sisters, but their friends drop in and taunt her; glances filled with disgust flit back and forth between everyone in the scene. In *Sound of the Mountain* (*Yama no Oto,* 1954) the young wife and her sister-in-law are dissatisfied with each other but keep silent about it, and merely avoid looking into each other's eyes. This emphasis on eye behavior is a superlative technique that cannot be rivaled in literature, theater, or painting. In this respect, Naruse achieved a high level of cinematicity, one that is different from Ozu's.

Naruse and Ozu were not the only directors to artistically sublimate this Japanese psychological trait. Directors Teinosuke Kinugasa and Mansaku Itami and the actor Sojin Kamiyama, among others, have written essays on this. Of particular interest are the following statements from *A Code of Acting Directions (Engi shido soan)* in volume two of *The Complete Works of Mansaku Itami (Itami Mansaku zenshu)*.

"In. . . nonverbal acting, there is nothing more important and effective then eye behavior. . . . When performers assimilate the feeling of a role, their eye movements and the direction of their gaze turn out exactly as the director wishes, even when he gives no particular instruction.

"When the player does not understand the feelings of the character at the time, if the director gives accurate and elaborate instructions on eye behavior, the player will seem to have understood them.

"At times when it is difficult to explain the feelings of the character, say, when the explanation would become so complicated that it would be better not to do it, as with children, I would rely on the player's confidence in me, and, without giving any reasons, would frequently specify mechanically the exact order of eye behavior as regards direction and distance and movement. In the final performance it appeared as if they understood each and every thought."

This is one example in Japanese film theory where eye behavior is placed at the core of a performance. The Japanese aversion to direct eye contact is probably related to their wish to avoid confrontation. In the past when the vast majority of people were paddy farmers—an occupation where cooperation is absolutely necessary—disputes were frowned upon or were deftly sidetracked to effect a compromise, and so the habit of averting one's gaze can be considered a reflection of this social pattern. This does not mean that the Japanese are always peaceful and always good at compromising, but confrontation within one's own social circle was avoided as much as possible. This is reflected in many extremely pleasing Japanese films where almost no dramatic conflict occurs, and we are merely shown kindred spirits looking at the same beautiful scenery together.

196

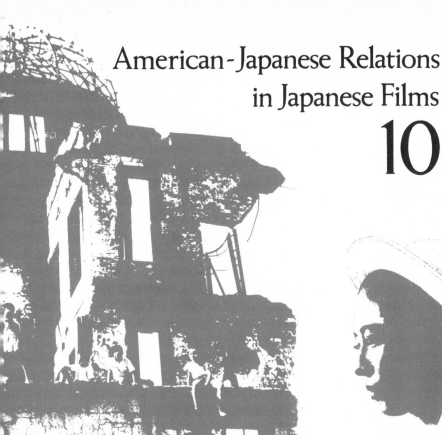

American-Japanese Relations
in Japanese Films
10

1. THE BOMB

The first film to portray the devastation wrought by the atomic 197
bombs dropped on Hiroshima and Nagasaki was a Nichiei documentary made shortly after the blasts. Although the film was supposed to have been confiscated by the U.S. Army and taken to America, it later appears that the production staff had concealed some of it. When this was shown in 1952, the year the Occupation ended, many Japanese saw for the first time some of the effects of the holocaust.

In the Occupation years it was strictly prohibited to criticize America's role in the tragedy, and the only way the subject could be broached in film was sentimentally, as in *The Bells of Nagasaki* (*Nagasaki no Kane,* 1950), the first feature-length Japanese film on the A-bomb, based on the best-selling memoirs of Dr. Takashi

Nagai, a former professor at Nagasaki Medical College who died of radiation-induced leukemia in 1951. Dr. Nagai was a Roman Catholic who regarded the atomic blast as a heaven-sent trial to be endured, and the film version concentrates on Dr. Nagai's own perseverance in the face of tragedy. Its director, Hideo Oba, circumspectly presents the explosion through the eyes of young evacuees, who see it as a mushroom cloud rising between distant mountains. Thus, the extent of the devastation was avoided, as was any criticism of America for dropping the bombs. However, this latter prohibition may not have been altogether necessary in postwar Japan since many Japanese shared the feeling that war is cruel, that the Japanese military committed various atrocities, and that Japan was also to blame for starting the war.

While *The Bells of Nagasaki* attempted a faithful portrayal of a human being's resolve in the face of approaching death, Tomotaka Tasaka's *I'll Never Forget the Song of Nagasaki* (*Nagasaki no Uta wa Wasureji,* 1952) was pure sentimental rubbish. The heroine (Machiko Kyo), the beautiful daughter from a good family, is blinded during the Nagasaki blast and consequently loathes all Americans. Along comes a young American, symbolizing the pilot who dropped the A-bomb, who is sincerely contrite and seeks forgiveness. Eventually, she discards her hatred and falls in love with him, a gesture that symbolizes forgiveness of him and of America.

The film, with its absurd theme of "let's forget our grudge about the Bomb," served only to embarrass the viewer. Its lack of reality may be attributed to the director, who himself was a victim of Hiroshima and had been hospitalized for a long time. However, his major theme—complete and utter loyalty and humanism consisting of a deep love for one's countrymen—without the ingredient of objectivity, quickly degenerates into shabby submissiveness to one's fate. The film only too clearly revealed the gullibility of some Japanese.

Japan's first, real anti-Bomb film was *Children of the Atom Bomb* (*Genbaku no Ko,* 1952), in which penitence is finally transcended, and the director, Kaneto Shindo—through flashbacks of events before and after the Hiroshima blast—paints a lyrical portrait of the quiet endurance of the living. In no way a contrite, romantic melodrama, Shindo raises, for the first time, the important issue of Japan's responsibility in forsaking the living victims of the holocaust. The film was released during the Korean War of 1950–53, when threat of another atomic bomb attack on North Korea or China loomed, but it was not sufficiently powerful to start an anti-Bomb movement. To fill this gap came Hideo Sekigawa's *Hiroshima* (*Hiroshima*, 1953) (which was financially backed by the Japan Teachers' Union).

Sekigawa strove to reconstruct, as faithfully as possible, the horror of the holocaust, and this contrivance was its chief failing. Despite memorable, tragic scenes, such as the one where scorched victims dive into the river for relief (later included in Alain Resnais's *Hiroshima Mon Amour*), on the whole it lacked the polish of an artistic statement. Nevertheless, Sekigawa's simple, forthright approach struck a responsive chord in many Japanese, temporarily uniting them in their antiwar sentiments.

Hiroshima crystallized anti-Bomb sentiments better than *Children of the Atom Bomb,* which changed the Bomb from a historical to a present-day problem by raising the issue of the victims suffering from radiation sickness. This issue was also treated in several later Japanese films, notably Tadashi Imai's *A Story of Pure Love* and Fumio Kamei's documentaries, *It's Good That We're Still Alive* (*Ikite Ite Yokatta*, 1956) and *The World Is Terrified* (*Sekai wa Kyofu Suru*, 1957), but due to their old-fashioned, run-of-the-mill approach there is no way of ascertaining the directors' views of the significance of the Bomb.

Kurosawa deals directly with the significance of the Bomb in *Record of a Living Being* by treating it for the first time as a psychological force devastating human life from within, rather than simply as an outer force of destruction. As mentioned in Chapter Seven, the small entrepreneur was prevented from emigrating by his family, and his resulting insanity could be considered the degenerative end of his fear of the Bomb. Moreover, the family, a primary source of spiritual strength for the Japanese, is first devastated from within by dissension and later symbolically ruined when its head, the father, goes mad.

Record of a Living Being can also be further interpreted in the context of the nation. Kurosawa may have been questioning the issue paradoxically: everyone fears an atomic holocaust but no one wants to flee from it because of his attachment to his country.

Even in the face of possible annihilation of the human race, people go about their business in the usual way. When offered the chance to escape they may become aware of the situation but are thrown in a quandary whether to leave or stay. Although Kurosawa does not state this theme explicitly, he seems to be saying that as long as people are completely satisfied with life in their country, they will not be able to come to grips with the issue of the Bomb. Viewed in this light, Kurosawa does not necessarily—as stated in Chapter Seven—confuse the issue of the Bomb with a family problem. The latter only arises out of love for one's own country. The real confrontation for him is between nationalism and the terror of the Bomb.

The significance of the Bomb was also taken up by Kaneto Shindo in *Lucky Dragon No. 5* (*Daigo Fukuryu-Maru*, 1959), based on a real incident concerning a Japanese fishing crew contaminated by fallout in the Bikini Islands. Shindo presents the Bomb as a quiet menace that infiltrates our daily lives. While *Lucky Dragon No. 5* cannot be counted among his masterpieces, it is a powerful work devoid of romantic embellishment and flashy sensationalism of any kind. It is a simple, straightforward portrayal of the struggle between human endeavor and the contaminating influence of the Bomb—a struggle that can only be won if all human beings work together. Later, Shindo again depicts this struggle in *Lost Sex,* about a man who becomes impotent as a result of atomic radiation.

2. THE *RASHAMEN* GENRE

The word *rashamen* is a derogatory term applied to a Japanese woman who becomes the mistress of a Westerner. The modern equivalent is *onri* ("only"), which in the immediate postwar period referred to a Japanese woman who devoted her attentions to *only* one GI. Joint American-Japanese productions turned out movies about such love affairs frequently after the war. *Sayonara* (Marlon Brando and Miiko Ko), *Teahouse of the August Moon* (Glenn Ford and Machiko Kyo), and *Flight from Ashiya* (George Chakiris and Eiko Taki) are the best-known examples. While they were successful abroad, in Japan these films were miserable failures. It was almost as if Japanese audiences felt sorry for the

Japanese men in such films. Hence, this kind of joint production came to be called *rashamen* movies.

Rashamen was indeed a fitting term because such films made Japanese viewers uneasy, bringing home the parallel that Japan's relationship with America had probably been that of geisha and patron. However, the Japanese themselves were not above making similar movies subsequent to the Sino-Japanese War of 1937, and a perfect example is *Vow in the Desert* (*Nessa no Chikai*, 1940). The hero of this, a Japanese engineer, is part of the work force building a road from Peking to Mongolia. Although he claims the road is for the Chinese people, it is obviously intended for military use, and communist guerrillas are constantly attacking it. The engineer's sweetheart, the daughter of a rich Chinese in Peking, tries to turn her people against these guerrillas by convincing them of the good intentions of the Japanese. She was played by Yoshiko Yamaguchi, a Japanese actress who went by the Chinese name of Li Hsian-lan (or Ri Koran, as the Japanese pronounce it), whom audiences of the time thought was Chinese. Her lead was the famous *nimaime*-type actor, Kazuo Hasegawa.

This love story between a Japanese man from the conquering side and a Chinese woman from the conquered side symbolized the need for cooperation. Moreover, it rationalized events because it allowed the conqueror to think that because he loved the conquered, no force had been used to bring about submission. The conquered side, however, felt both the physical pain of losing and the psychological pain of serving the conqueror. The old concept of the man conquering the woman in sexual intercourse may also have played a part here, revealing the strong hold of the idea of male dominance despite modern ideas of sexual equality.

Other Japanese films dealing with the same theme but with different renditions include *Song of the White Orchid* (*Byakuran no Uta*, 1939), *China Night* (*Shina no Yoru*, 1940), and *Suchow Night* (*Soshu no Yoru*, 1941). There was even one made about a Japanese man and an Ainu woman—the equivalent of a love story between a white settler and an Indian woman in an American cultural setting. In postwar *rashamen* movies Japanese and American roles were simply reversed, with the Americans on top instead of the Japanese.

For some time after the war Japanese film producers also made *rashamen*-type movies ostensibly to promote goodwill between America and Japan. One curious example is the previously mentioned *I'll Never Forget the Song of Nagasaki*. Strangely enough, for this film an ultra-right scriptwriter, Tsutomu Sawamura, who had promoted militarism and praised the war effort in prewar and war-time scripts, worked with the director Tomotaka Tasaka, whose artistic war-time masterpieces like *Five Scouts* and *Mud and Soldiers* emphasized the human side of Japanese soldiers.

When these two made a thoughtful film about the Bomb, they came up surprisingly with a love story between an American man and a Japanese woman. In effect, their submissive attitude toward the prewar Japanese military was simply transferred to a postwar, powerful America. The film's sentimental message was that America's guilt in the sufferings of the Japanese would make America assume a soft attitude toward Japan. In other words, it is like the petulant wife, who, after being soundly beaten by her husband, feels his love for her even more. In this masochistic way of bringing up the subject of the Bomb, it was thought that America's love for Japan, which does not bear any grudges, would increase.

That men with such masochistic dispositions could make some of the best Japanese war movies is enough to shatter the manly, military stereotype, one that is mainly propped up by submissiveness. In this way a large number of loyal Japanese militarists during the war became equally loyal pro-American supporters after the war. They had not seen the error of their ways, nor had they suddenly been converted to a new way of thinking; rather, they were like the widow who will marry any man she can get.

After *I'll Never Forget the Song of Nagasaki* this submissive stance toward America vanished completely from Japanese films about the atomic bomb, as did Japanese *rashamen* movies themselves in the 1960s. In 1961 America turned the *rashamen* theme around in *Bridge to the Sun,* about a Japanese diplomat (James Shigeta) who marries an American girl (Carroll Baker). The hardships they endure in war-time Japan are depicted realistically and Carroll Baker cut a gallant figure in the fields in her *mompe,* baggy pants worn by Japanese women during the war. The director, Etienne Perrier, was a Belgian and an independent director in

France. From France also came Alain Resnais's *Hiroshima Mon Amour*, another film that reversed the *rashamen* model.

Resnais's story concerns a French actress (Emmanuele Riva) who comes to Hiroshima to make an antiwar movie. Her love affair there with a Japanese man (Eiji Okada) brings back painful memories of her own war experiences. In both films the mature presentation of the contact between two equal individuals from different cultures served to emphasize the unreality of typical *rashamen* movies, where the man supposedly comes from a superior country and the woman from an inferior one.

Perhaps because Japan's relations with China in the 1940s and with America in the postwar years were unequal, Japanese films could only portray love stories like *Vow in the Desert* and *rashamen* movies. Friendship between Japanese and Chinese or Americans of the same sex on an equal basis still seems unreal to Japanese audiences today, even though the young do not have any inferiority complex toward Americans, and a love story between an American man and a Japanese woman, albeit annoying, still appears more real.

In Japanese films of the 1960s, three films appeared that reversed the *rashamen* theme. While American movies continued to depict Japanese-American friendship by a love story between a Japanese woman and an American man, Japanese films reversed the trend by pitying Americans instead of being pitied by them. The first was *Black Sun* (*Kuroi Taiyo*, 1964) by Koreyoshi Kurahara, about the relationship between a Japanese youth and a black American soldier. The Japanese, a jazz aficionado, admires American blacks for their talent in jazz. He meets a black soldier, a farm boy who knows nothing about modern jazz, and when shown photos of black musicians, simply says, "Those guys are really making it in white society." The young Japanese is disillusioned but gradually comes to feel friendship for the soldier. In one scene the Japanese, who seems to be going mad, puts white powder on the black's face and they parade through the streets like *chindonya*, Japanese street musicians who advertise store openings and the like. They are eventually chased by American MPs and Japanese police, their common enemies, and this episode seals their friendship.

The second divergence from the *rashamen* syndrome is Hiro-michi Horikawa's *Farewell to the Gang in Moscow* (*Saraba Mosukuwa Gurentai*, 1968), where jazz again becomes an important element. The hero (Yuzo Kayama), a pianist and ex-impresario, occasionally gets his old group together for a jam session in some hole-in-the-wall coffee shop. One day a tall, lanky American arrives with a letter of introduction from a mutual Japanese friend in New York. The American is a soldier in Vietnam on leave in Tokyo and since he can play the piano, Kayama lets him join their session. "You're pretty good," he says, "but your jazz is a monologue. True jazz has to be a dialogue." The American takes offense. "When it comes to jazz, an American should know more about it than you." The drummer in Kayama's group retaliates that jazz is no longer the exclusive domain of Americans, and the American leaves in a huff.

On a rainy day before the American is due in Vietnam, however, he comes around again and asks Kayama to let him play. Kayama complies, and after the American finishes Kayama acknowledges the plaint of a certain anger and pain in his solo performance and expounds on the philosophy of jazz. "Yeah. . . . You *can* do a solo dialogue with jazz. . . . You just answer yourself. . . . That's what your performance was. . . . Don't forget what you did today." The young American is deeply moved, and bows politely and leaves.

A Japanese teaching an American is rarely depicted in postwar Japanese movies. It is plausible here since the Japanese is a top pianist and the American still a fledgling. However, without the background of the Vietnam War it would lose its reality for Japanese audiences. That war allowed the Japanese to discard their old inferiority complex, even if they were not deluded into thinking they were morally superior. When Kayama looks pityingly at the American going to Vietnam, he shows the extent to which the postwar Japanese have regained their self-confidence.

In the film Kayama goes to Moscow to introduce Japanese jazz to the Soviets. There he makes the acquaintance of a Russian youth alienated by Soviet oppression, who can only find relief in playing his trumpet at a·cafe where he hangs out with the rest of his gang. Kayama goes there and forms a trio with a bass-playing American tourist he meets in Red Square and a Japanese diplomat who plays the clarinet, and through their jam sessions he teaches the Russian kids what jazz is all about and establishes international solidarity.

While fairly sentimental, the film is nevertheless epoch-making for it allows a self-confident Japanese to pity a Vietnam-bound American and a freedom-seeking Russian—and, by analogy, to pity the two most powerful nations in the world.

The third example of the reversal of the *rashamen* theme is Yoshitaro Nomura's *Oh, Your Love!* (*Aa Kimi ga Ai,* 1967). The story is about a young, respectable doctor and his older sister, who had supported his education by working in an office in the port of Yokosuka. One day the brother learns that his sister has an American boyfriend, a sailor, presently on duty off Korea. A letter arrives from him and the sister asks her brother to read it as it is in English. In the letter the sailor asks her to marry him; however, her brother lies and says it is from a fellow sailor informing her that her sweetheart was killed in action. Later, in order to convince her, the brother goes to the U.S. Naval Headquarters and gets a fake notification from an officer who frowns on fraternization between enlisted men and Japanese women. Thereafter, his sister turns to the bottle, ruining her health, eventually having to convalesce in the country. Her brother sends her money until one day, as if to expiate his guilt, he confesses to a forgery, thereby ruining his future, and leaves the city to live together with his sister.

Despite its melodramatic overtones a thought-provoking political analogy can be made from the film. The brother represents progressive Japanese intellectuals who are humiliated by Japan's subordinate and dependent position vis-à-vis America, reinforced by the sister's affair with an American. The submissive attitude beneath *rashamen* movies—and the feeling of the people in general—is represented by the sister who does not care if people look down on her for being a GI's girl since she is better off through her relationship with him. Her humiliated brother adopts an anti-American stance by forcibly severing her relations with the American, resulting in his sister's misfortune. The only thing he can do for her is to give up his successful career and take care of her. The tragedy reflects Japan's political dilemma, its ambivalent position vis-à-vis America. The author of the original novel, Ayako Sono, seems to be posing the following question to progressive Japanese intellectuals: "I can recognize a justifiable emotional basis for your anti-Americanism; however, are you really sure that if you came to power, the Japanese people would be better off?" This analogy might be a bit strained, however, because although the American sailor never makes an appearance, he is supposed to be as pathetic as the sister and brother, not someone who can be relied on.

The Japanese, who had been pitied by Americans ever since the Occupation, are now pitying Americans. This may have pleased many Japanese, but reality is sacrificed here because it is doubtful whether American soldiers were really that pathetic or whether Japanese gained moral superiority by pitying them. Perhaps one could make friends with the frail, lanky American soldier in *Farewell to the Gang in Moscow*; however, that boy, with tears in his eyes, is on his way to Vietnam to kill, and that in itself makes him an unlikely object of pity.

Japanese films which depicted friendship for American soldiers through pity are actually based on the premise of self-pity, as in *Farewell to the Gang in Moscow,* where the self-confident pianist suffers from a nameless frustration and reveals that he is not so sure of himself after all. These movies are attempts to link Japanese sentiments of alienation with the most alienated segments of the American population. This can succeed if any feeling of superiority on the Japanese side is avoided, for friendship between alienated Japanese and Americans could develop through anti-establishment sentiments. An example is the warmth some Japanese felt for Vietnam deserters, or for the black American who claimed on Japanese TV that the American authorities dropped the Bomb on Hiroshima because the Japanese were not white, and that the common enemy of blacks and Japanese alike is white racism. When such feelings of friendship gradually spread and solidify, the *rashamen* genre might become a thing of the past.

The attitude upholding this genre will not die overnight, however, judging from the Japanese view of other Asian countries with whom Japan is supposed to have friendly relations. Japan's "friendship" for them has already been demonstrated in several joint movie productions with Thailand or Hong Kong. Without exception these films are love stories of a Japanese man and the foremost beauty there. Their Japanese heroes do not care a fig

206

for Japanese women, and by offering their love to Thai or Chinese women, reveal Japan's sincerity of intent toward Thailand or Hong Kong. However, these movies could also be postwar editions of *Vow in the Desert,* in which imperial Japan offered its love to China.

11

Developments
in the 1960s

1. THE BACKGROUND: HANI AND MASUMURA

208 An important transition period in Japanese film history occurred in the late 1950s, signaled by a new approach to direction and film-making. This was first apparent in *Children in the Classroom* (*Kyoshitsu no Kodomotachi*, 1955), a short documentary made at Iwanami studios for the Ministry of Education. Its director, Susumu Hani, was relatively unknown then and its documentary-style of presentation introduced a fresh approach to film. Critics applauded this innovative piece of work, and the following year Hani, who had become famous overnight, made a similar documentary, *Children Who Draw Pictures* (*E o Kaku Kodomotachi*, 1956), which was billed with a feature, a rare distinction.

These two records of classroom behavior may seem ordinary today because Hani had anticipated the methods used in television and other documentaries. However, when they were released, audiences were struck by how natural the children were, leading one critic to assume that a camera had been hidden in another room for the filming. However, Hani had set up the camera in the children's classroom, made friends with them, and they gradually overcame their nervousness and appeared completely uninhibited in front of the camera.

After this success Hani went on to make *Bad Boys* (*Furyo Shonen*, 1961), a full-length feature about juvenile delinquents on the streets of Tokyo, in detention areas, and in reform schools. In it Hani combined his new documentary style with the use of amateurs, even incorporating some of their own experiences. This came about completely accidentally because one day the boys did not bring their script and refused to say their lines as directed. At this juncture Hani explained the situation they were filming and asked the boys what they themselves would say. They responded enthusiastically and determined their own lines, gestures, and movements, which Hani then proceeded to incorporate. The documentary impression was thereby strengthened, as though Hani had filmed their actual behavior with a hidden camera. Moreover, his camera angle was always perfect and he gave equal weight to all the necessary shots, thus creating a feature film with a refreshingly new texture.

In the feature and the short documentaries, Hani's main concern was not to project what was in the script but to reflect reality as accurately as he could. (Film realists also share this love for realism, but they usually resort to fictionalizing after choosing what they consider to be "realistic images.") Hani's approach was to use the ideas of the subjects themselves, nonprofessional performers, and not to rely solely on his own imagination. He did not see himself as a director "ordering" his performers but as a friend, and the camera simply caught the results. Since the recorded happenings were imbued with an air of amiability and harmony, some viewers were even disappointed at the lack of a harsher aspect of reality. Nevertheless, until *Bad Boys*, human behavior had never appeared so genuine in a feature film, and Hani used this approach again with tribal black Africans in *The Song of Bwana Toshi* (*Buana Toshi no Uta*, 1965).

Between *Bad Boys* and *The Song of Bwana Toshi*, Hani made a "pure" feature, *She and He* (*Kanojo to Kare,* 1963), in which the main roles were played by professionals. As in his documentaries, he still attempted to capture reality in all its complexity, even down to the actual surprise he experienced while filming, presenting ambiguity as ambiguity while intimating that something very important lay therein. The theme of *She and He* is relatively simple, a comparison between the desolation of human relations in a modern apartment building and the closeness of the poor in a ragpickers' slum, and Hani made superb efforts to capture the feeling of loneliness experienced by the apartment dwellers. The seemingly meaningless shots of the walls inside an apartment, the urban scenes, the daily conversations and activities of the characters all take on a fresh texture and seem to be telling the viewer something.

Before the filming Hani and his scriptwriter, Kunio Shimizu, only had a general format, adding lines as they went along. Words limit meaning, and Hani consciously avoids a theme that can be conceptionally summarized by words. He focuses on presenting feelings and desires themselves, for to him the essence of human beings lies in those needs that cannot be verbalized—a new perception.

A second important change in Japanese cinema of the late 1950s was the birth of a new young hero and the development of a lighter, faster tempo in editing, as shown by Yasuzo Masumura's first three films, made in 1957: *Kisses* (*Kuchizuke*), *A Cheerful Girl* (*Aozora Musume*), and *Warm Current* (*Danryu*). At the time of its release, film critics ignored *Kisses* because it seemed to conform to the well-worn genre of films about youth (*seishun eiga*). However, as was later evident, Masumura rejected the old formulas of the genre, and his hero was neither mild-mannered, romantic, nor especially good-looking, but rather audacious and perpetually angry. He was not the first Japanese version of the angry young man—rich, profligate youths had to some extent raised hell before him—but he was the most significant because he was a poor boy from the masses. In contrast to previous youthful heroes, he gives vent to his frustrations through exaggerated actions rather than through languishing melancholically, for sympathy was the last thing he wanted. Thus, there are no atmospheric props or sentimental effects in *Kisses,* and the young hero is going to fulfill his thwarted needs through action alone. Adults who do not understand him are simply caricatured by the director, who is announcing his desire to make new films for and with the younger generation.

The freshness in *Kisses* becomes all the more vivid in *A Cheerful Girl*, where it takes on the garb of light comedy. Then Masumura did a remake of *Warm Current*, Kozaburo Yoshimura's prewar masterpiece that had come to be regarded as a classic love story. By increasing the tempo to the violent pitch of an action film, however, Masumura succeeded in surprising the audiences and in making them laugh. The characters were neither foolish nor absurd, but as they all behaved so frankly and acted so openly, the comic effect was further heightened. There was also a thrill in their audacious frankness, as in the scene where the heroine sees her boyfriend off at the crowded railway station and shouts, "I don't care if I only become your mistress; I'll still be waiting for you."

The scriptwriter for *Warm Current*, as well as *A Cheerful Girl*, was the relatively unknown newcomer, Yoshio Shirasaka. When he joined forces with Masumura to produce such bold, iconoclastic films, the viewing public had the premonition that a new age had dawned in Japanese cinema. In 1958 the Masumura-Shirasaka team came out with *Giants and Toys* (*Kyojin to Gangu*); Shohei Imamura made his directorial debut with *Stolen Desire* and *Endless Desire* (*Hateshi Naki Yokujo*); and newcomers like Kihachi Okamoto and Tadashi Sawashima were also attracting attention. All these new directors favored active characters brimming with vitality, and adeptly depicted exaggerated action—close to that in musicals—and a fast, energetic tempo. Their methods often induced laughter from their audience and thus sharply contrasted with the old directorial school, whose effects were emotional, passive, and introspective.

At first these new directors had more common points than differences; however, each would later develop his own methodologies. As for Masumura, this was already evident in *Giants and Toys*, where the hero continually resists becoming a mere cog in the mechanism of modern society. A sense of anguish already begins to show through the laughter, and in his later films this deepens together with the almost abnormal and wild behavior of his characters—people trying to overcome adversity. Masumura went on to portray people with stronger egos, and through their apparently mad behavior, he forces Japanese viewers to ponder about the true nature of human beings.

Masumura antagonized some critics who claimed that he sacrificed reality, emotion, and atmosphere for exaggerated behavior. He retaliated in an essay, saying that these qualities had been overvalued in Japanese film previously. In films with "reality," social pressures were delineated in detail, and while they made the viewer aware of "the evils of society," they suggested only resignation. When the film-maker sympathized with this resignation and shed gentle tears over the defeated, his films were praised for their "emotion" and "atmosphere." Masumura refused to recognize this denouement, stating that he ignored social environment on purpose so as to portray people who act like maniacs, thereby calling attention to the ego and expressing himself by exaggerating it.

Masumura claimed that he had learned the above during his study at the Centro Sperimentale in Rome some years before. However, here it is worthwhile examining the influence of the controversial "sun tribe" (taiyozoku) films which preceded Masumura and in which the ego was emphasized. The sun tribe referred to teenagers who hung around beaches during the summer vacation. They were made famous by novelist Shintaro Ishihara's early works, three of which were made into movies in 1956: Season of the Sun (Taiyo no Kisetsu), Punishment Room (Shokei no Heya), and Crazed Fruit (Kurutta Kajitsu). All three films created a stir because they were rather raw and lurid portrayals of the delinquent behavior of rich, aimless youths, and many felt they had a bad influence on the public at large. Consequently, tighter censorship was considered necessary, and the Japanese Board of Censors, Eirin, was forced to disassociate itself from the film industry and become independent.

In those days Shintaro Ishihara's message seemed to be: rather than worry about the whys and wherefores of society, first run wild and steep yourself in life's intoxication. While Season of the Sun, directed by Takumi Furukawa, was simply a timely exposé of juvenile delinquents, Punishment Room was a fairly powerful, original film, since director Kon Ichikawa appended a serious, moral question lacking in Ishihara's novel—namely, how can the older generation cope with the aimless protest of the younger generation? *Crazed Fruit* was the first really faithful adaptation, for director Ko Nakahira captured the sense of intoxication of the original and expressed Ishihara's premonition that these rich youths, who had been raised without restraints, were the harbingers of an age of rapid economic growth and free sex.

In an essay entitled *Is This a Breakthrough? The Modernists in Japanese Cinema* (*"Sore wa toppako ka? Nihon eiga no kindaishugishatachi,"* *Eiga hihyo,* July, 1958), Nagisa Oshima, an assistant director at the time, summed up the reverberations of the "sun tribe" films as follows: "In July, 1956 Ko Nakahira said that the sun tribe had been praised in *Season of the Sun* and criticized in *Punishment Room.* However, I had merely sneered at them until [his] *Crazed Fruit* made its appearance. Then I felt that in the sound of the girl's skirt being ripped and the hum of the motorboat slashing through the older brother, sensitive people could hear the wails of a seagull heralding a new age in Japanese cinema. In May of the following year, 1957, Yoshio Shirasaka's script for *The Betrothed* (*Nagasugita Haru*) portrayed healthy, rational youths. He proved that a superbly written script can transcend the ability of a director and determine the style of the film itself. I was then aware that people could no longer talk about Japanese film if they continued to ignore this new wave. In July, 1957, Yasuzo Masumura's *Kisses* used a freely revolving camera to film the young lovers riding around on a motorcycle. I felt now that the tide of a new age could no longer be ignored by anyone, and that a powerful irresistible force had arrived in Japanese cinema."

2. THE REBEL AND THE CRIMINAL: OSHIMA

Nagisa Oshima was only twenty-seven when he made *A Town of Love and Hope* for Shochiku's Ofuna studios in 1959. Before the war it was not unusual to be made director at an even younger age, but after 1945 the length of apprenticeship of an assistant director increased and the rules of seniority tightened so that it was exceedingly rare to direct one's own film before the age of thirty. In 1959, however, with the decline in popularity of Shochiku's well-acknowledged forte, the "women's melodrama," the studio decided to try to rejuvenate itself and took the unprecedented step of appointing Oshima director over his older colleagues.

Shochiku's president then, Shiro Kido, took a personal hand in production, and it was he who selected Oshima's script, *The Boy Who Sold His Pigeon*, later changed to *A Town of Love and Hope*, over several others that appeared in a magazine produced by the studio's assistant directors. Kido saw that it had the makings of a film in the Ofuna *shomin geki* genre of humanistic stories on the lives of average city dwellers. He took great pride in this genre which he had shaped and guided, beginning with the films of Ozu and continuing to those of Keisuke Kinoshita. Its strength lay in the fine vignettes of the people's sentiments, and its directors were sympathetic to the laments of the weak and helpless but were also aware of life's small joys. Although they tackled society's contradictions with a sigh, most of the time they settled problems through the bonds of family love.

A Town of Love and Hope is set in the factory town of Kawasaki, south of Tokyo, where Oshima himself had lived. Due to poverty the hero, a young teenager, practices a con game of sorts by reselling a homing pigeon. After he sells it to the teenage daughter of an executive of a large company, he befriends her, and upon leaving school manages to apply for a job in her father's company with the help of the girl and his teacher. He passes the company entrance examination but is refused employment when his delinquent act of selling a homing pigeon is discovered. Angered that his innocent con game is considered such a crime, the boy vows to continue it, aware now that he is rebelling against society through it. The girl, however, is furious with him because she thinks the boy has betrayed her. She buys the pigeon again, sets it free, and has her brother shoot it with a rifle, thus symbolizing the end of the short-lived friendship between a rich girl and a poor boy.

In the original script another scene followed this in which the teenagers agree not to let their friendship end on such a sour note, and there was the brave, heart-warming message that together they would build a more genuine society. However, Oshima's film ended with the slain pigeon falling—an image which pierced the viewer to the core. It was a compelling ending because the viewer, who had been an objective, detached observer, was suddenly and forcefully confronted with the question: Where do you stand?

Shiro Kido had expected the film to pivot on the humanism of the rich girl and thus feature the theme of love and hope in the form of cooperation between labor and management. However, when confronted with the finished version he was reportedly furious with Oshima, exclaiming, "This film is saying that the rich and poor can never join hands," and he promptly labeled it a leftist film. This was the first time Oshima found himself at odds with his studio, and for six months he was suspended from filmmaking, the film only being released at a few out-of-the-way theaters in Tokyo.

The essence of Oshima can already be discerned in *A Town of Love and Hope,* particularly in the hero's "double" reaction upon being taken to task for his "delinquent" behavior. Previously, he had been rather noncommittal about selling his homing pigeon. Now, however, he not only flaunts it one last time but also destroys his pigeon coop. If he apologized for his act, he would have to admit that what he was forced into doing earlier was wrong, something his self-respect would not permit. Nor would it allow him to continue selling his pigeon, for then he would be stuck with the juvenile delinquent label for good and his protest would go unnoticed. In order to become a true rebel against society, he angrily demolishes his means of delinquent behavior. He rejects not only mending his ways but also the image of a pitiable juvenile delinquent. By simply asserting, "I am myself," he brings up the issue of the autonomy of rebellion.

A good boy who mends his ways will probably have no strength left to rebel against injustices, and a boy who protests by evoking pity is merely playing on the sympathy of others. The boy in *A Town of Love and Hope* does neither, and thus manifests his intense self-respect and his resolve to dispel the sense of humiliation upon being called a juvenile delinquent. In the image of this boy, especially in the intensity of his self-esteem, lies an indisputable self-portrait of Oshima himself.

In spite of the fact that *A Town of Love and Hope* only played in small theaters, the controversial contents gave Oshima a chance to work on his second film, *Cruel Story of Youth* (1960), which stirred up controversy in the mass media. Its resounding success even prompted other studios to follow Shochiku's lead and appoint younger men as directors.

In contrast to the hero of *A Town of Love and Hope*, the boy in *Cruel Story of Youth* actually becomes a delinquent since he uses his girlfriend to extort money from adults. Yet this film is clearly distinguishable from the "sun tribe" and other juvenile delinquent movies because the young couple are portrayed neither as sad victims of society nor as daring rebels. In a society as evil as this one their rebellion merely takes the form of meaningless delinquency, which is what is "cruel" about their story. It is as if the promising rebel in *A Town of Love and Hope* can only assert himself later through delinquent behavior.

In terms of accomplishment, *Cruel Story of Youth* is one of Oshima's best films, for its style is closely related to its theme of cruelty. There is not one scene in the sunlight, and since almost everything is shot under a leaden sky, something red, like flowing blood, creates a striking impression when seen through a telescopic lens, burning sensually amid all the gray. Moreover, long shots conveying heavy oppressive images are interspersed with shots taken by a roving, hand-held camera, thereby creating a jarring effect. Both these original, contrapuntal cinematic techniques brilliantly capture the tense relationship between a stagnant, bottled-up social environment and a young couple who are beaten bloody while looking for an escape hatch.

It is said that Oshima's frequent use of the hand-held camera in this film is an imitation of Jean-Luc Godard's *Breathless* (*A Bout de Souffle,* 1958). However, looking more closely, the psychologies behind their usages are almost antithetical. Godard's hand-held camera exhibits an artless ease that seems to be following the wind. This is Godard's nihilism, bound to a method of fragmentation, whereby camera shots which are expected to be uninterrupted are willfully interrupted. Oshima's hand-held camera, on the other hand, is a cinematic expression of the endless, painful writhing of the young couple seeking a path to active resistance. Since he is attempting to capture their silent, agonizing struggle against an oppressive environment, he does not want to observe them objectively, as a third person, through a mounted camera. Rather, he is trying to apprehend their irritation through jittery camera moves that echo their own moves, thus becoming one with them.

216

This is also the reason for his persistent use of long, revolving shots with a hand-held camera.

Through *Cruel Story of Youth* Oshima became the darling of the age, and he followed it up with *The Sun's Burial,* which also aroused controversy in the mass media in 1960, prompting Shochiku to promote more young directors, like Masahiro Shinoda and Yoshishige Yoshida. One reason for Oshima's popularity was that he himself always acted as a member of the new generation, arguing loquaciously for his contemporaries. Another reason lies in his talent for capturing the spirit of the times. It was in 1960 that the *Anpo* struggle against ratification of the U.S.–Japan Security Treaty took place, and *Cruel Story of Youth* came to symbolize the anger of college students who were against military ties with the U.S., an apparent violation of their postwar constitution. Although *The Sun's Burial* and *Cruel Story of Youth* were not directly connected with this political struggle, they ignited all the latent feelings toward it—the initial excitement and the despair and resentment that came with defeat.

The Sun's Burial was shot on location in Kamagasaki, Osaka's biggest slum, which Oshima presents as a place where men bare their fangs and fight like wolves with their fellow beings. The story unfolds like a scroll painting of hell, with the director saying: Rip away the facade of peaceful, modern Japan and you will find a dog-eat-dog philosophy. At the same time, he exhibits a romantic yearning for a situation in which human beings can express the violent side of their natures, exhaust it, and plunge suddenly into an abyss of annihilation.

This is a film where only the strong survive, and even the strong perish at the slightest show of weakness. The dead are then disposed of as though they are insects. If there is a message here, it is probably simply that human beings have to be strong. Each scene is filled with Oshima's assurance that "I am strong," and it is extremely hard to tell whether he is self-confident or self-intoxicated.

The setting sun, photographed in red-orange tints, dominates the screen, slowly sinking behind what seem to be the ruins and black-market area of Kamagasaki in 1945. In that image of the fat, setting sun I see Oshima's self-projection, as though he is saying grandly and contentedly: "I will shine to my utmost over this scene of tragic sorrow." Braced by such an expansive feeling of self-esteem, or conceit, he may have felt a heroic urge to tackle more difficult situations, and the result was *Night and Fog in Japan,* which he began working on soon after.

The idea for *Night and Fog in Japan* ran outside the currents of Japanese commercial films and was only considered by Shochiku because of the failure of their traditional films compared with the unorthodox hits, *Cruel Story of Youth* and *The Sun's Burial.* Oshima, it seemed, could save the situation, especially since his projected film focuses on a political debate between students who had participated in the *Anpo* struggle of 1960. Although the intensity of those days had been replaced by calm, studio heads estimated that a film portraying this recent, vivid event would still be controversial, and Oshima was given permission to go ahead.

Night and Fog in Japan begins with the marriage of a couple who became acquainted during the *Anpo* demonstrations a few months earlier. At their reception a member of the Japanese National Student Organization (*Zengakuren*) gives a volatile speech highlighting the internal dispute between the mainstream faction of the student movement and the breakaway factions opposed to its leadership. A heated debate ensues, and each person present argues for his or her view on how the struggle should be waged thereafter. The debate then takes an unexpected turn.

The groom, a newspaper reporter, had been an active member of the student movement of 1952 against the Subversive Activities Prevention Bill, a conservative measure aimed to stem the sometimes violent leftist demonstrations of the day. (This bill was later passed and is similar to the Anti-Riot Acts of America.) His former comrades are also present at the wedding and, drawn into the confrontation of the present-day students, they begin to revile the internal tyranny and corruption of the student movement's Stalinist leadership in the 1950s. An endless, violent exchange erupts over common issues within the student movements of these two generations.

The generation of university students who waged the Molotov cocktail struggle in 1952 belongs to that of Oshima and his co-scenarist, Toshiro Ishido. Their self-portraits are filled with such emotion-packed, dialectical exchanges and the resentment they express is so powerful that a screen parallel cannot be found anywhere else.

In his usual way Oshima used the journalistic and political approach rather than the artistic because he first mulled over what the most important statement he could make in 1960 would be and then produced an opportunity to deliver it. Most film-makers quietly brew one idea or theme and express it when they are sure of themselves. For Oshima, however, art is not born of meditation. It is a product of intentional action in a state of tension, amid an awareness of the full exertion of one's powers for the most urgent issues.

This kind of approach might lead to immature propaganda films; however, in Oshima's hands it creates an original work of art. This is because while he is engrossed in making an urgent political and social statement, he also reveals his own, innermost sentiments. This was especially true of *Night and Fog in Japan,* for here his passionate portrayal of the form the 1960 student movement should take becomes a tale of his own youth as a political activist, and thus he realizes both his concept and approach in a state of high tension.

The political theories debated in *Night and Fog in Japan* may have lost their relevance, but it is still one of the most beautiful films about youth in the history of Japanese movies. In contrast to the blue skies, sports activities, and sentimental love scenes usually associated with the genre, youth is portrayed here in the darkness of night, as a time of endless arguments and self-loathing and humiliation, a season of unabashed, naive lust for power and a burning sense of shame, and, above all, as a ceaseless quest for absolute justice. Here, indeed, lies the true power and beauty of youth.

Regardless of the beauty of *Night and Fog in Japan,* it was not a financial success, and Shochiku withdrew it from circulation before its first run was completed, so abruptly in fact that political pressure cannot be ruled out. Moreover, the studio's refusal to lend a print of it to research groups or individual theaters reinforced this suspicion, leading to a furious quarrel between Oshima and Shochiku.

At this time Oshima married the actress Akiko Koyama, and a grand reception was held. There, in front of a large gathering, which included several Shochiku heads and numerous journalists, the groom and some of his friends delivered speech after speech denouncing Shochiku. As a result, the rift was irreparable and Oshima and a number of his colleagues formed their own independent production company, which was called *Sozosha* (Creation Company).

Oshima's first independent production was the superb but overly conceptual *The Catch* (*Shiiku*, 1961), based on the novel by Kenzaburo Oe. Since author, scriptwriter, and director were all at odds as to what the novel was about, the film was irritating and confused. The following year Oshima was invited to Toei studios, where he made *Shiro Tokisada from Amakusa*, and three years later, with Shochiku financing, he came out with *Pleasures of the Flesh*. While the former had an urgent statement, it lacked emotion and fresh sentiment, and the latter simply had no message. Despite these failures, in the interim Oshima made some excellent TV documentaries like *The Forgotten Imperial Army* (*Wasurerareta Kogun*, 1963), considered one of Japan's best, and *A Tombstone to Youth* (*Seishun no Ishibumi*, 1964). Then, in 1966, with *Violence at Noon*, Oshima emerged with another feature film that was a masterpiece.

Based on a short story by Taijun Takeda (and scripted by Tsutomu Tamura), *Violence at Noon* concerns a brutal rapist-murderer and the complex male-female relations among all those who had known him. It is Oshima's first incisive probe into the problems after youth. Ever since *A Town of Love and Hope*, he had shown stories of youth usually revolving around crime. Even in the political *Night and Fog in Japan*, the confinement of a youth who is accused of being a "spy" became an important issue. Yet all those crimes could be forgiven on account of the youthfulness of the perpetrators, or overlooked because of poverty, or even considered the proof of youthful purity in contrast to an evil society. In 1966, however, Oshima was unable to repeat his criticism of society from the privileged standpoint of youth, and could no longer judge others with the premise that he alone was innocent. The main character in *Violence at Noon* is a real adult criminal, one who cannot be forgiven. He may be abnormal, or a pervert, but he is nevertheless a result of the sick societies that adults create.

The film is set in a mountain village in the Shinshu (north-central Honshu) region of Japan just after World War II, where several young people attempt but fail to run a collective farm (an ideal society). As they are from different social classes, eventually they go their separate ways. The collective farm episode is treated as a recollection, and there is a touchingly pathetic glow to it. Intercut are scenes depicting the state of confusion of these grown men and women, who have not progressed at all since their youth. The internal disintegration of these adults is portrayed with a poignancy that is both ominous and compelling, intimidating those who try to live at peace with themselves.

3. EVANESCENCE AND HUMOR: SUZUKI

In the late 1950s and the 1960s Seijun Suzuki was a director for Nikkatsu studios, dutifully churning out the modern action films they specialized in at that time. However, in the 1960s his farcical treatments of these popular films both gave him a large following and incurred the displeasure of his company, which fired him for making "incomprehensible" movies. As a result Suzuki became a counterculture hero among antiestablishment youths, who would stay up late to see revivals of his masterpieces at all-night showings in the Tokyo area.

Since Suzuki's best films were farces, he can be called a *gesakusha*, a humorist whose roots date back to the popular comical literature of the Edo period, for example, *Shank's Mare* (*Hizakurige*) by Ikku Jippensha (1765–1831). There have been other film-makers in this tradition who scorned the phony seriousness of the respectable, and together with "tendency" and nihilistic film directors, they formed an antiorthodox group. This was really the main current of early Japanese cinema, for the film world was not considered respectable until the late 1930s, and within the rigidity of Japanese culture, still bound by an academic attitude, it formed an influential counterculture force.

Many were discontent with the lowly status accorded to film and actively sought to raise it to the level of literature or painting, and gradually Kenji Mizoguchi, Yasujiro Ozu, and Akira Kurosawa were added to the list of representatives of Japanese culture. These film artists tended to stress moralistic themes and

221

valued a serious and rigorous approach to cinematic technique. On the other hand, Suzuki and those who intentionally stressed the countercultural aspect used antimoralistic and antiestablishment themes, and in technique cherished a light touch, aiming for an unconventional style.

Even serious directors such as Mansaku Itami and Sadao Yamanaka participated in the *gesaku,* or humorous side of the counterculture, by ridiculing Bushido, thereby embarking on new ground in the period drama genre. In fact, there was so much jest and playful parody in some of Yamanaka's films that a prewar critic claimed they lacked any intellectual thought. This judgment depends, of course, on the definition of "thought." In *Sazen Tange and the Pot Worth a Million Ryo* (*Tange Sazen—Hyakuman-ryo no Tsubo,* 1935) Yamanaka turns a Japanese superman into a lovable, unemployed man in Shitamachi, the old district of Tokyo. Here, as in his tragic masterpiece *Humanity and Paper Balloons* (*Ninjo Kami-fusen,* 1937), there is a rejection of heroism for a philosophy in which strength is juxtaposed with gentleness. This was not an inherited artistic tradition but a consistent endeavor to shatter old stereotypes, and surely such an original creation is worthy of the appelation "thought."

Yet since Yamanaka turned into a serious artist, it would be difficult to name him as the prewar predecessor of a light humorist like Seijun Suzuki. A better choice would be Masahiro Makino, who also specialized in popular entertainment pieces— usually swordfighting, or *chambara,* films, for while Makino was not exactly a humorist, he, like Suzuki, injected a playful mood into an action genre. During Makino's long career he created a number of excellent films, such as *The Street of Masterless Samurai, Genealogy of Women* (*Onna Keizu,* 1942), *A Horde of Drunken Knights* (1951), *Jirocho—The Record of Three Provinces* series (*Jirocho San-goku-shi,* 1953–54), and *An Account of the Chivalrous Commoners of Japan* series (*Nihon Kyokaku-den,* 1964–65), interspersed with pieces of rubbish. Still, his best films consistently feature the dreams of the weak and the illusions of the defeated, like those of humorists, since they were meant for the common people. Thus, Makino gave them a hero, the superman, and under his warm, sensitive direction, the viewer saw that these supermen who paraded their heroism were actually enjoying their shows of

222

strength themselves. They were play-acting, and when this mood of jest suddenly surfaces, we also recognize that it is nothing but a dream of the weak.

Although the phrase "nothing but a dream" is apt to mean nothing of value, the nuances in Makino's best films are better described "as fleeting and beautiful as a dream," and "as rambling as a dream." In the course of life we taste the bitter dregs of regret, and in order to dispel them and induce a blissfully ignorant sense of relief Makino gives us a hallucination of violence. His best films are the dreams of weak people, and while they may appear foolish to those who follow the strong—or who are under the illusion they themselves can become strong—to human beings who recognize their own weakness they are a joy to watch.

In the 1960s Seijun Suzuki took Masahiro Makino's dreamlike quality and made it even more evanescent. He then counterbalanced it with the farcical humor of a true *gesakusha* and introduced original cinematic techniques. This development was largely due to a unique brand of romanticism that he shared with his war-time generation of university students with a literary bent, many of whom, like Suzuki, were drafted during the large student mobilization in 1943 and sent to the front.

The generation preceding Suzuki's had received a Marxist baptism in their youth, and their artistic or literary expression tended to be based on ideas of social justice. We see them in the film world in the likes of Tadashi Imai and Satsuo Yamamoto, and Akira Kurosawa's and Keisuke Kinoshita's sympathy for the underdog is founded on the same premise. On the other hand, the postwar generation after Suzuki had been exposed to various schools of thought and had witnessed their shortcomings, such as Marxism degenerating into Stalinism. Consequently, self-assertion for them took precedence over social justice and, like Nagisa Oshima, they soon progressed toward opposition to oppression in any shape or form.

The war-time generation had only militarism, and literary youths such as Suzuki came to hate its senseless, coarse nature. Their only recourse was to read the Japanese classics, since most European and American works of art and literature were condemned as products of the enemy. In such an environment their thinking inevitably became more abstract, as it was better to take the philosophical view that life was based on fate rather than attempt to interpret reality. Their soldiering experiences and Japan's subsequent defeat reinforced this view, as it made more sense to disregard reality than participate in it.

Suzuki himself summed up this philosophy in an interview which appeared in the second issue of the magazine, *Cinema '69*.

"Shall I call it 'image?' Anyway, I think that what remains in our memory is not 'construction' but 'destruction.' Making things is not what counts. The power that destroys them is. For example, when Chusonji, the famous Buddhist temple grounds at Hiraizumi, was still standing, travelers would simply pass it by. I think they only began to notice it was there after it was in ruins. What is standing now isn't really there. It is just something reflected in our eyes. When it is demolished, the consciousness that it is, or was, there first begins to form. Thus, even in terms of civilization and culture, the power of destruction is the stronger. Consequently, I don't like films such as *Sun over the Kurobe Gorge* [about a dam]. I just don't like construction. I look down on it, actually. Everyone says that it is better to be asleep. That way you can do what you want. That blissful Japan really lives. Power exists, too. But we don't have to put on a red helmet [like student activists] to resist it. I'm saying it's better to do nothing at all. That way the ones to be worried will be those in power."

When Suzuki advocates the influence on culture of things destroyed by using the ruins at Hiraizumi as an example, the literary student of Japanese classics emerges because these grounds were built during the Heian period (794–1185). The influence of the famous thinker Hideo Kobayashi is also present. Kobayashi's concept of evanescence (*mujo-kan*) was the most influential ideology during World War II. By stressing the mutability of all things, he made young, intelligent men accept death and destruction on the battlefield.

For Hideo Kobayashi, Japan's defeat was merely a continuation of mutability, and he thought people should forget the horrors and sufferings and simply adjust to the present. For those like Suzuki, though, this would mean a betrayal of their grim youth. They had believed in the doctrine of mutability and had actually experienced it poised between life and death on the battlefield; when they returned from the war they felt that others should know it, too, in particular, its aspect of annihilation. Furthermore, when people began to talk of an age of construction following the previous one of destruction, Suzuki and his generation probably felt betrayed once more. Their feelings can be likened to film directors of the immediate postwar generation—Kei Kumai, Kiriro Urayama, and Masahiro Shinoda—who had firmly believed in postwar democracy only to be betrayed by reactionary movements like the red purge and the Self-Defense Force.

Besides destruction, humor is also an important ingredient of mutability for Suzuki, as is evident in his answer (in *Cinema '69*, no. 2) to the question: Why do the murder scenes in your films appear to be comical?

"When you go to war you get that feeling. It is inexcusable to say so, but it *is* humorous. For example, when someone got wounded at sea, he was rescued by an Imperial Navy ship from which a rope was thrown down. He tied it around his body, and they pulled him up. But since the rope swung back and forth, he kept banging into the side of the ship. The men that got pulled up had lumps all over their bodies, and they looked so funny.

"Once there were about ten dead men among those rescued, and all naval officers from ensign up were ordered to assemble. When we got to the deck, there was a bugler there and the corpses were placed below. Two sailors would come and get a hold of each one at the head and feet. The bugle would sound and they would throw the body into the water. Each time we heard the sound of the bugle, it was followed by that of the body plunking in the water. The tata-tata of the bugle and the plunking sound didn't go together at all. It was really funny."

For outside observers such as Hideo Kobayashi, the road to annihilation was beautiful as long as it was touched by a tragic or pathetic glow. However, for Seijun Suzuki, who had lived amid annihilation, it was necessary to view oneself objectively, even to the point where mutability appeared pathetic and humorous at the same time. Furthermore, it was even necessary to discover a certain masochistic pleasure in the abnormal nature of an experience that shook one's core, and for this reason Suzuki's best films take on the semblance of a masochistic cartoon.

Suzuki's masochistic attitude was probably reinforced by his postwar job as a director in the commercial film world. Before his own style emerged with *Wild Youth* (*Yaju no Seishun,* 1963), he made twenty-seven B pictures, which were routine job assignments. If he had made his directorial debut at Shochiku, where he served his apprenticeship as an assistant director, he probably would have been turning out "women's melodramas" just as assiduously. Since he did not like "construction" themes, he was fortunate that the studio's specialty was modern action films, but he would have tackled anything. He was able to accept the assignments because he saw humor in situations where the characters were faced with death. However, as in the case with compliance in the face of death on the battlefield, quietly grinding out films dictated by studio policy was by no means an easy, pleasurable task. In *Cinema '69,* no. 2, he had the following to say about it.

"Actually, making movies was painful work, as I often said to my wife. I had already wanted to quit four or five years before. I told her I hated this foolish, painful process. She told me I shouldn't say such a thing . . . that if I talked that way, it would come true. And it eventually did. [This alludes to his unfair dismissal from Nikkatsu in 1968.] For me, it was a relief. I felt that way from the very start."

Despite Suzuki's distaste for film-making, he eventually developed an original style that is well illustrated in the following scenes from the *yakuza* movie, *Kanto Wanderer* (*Kanto Mushuku,* 1963).

226 The hero (Akira Kobayashi), a bouncer at a gambling den, lives by the chivalrous code of *ninkyodo* and, out of a sense of honor, is forced to tackle two roughnecks who intend to pick a fight in the den. When the bare-chested hero suddenly swishes his sword and the two *yakuza* fall with a thud, everyone flees and all the *shoji* (paper-covered sliding doors) of the large room fall away in a wafting motion. The surrounding corridor is then revealed, bathed in brilliant red light. The scene changes in the next shot, and the screen is filled with snow. In the midst, shaded by a Japanese paper umbrella, the hero is striding forth to fight his enemies single-handedly.

The above scenes were so unexpectedly theatrical that they made the other scenes—which had by no means been subdued— credible, thus heightening these two splendid poses of the hero.

While the viewers were startled and absorbed by them, they could not help laughing at themselves for having been taken in by such abrupt histrionics.

Berthold Brecht also made use of abrupt histrionics. During a realistic play, he would suddenly insert expository lines piecemeal through songs, make use of masks, have the actors make machine-like movements, and so on. He himself called these devices alienation effects (*verfremdung effekt*), which would restrain audience empathy, thus maintaining objectivity throughout.

At first glance the abrupt histrionics in Suzuki's films from *Kanto Wanderer* on seemed to be a further elaboration of Brecht's alienation effects. However, whereas Brecht used them to reject empathy and negate catharsis, Suzuki employed them to enforce the pathetic beauty of the actor's pose to induce empathy. The resulting surge of emotions did not erupt into a tragic catharsis, though. While these theatrical poses were rich in pathos, they were nothing more than beautiful fragments, as fleeting as the sparks of fireworks in the night sky. Moreover, these poses were comical, not so much for satirical reasons as for relief, because for Suzuki humor serves as the only salvation for those who know mutability, the transience of all things.

Suzuki was obsessed with the idea that all human endeavors are foolish; yet if one affirms this foolishness, it becomes all the more interesting. Thus, he sought meaning in the humor of mutability, and in his films humor replaced catharsis.

In terms of the humor of evanescence, Suzuki's most remarkable film is *Tokyo Drifter* (*Tokyo Nagaremono*, 1966), for its flamboyant use of color, and its comical, eccentric tempo practically turned it into a pop art display. It was based on a popular song of the same title, and its absurd but amusing story developed along the lines of a potboiler. The hero, a modern *yakuza* played by Tetsuya Watari, is sent wandering in the provinces because of a dispute within his gang in Tokyo. Whenever he strikes a dramatic pose—drawing blood during a fight, or standing still in a deserted snowy field, or suddenly setting off on a journey—the title song comes on the sound track. The rhythm with which these poses occur is not consistent; they resemble flashes of transient beauty and humor upon the screen of a revolving lantern.

Suzuki's perception of mutability is best demonstrated in

Violence Elegy (*Kenka Ereji,* 1966), a memorable masterpiece in the tradition of the *gesakusha*. The story is set in the provincial areas of Okayama and Aizu in the 1930s, during the rise of militarism. In the beginning the hero, Kiroku Nanbu, a somewhat delinquent teenager played by Hideki Takahashi, is lodging at a relative's house in Okayama and going to high school there. The daughter of the house, a Christian, is also a student, and he has a crush on her. His platonic love differs considerably from that of more literary youths, for Kiroku is seized with sexual desire. He can only find release through fights with other teenagers like himself, or by daydreaming of the sublime love a knight offers a noble-woman. Once quieted, his sexual urge soon reappears, so he is continually fighting and becomes very good at it.

As Kiroku is a pure-hearted youth, his pride won't allow him to be satisfied with mere teenage gang fights, and so he even assumes a rebellious attitude toward his school. After he makes fun of the military instructor during a school drill practice, he is forced to leave Okayama. He goes to live with relatives in Aizu and continues to rebel, but since the school principal there likes youths with spirit, his rebellion does not end as an open dispute. Instead, he assembles his classmates and fights students from a neighboring school.

Although he enjoys such battles, he also realizes they are child-ish. One day in a coffee shop he exchanges glances with a middle-aged man with a piercing look. While wondering who he is, news is announced of the famous February 26 Incident of 1936, an attempted coup d'etat by one faction of the military. Kiroku later discovers that the older man is Ikki Kita, a right-wing thinker implicated in the incident and eventually executed. The film ends with Kiroku setting off for Tokyo to get into a bigger fight, no doubt the Sino-Japanese War, which began the next year (1937).

This somber, ironical ending to a film full of wild, entertaining fights, fantasy, and humor, was added by Seijun Suzuki himself since it was not in the original novel nor in the script by Kaneto Shindo. One especially remembers the scenes depicting the young hero's sexual frustrations. In one of them, he is alone at home and has an erection; he gleefully alleviates his distress by pound-ing on the keys of his platonic love's piano with his penis. In another, he is seized with the burning pangs of sexual anguish,

228

dashes outside, beats up some nearby toughs, and then returns to his room immediately, feeling refreshed in body and mind. Yet such exceedingly funny scenes are all tied together in the short, serious one in which Ikki Kita appeared, and this casts an eerie sense of uneasiness and a certain air of romanticism to the film.

The above effect could be attributed to the personage of Ikki Kita himself, for he had fanned the flames of revolutionary ardor in several young military officers with his doctrine of national socialism. However, since Suzuki detested the constructive, interest in ideology would not have been his reason for inserting the scene. He probably saw in Kita a pathetic symbol for human beings rushing headlong to their deaths in the coming world war. The many humorous episodes of the hero himself, before he meets Kita, probably presuppose a distant vision of annihilation, and are thereby beautiful. Here, as if by chance, we get a fleeting glimpse of the serious side of Seijun Suzuki.

4. SEX AND VIOLENCE

In the 1960s the subject most often treated in Japanese film was violence, with sex a close second. Nikkatsu's violent action thrillers and Toei's *yakuza* movies were the dominating genres, and the prolific "pink" movies—low-budget, soft-core pornography— eventually surpassed the yearly output of the five major film studios. With the exception of the Soviet Union and the People's Republic of China, the increase of this phenomenon was worldwide and even encompassed socialist nations of Eastern Europe. Two reasons cited for this trend are the lifting of censorship and a competitive commercialism, although commercialism can be discounted since artistic films also projected sex and violence.

The trend is evident in films made by Japan's leading directors of the 1960s—Shohei Imamura, Nagisa Oshima, Susumu Hani, Masahiro Shinoda, Yoshishige Yoshida, Seijun Suzuki, Yasuzo Masumura, and Koji Wakamatsu. It is also evident in the films of foremost European and American directors—Godard, Bergman, Fellini, Antonioni, Pasolini, Richardson, Schlesinger, Buñuel, Penn, and Nichols. All of them undoubtedly have their own reasons for following this course, as will be evident from a brief examination of the views of Japanese directors on sex.

For Imamura, sex is the act of a child seeking to nestle in the security of the womb. It symbolizes the lost sense of communalism that existed in the villages of old. In *Intentions of Murder,* the outwardly, tyrannical husband creeps into his wife's bed at night crying, "Mommy," in a childishly beseeching voice. The only spiritual source of support for the prostitute in *The Insect Woman* is the memory of the maternal love she had for her dead idiot father. In *The Profound Desire of the Gods,* a cloistered island village is spiritually controlled by a political leader who takes a *miko,* or temple priestess, as his mistress, and sex is the essential bond holding the community together.

In the work of Oshima, sex takes on a more aggressive aspect. The young couple in *Cruel Story of Youth* strive to free themselves from society's restrictions, and the first liberty they reach for is sexual. In *Pleasures of the Flesh* an unhappy, dissatisfied youth lays hands on a large sum of money and begins to sleep with all sorts of women. *Violence at Noon* concerns a degenerate who only obtains sexual satisfaction through rape, and is a symbolic probe of the violent, irrational results of sexual repression. This problem is treated more concretely in *A Treatise on Japanese Bawdy Song,* about the wild sexual fantasies of frustrated college students, and in *Death by Hanging,* an analysis of the sex crime of a Korean youth born and living in Japan.

Oshima's treatment of sex led him to differ from leftist directors of the 1950s because, unlike his predecessors, he regarded psychological repression to be as important an issue as economic poverty. In contrast to their portrayal of the normal, healthy masses, Oshima's later films on repression presented characters who were spiritually sick or psychologically perverse. His main theme then became an attempt to liberate the self from this deformity through sudden violent acts, and in such situations sex served as the most vivid symbol of liberation.

In Hani's films, sex is a key to development, for they are generally stories of how a youth breaks out of the small hard shell of the ego to form deeper relationships with others. In his greatest work, *The Inferno of First Love* (*Hatsukoi Jigoku-hen,* 1968), sex is treated as the adventure of a young soul, and sexual development is equated with human development, that is, maturation. Early in the film the boy's masturbation is portrayed in a particularly vivid manner. Then the director follows each microscopic step in his psychological process toward an attempt at sexual union with a girl.

Yoshida continually ponders whether it is only through sex that human beings can cast aside their respective egos and effect a union, and if so, what they discard thereby. In a superior early film, *Akizu Hot Springs*, the heroine gives her body to an unfortunate youth, but as time passes she is so revolted by his philistine character that she commits suicide. In his later films the heroine, usually played by his wife Mariko Okada, continues to languish while searching for sexual fulfillment. She is usually a proud woman, and the more pride she has the less she can bear the thought of having sexual relations with a worthless man and surrendering to him psychologically. At the same time, however, she needs men to liberate herself from the insecurity and loneliness of a strong ego. Through such a woman Yoshida relates the dilemma of individual autonomy and the need for social bonds, and for him sex becomes the best symbol. In his masterpiece *Eros Plus Massacre*, the search for individual autonomy through free love ultimately fails because the people concerned inevitably try to monopolize one another.

For Masumura, sex is the very lust for life itself. In *The Red Angel* (*Akai Tenshi*, 1966), set in China during World War II, the army nurse (Ayako Wakao) is swept into sexual relations with Japanese soldiers who are on the brink of death. From its content, this fine film might be confused with pornography; however, through the fierceness of its expression, sex becomes the symbol of the will to live even in the direst circumstances. A young man who has lost both arms in battle pleads with the nurse to masturbate him, and she obliges. The field doctor, despairing at the lack of facilities, takes drugs and becomes impotent, and the nurse helps him recover by giving him her body. In the end her efforts are to no avail: the armless soldier commits suicide and the doctor has himself sent to the front to be slain by the enemy. Her zest for life is unable to save them because they are trapped within a social code that stresses glory on the battlefield and regards weakness with shame.

Shinoda's view that sex is the purest of pleasures is best illustrated in *With Beauty and Sorrow* (*Utsukushisa to Kanashimi to,*

1965) and *Double Suicide* (*Shinju Ten no Amijima*, 1969). In these films he portrays men and women who, by their own acts, create a situation in which the only way they can enjoy sexual pleasure is to pay for it with their lives. His lovers rush headlong to their fate. Resolved to die, they ignore all social convention and are thus able to enter the realm of ecstasy. This is pure aestheticism, where the beautiful is valued more than life itself, but in Shinoda's films fulfillment is not complete. It seems that he puts greater emphasis on the determination to pursue pleasure than its attainment.

In the work of Wakamatsu, "the determination to pursue pleasure" has none of Shinoda's aestheticism, and it is sadism pure and simple. In *The Embryo Hunts in Secret* (*Taiji ga Mitsuryo Suru Toki*, 1966) and *Violated Women in White* (*Okasareta Byakui*, 1967), Wakamatsu does nothing more than create a world where men cruelly abuse women, half killing them in the process, and their anguished faces deny that pure pleasure is possible in this world. Wakamatsu also shows us that the more one engages in sadism, the more it turns into something resembling a fairy tale, whose allure turns into antipathy toward reality.

In the films of Tetsuji Takechi sexual relations are usually an allegory for the relation between the rulers and the ruled in politics. In *Black Snow* (*Kuroi Yuki*, 1965) and *A Tale of Postwar Cruelty* (*Sengo Zankoku Monogatari*, 1968), the powerless position of Japan vis-à-vis America, and of the Japanese populace in relation to its rulers is represented by the outraged Japanese women and the G.I. rapists.

232

This sexual wave in films of the 1960s is the vehicle for many messages, depending on the director, but the question remains why all these directors used sex to express their message.

Despite thematic differences, the above directors were all trying to grasp the nature of feelings that lie deep in the human psyche. Moreover, fundamental human problems, such as the relationship between rulers and ruled, the power-wielder and slave, harmony and confrontation, freedom and loneliness, can all be seen within the sexual relationship between a man and a woman. These problems are usually defined in a social or political context and treated accordingly. However, it then becomes extremely difficult to investigate them without using existing morality, and the investigator is hampered by hackneyed notions of social justice, traditional or modern, and cannot consider the raw passions and sentiments of the individuals involved. On the other hand, in the context of the complicated sexual relations between a man and a woman, it becomes possible to objectively investigate the will to dominate and submissiveness, as well as the loneliness attendant on the thirst for freedom, and to portray such problems realistically.

While it is difficult for an individual to grasp entities such as society and government, sex is a sensual experience. Accordingly, in contrast to social and political problems which are usually considered intellectually and lead to consent or indignation, sexual problems are confronted at a gut level and bring about a struggle between what one thinks and what one physically demands. Problems that activate such an internal struggle cannot be solved by the precept of "social justice," for they boil down to the question of what one is really searching for in life. This question is made tangible by treating it from the emotional angle in the dimension of sexual demands. In this manner, both the film's creator and the viewer can feel the struggle within themselves and can begin to grope for an answer in the twilight zone between this sexual dimension and intellectual abstractions such as freedom, the will to obtain power, the consensus of the community, and so forth.

In the late 1950s and 1960s the only effective films seemed to be those that fulfilled such gropings. Directors who appealed solely to social justice may have achieved some understanding of that precept, but could not move their audiences. These new directors, on the other hand, perceived the necessity of starting from the dimension of sexual demands and developing their individual themes accordingly.

While films with sex activated an internal struggle between what an individual thinks and what his body demands, films with violence anticipated the struggles in the 1960s in modern societies, struggles to express the passionate needs of diverse groups. In the past, social, or at least group, solidarity was stressed in Japanese cinema, and this was particularly evident during the war. Depictions of sexual love were completely absent and those of romantic and conjugal love exceedingly rare. In their place,

Japanese audiences were subjected to the camaraderie among soldiers, the self-effacing fraternity between neighbors, family love, love of one's birthplace, and, of course, love of the fatherland. At a time when the Japanese nation was exerting an enormous amount of violence abroad, "spiritual healthiness" and social harmony were demanded by the government through the cinema.

A similar situation has probably existed in other war-time nations. The first notable exception was the U.S. during the Vietnam War, for then the mass media, television in particular, gave considerable coverage to the violent Black Power and antiwar movements that sprang up within the country itself. Television may have also influenced these movements, since it transmitted coverage of the Vietnam War to U.S. citizens.

This war highlighted the fact that members of developed societies, such as the U.S. and Japan, are not simply satisfied with local news and domestic affairs in the age of mass media. News of a war within a confined area of a distant country is transmitted almost immediately and can instigate a domestic, ideological debate. Even within one's own country, struggles concerning specific problems in certain geographical regions can become nationwide matters. Consequently, citizens soon know that confrontations are being conducted with a naked show of force, and they can no longer believe that their society is based on a kind of "brotherly love." The desires and intentions of diverse groups are often communicated through power plays in which violence is not an abnormal effect but part of the main thrust. Given such a social climate the inevitable escalation of violence in Japanese films, beginning in the early 1960s, cannot simply be due to "post-war decadence." This escalation also anticipated the Japanese consciousness, for the public did not realize the violent turn of events in their society until 1967, when student activists began hurling rocks and brandishing wooden poles at riot police. Japanese film-makers, sensitive to the inevitability of violence in contemporary society, produced modern action thrillers and *yakuza* movies to replace period dramas in the theater circuit.

The period drama was once the only genre where violence was used as a mode of expression. However, even though the swordplay could be termed violent, the stories, depicting a society with a rigid hierarchy, were like fairy tales to modern, mobile Japanese.

234

Furthermore, no matter how much violence occurs in a period drama, disrupting effects are minimized and the social order is never in danger of disintegration. On the contrary, when a noble samurai cuts down a villain, violence is employed to support the status quo.

In modern action and *yakuza* films, although the gangs are ruled by their own hierarchy, the plot develops on the basis of its gradual disintegration. Despite the underworld theme, the modern viewer feels closer to this type of society than to feudal society. The attraction of modern films with violence, therefore, rests on the realistic portrayal of the relations between diverse groups. Indeed, the significance in these films seems to be how an individual can act with grace amid conflicting power groups.

Another explanation for the proliferation of sex and violence movies lies in the major change in audience composition between the 1950s and 1960s, although this also reflects the sensitivity of film-makers to changing conditions.

In the 1950s the inherent social value of film lay in its rare ability to transcend differences in age, sex, social class, and education, giving its audience a common emotional experience. Even though Kurosawa's *Ikiru,* Kinoshita's *Twenty-four Eyes,* and Imai's *Darkness at Noon* leaned toward the tastes of progressive intellectuals and women, they still managed to appeal to the emotions of the public at large. *Ikiru*'s morbid theme—a main character fated to die of stomach cancer in six months—pulled the heart strings of those who hoped to steer through the dark, dismal postwar days by clutching at their old work ethic. *Twenty-four Eyes* seemed to crystallize the feelings of pacifism in the Japanese audience, which included housewives and intellectuals, the bourgeoisie and the proletariat. *Darkness at Noon* was based on Hiroshi Masaki's book *The Judge (Saibankan),* in which the judicial system rather than the accused parties was indicted in a famous murder case. The book was a best seller, but the author's plea only became a public issue after the movie, which succeeded in persuading the common people of the well-founded criticism by a group of intellectuals.

In the 1950s the cinema was still the most influential medium in Japanese society compared to literary works, which had select readers, and popular songs, ballads (*naniwa bushi*), and other performing arts, which would not accept contemporary themes. In the 1960s, however, with the popularity of television, housewives stopped going to movies and "women's melodrama" (sentimental love stories) and the home drama genres were dealt a death blow. Even "human dramas" like *Twenty-four Eyes* rapidly lost appeal. Spurred by interest in foreign language study, especially English, and the dream of traveling to the U.S. and Europe, even the young unmarried women stopped going to movies and the only major film-going group became young bachelors working in Tokyo.

A change in housing patterns following a heavy influx of young workers and college students from the country, which began in the 1950s and skyrocketed in the 1960s, meant that entertainment areas of large cities (and in Tokyo these are situated near every major train station) became packed with wooden housing units for young bachelors, bartenders, cabaret hostesses, and so on. When these people got married, they usually moved to the suburbs, and since that meant a two-hour daily commute, it was extremely difficult for them to keep up the habit of going to the movies. Thus, the movie theater audience came to consist largely of young bachelors who loved erotic and violent films, whose continued success in turn kept older men and women from movie theaters.

Consequently, the Japanese audience in the 1960s was divided into two main groups: television viewers and cinema viewers. The former were usually small families flattered by television dramas that lauded home and hearth. For the most part they were satisfied with life and liked "things as they are." Cinema viewers, on the other hand, preferred sex and violence, since they were all young bachelors dissatisfied with life and society. In movie theaters, where real women could not be found, erotic and violent stimuli escalated and aggressive and self-destructive impulses ran amok. Although unmarried women who doted on foreign movies were a marginal factor, upon marriage the vast majority of them would probably be content with television home dramas.

Naturally, television, despite its appeal to the contented, had its share of incisive documentaries on shameful realities about "things as they are"; conversely, despite a basically discontented audience, some films (which were often financed by big business)

236

affirmed "things as they are" in the form of praise for Japan's postwar prosperity. Still, regardless of these exceptions, television created a world of hypocritical goodness, and the cinema, one of hypocritical evil. These different approaches to reality are accurate gauges of audience reaction and can be considered two distinct cultures which are independent and do not interact. The cinema of the 1950s—a grand culture embracing people of different ages, sex, social class, or education—had been split into a "tube culture" and a "screen culture."

This split corresponds to the two-tiered structure of the Japanese population whereby television appeals to the fixed populations of town and country, and the cinema to migrant workers and students from regional areas. Just as the double structure of the economy, which pits large enterprises against smaller ones, does not necessarily appear as a clear-cut case of class conflict, the two populations do not seem to be divided by social class or status. However, judging from their preferred media, their psychological make-ups are obviously different. In contrast to television's happy families, modern action and *yakuza* movies praise the lone wolves, with emotions wavering between loneliness and camaraderie. Despite the close ties that bind members of a gang, these loners give the impression that such social bonds are only an illusion and cast them aside in favor of individual action.

This kind of hero appealed to the most alienated sector in the two-tiered population structure. In the 1960s the cinema had become their preserve, almost being a "mini" medium, since television had the larger audience. Although some may regret the loss of the cinema's capacity to transcend social classes, this new state of affairs made it possible for cinema to become the spokesman for alienated minorities.

While democracy is based on the principle of majority rule and happiness for the greatest number, it became increasingly evident in the 1960s that this principle was used to stifle the demands of minorities. Therefore, the defiance of those conscious of themselves as an alienated minority takes on greater significance, and only the cinema could articulate their existence. Just who "they" are is insignificant. For example, a junior high school graduate can be considered a minority vis-à-vis those with advanced education. On the other hand, college students could feel that they are alienated from the rest of society. Whatever the case, the standard, uniform labels of workers and masses no longer apply, and it is the task of cinema today to persevere with the expression of the needs of such minorities.

5. CINEMATIC GUERRILLAS

In the late 1960s a number of film-makers drew attention to the existence of alienated minorities by independently producing and showing documentaries of their struggles. The most famous was Shinsuke Ogawa, who became an independent after refusing to make sponsored PR films. His first effort was *Sea of Youth* (*Seinen no Umi*, 1965), a short documentary about some part-time students who began a protest movement against retrogressive reforms by the Ministry of Education. Capital was collected by the students themselves, and the object of the production was achieved when Ogawa took the film on tour and showed it to part-time student groups nationwide.

Ogawa became widely known as a result of his next documentary, *The Oppressed Students* (*Ansatsu no Mori*, 1967), about the long, bitter struggle of a small number of students who managed to occupy school buildings at Takasaki College of Economics. Ogawa later showed it at universities throughout the nation, and this record of the actual fighting as well as the passion of the students left a strong impression on viewers. In retrospect, it seems to have been a preview of the university riots throughout Japan in the late 1960s.

238

Ogawa also dug in with the farmers of Sanrizuka in Chiba Prefecture against the expropriation of their land for the new airport. He made *Summer in Sanrizuka: The Front Line for the Liberation of Japan* (*Nihon Kaiho Sensen—Sanrizuka no Natsu*, 1968), and over the next five years made five more feature-length documentaries while living with the farmers.

Through these independent productions and showings, Ogawa and others broke with precedent, for news in the past was made by mass communication networks and distributed by them to the general public. Since it cost money to come out with a big newspaper or to make films, people did not question this state of affairs. Only small newspapers and clublike little magazines—low-cost operations—could form a "mini communication network." However, if they dealt with news of a probing nature—too hot for the mass communication networks to handle—issue was taken with them and they could only be published through the strenuous efforts of a few people.

In the 1960s, however, through Ogawa and others it became possible to form a "mini communication network" through cinema, and since films could be shown to large audiences, this was a distinct improvement over the limited communication of a small magazine. Furthermore, ordinary citizens could become journalists by bringing their own cameras to a demonstration and recording it on film. Then they could show it privately. As such, making one's own news became the ideal and goal of the independent documentary film movement, and this capacity would only increase with further development in film techniques— unless the movement was suppressed for political reasons.

This film movement continued in the 1970s, and the greatest contributions made then were by Noriaki Tsuchimoto. Ever since he came out with *Minamata: The Victims and Their World* (*Minamata—Kanja-san to Sono Sekai*, 1971), he has continued to make feature-length documentaries in the fishing village of Minamata in Kyushu about the victims of mercury poisoning there—those who have died and those who have suffered severe ailments—and their struggle to receive compensation from the government and the industry which caused the water pollution. Whenever difficult problems arose during this distressful struggle, Tsuchimoto and his crew would make a new film as a means of solving them. Once when they learned that Minamata disease had broken out in a Canadian Indian reservation, they took their films to Canada to show to the Indians there.

12
Developments in the 1970s

240 Until 1960 the Japanese had thought of themselves as part of poverty-ridden Asia, so it was a shock when they found out that Japan had become one of the world's most affluent nations in the early 1970s. Since the early 1900s Japan had been more prosperous than other Asian countries, but the Japanese fear of being swallowed up by the imperialist powers of the time made them intent on catching up with or even surpassing the wealthy nations of Europe and the U.S. The belief in Japan's poverty was reinforced by the hard times after Japan's defeat in World War II, with the result that Japanese could not believe they could ever become as affluent as Europe or America.

This consciousness was apparent in most serious masterpieces, which frequently portrayed people striving in vain to escape from poverty. Some examples are Mizoguchi's *Osaka Elegy* and Ozu's *The Only Son* of 1936, Kurosawa's *One Wonderful Sunday* of 1947, and Oshima's *A Town of Love and Hope* of 1959.

By the 1970s, however, Japanese no longer considered themselves poor, and according to a survey taken in 1980, ninety percent stated that they thought they belonged to the middle class. While these views are only subjective, it is evident that even though poverty existed, its scope was greatly diminished. Accordingly, film-makers could not continue portraying the theme of escape from poverty. (A few leftists did by showing destitute workers waging a class struggle against the capitalists, but their works lacked reality and force.)

One of the ways this social change was manifested was in love stories, which from around 1910 through the 1950s usually depicted romance between the rich and the poor. The 1938 commercial success of *The Compassionate Buddha Tree,* where the rich son and his poor girlfriend cannot marry due to opposition from his family, was eclipsed by the 1953 melodrama *What Is Your Name?* about a poor girl who marries into a rich family but cannot forget her love for a poor boy she met during a Tokyo air raid. She eventually leaves her husband and goes through a series of hardships until she is reunited with the poor boy. This poor girl-rich boy theme in the love melodrama genre was even popular with artistic directors like Mizoguchi (*The Story of the Last Chrysanthemums,* 1939) and Yoshimura (*Warm Current,* 1939). By the 1960s, however, largely due to the decline of the old bourgeoisie after 1945, this theme was suddenly behind the times, and Kinoshita's *The Bitter Spirit/Immortal Love* (*Eien no Hito,* 1961), set in the 1930s, was its last masterpiece.

As the Japanese rose in affluence, other popular genres were also discarded, such as the mother films (*haha mono*), which had been big box-office hits throughout the 1950s. Ozu's *The Only Son* was an artistic work on this theme, in which a mother suffers hardships for her child's success. The poverty-ridden mother raises her son with high hopes, only to be disappointed in him as an adult. Kinoshita's *A Japanese Tragedy* was another, in which the mother finds that her son and daughter interpret modernization and postwar democracy to mean that they are no longer under any obligation to take care of her in her old age. Popular melodramas about mothers, on the other hand, often featured a poor woman who cannot marry a rich man but has an illegitimate child by him. Thereupon, either she undergoes hardships raising the child or the child is raised by the man's wife, and on reaching adulthood he is torn between the mother who gave birth to him and the mother who raised him. Whatever the case, these films served to praise the nobility of poverty-ridden mothers.

As a rule the 1950s produced hardly any films with a happy mother in the leading role. The mothers were played by middle-aged and older actresses, and the more miserable they looked the nobler they appeared. Even in Ozu's postwar films about relatively happy homes, it was the daughter who would be given the main role, and the story ended when she left home to marry. At any rate, as the number of poor mothers decreased, so did the popularity of mother films. In the television family dramas of the 1970s she reemerged as a beautiful fifty- or sixty-year-old heroine who enjoys home life. She is shown in one beautiful, expensive kimono after another, chatting so cheerfully that it disconcerts her mild-mannered husband and sons. Housewives who had previously cried when they saw miserable mothers on the screen now accepted these cheerful and beautiful middle-aged women as perfectly natural.

Another genre associated with past poverty, *yakuza* films, also headed for a decline in the 1970s. The hero of these films was usually a man raised in a poor environment, who then becomes an outlaw. In the end he would fight a just battle with the strong and evil for the sake of the poor and weak. Such a hero was only a myth, but he was loved by the Japanese, who were mostly poor and preferred to believe that they were honest while the rich were liars. It may seem paradoxical that *yakuza* movies were at their zenith in the relatively affluent 1960s. The rapid social changes then perhaps brought on a sense of insecurity, which the myth of "*yakuza* justice" served to allay. By around 1973, however, they suddenly lost their appeal, as if the viewer suddenly realized that *yakuza* movies were a fake, and film companies specializing in them turned out a few realistic versions of the *yakuza* world while waiting for a new fad to appear. The best of these was Kinji Fukasaku's *Battles without Honor and Humanity* series (*Jingi Naki Tatakai,* 1973–76), about cruel killings within one gang. Some were successful, but audiences soon tired of them by the end of the 1970s.

By then, as we have seen, several important genres that had previously been big box-office attractions lost their popularity, and the only series that survived the 1970s was *It's Tough To Be a Man (Otoko wa Tsurai yo)*. With two sure hits every year, director Yoji Yamada had the freedom to make individual masterpieces like *The Family (Kazoku,* 1970), *Home (Kokyo,* 1972), *The Yellow Handkerchieves of Happiness (Kofuku no Kiiroi Hankachi,* 1978), and *The Call of Distant Mountains (Harukanaru Yama no Yobigoe,* 1980). Yamada has so far made twenty or so films in the *It's Tough To Be a Man* series, and none have failed at the box office despite the same characters appearing in each and the lack of variation in the stories.

The famous comedian Kiyoshi Atsumi plays the role of the main character, Tora-san. He is a *tekiya,* an itinerant merchant who sells inexpensive merchandise at festivals and is a persuasive talker. Tora-san's relatives are all waiting for the day he finds a decent job, for although *tekiya* were common in the past, with Japan's affluence and the availability of more lucrative jobs, they have virtually disappeared. Tora-san is therefore a lonely figure who does not intend to give up his trade, and in the highly regulated and bureaucratized modern society he is probably the last free spirit left. At times when he can no longer bear the loneliness of traveling, he returns to his home in the Tokyo area to see his aunt and uncle and his younger sister and brother-in-law. There he always falls in love with a beauty, and after suffering a broken heart, he sets out on his travels again.

The appeal of this series lies in his free spirit and in Tora-san's home, Katsushika Shibamata, which used to be a small town on the outskirts of Tokyo but is now incorporated into the burgeoning metropolis. It is like a neighborhood in the Japan of the past, where neighbors help each other out and freely enter and leave each other's homes as though they are all members of the same family. This way of life has been steadily disappearing in Japan's modernized cities, but is miraculously preserved in this film version of Katsushika Shibamata. It is this idealization of the old neighborhood that captures the heart of modern Japanese audiences.

This series allowed Yamada to become the only director in the 1970s to maintain a steady stream of successes and a reputation for artistic and social responsibility. A socialist, Yamada's main theme in all his works is not the class struggle but the maintaining of warm, human relations within families and communities in danger of collapse in an industrialized society.

The extinction of many film genres in the 1970s also altered the old dichotomy between the *tateyaku* and *nimaime* roles. The male lead in *The Yellow Handkerchieves of Happiness* and *The Call of Distant Mountains* was Ken Takakura, a *tateyaku*-type actor who had won fame through *yakuza* movies of the 1960s. As he came slashing his way into the villains' den for the sake of the good but weak, he was greeted with applause by college student audiences, aroused by the campus struggles in 1967 and 1968. In these later films by Yamada, however, Takakura takes the role of a man who has just served out his prison sentence for murder. He becomes a wanderer, in search of a peaceful life. In both films Takakura's shyness in confessing his love for a woman he meets, which due to *tateyaku* tradition he does awkwardly, still breaks the taboo that a noble man does not love a woman. Yamada's sound judgment even succeeded in bringing some women viewers back to movie theaters.

The *nimaime*-type of leading man also remained successful in the 1970s, albeit so changed that he can only be recognized after a brief diversion into the development of artistic porno films. As mentioned earlier, Japanese movie audiences decreased heavily in the 1960s, from a total attendance of 1.2 billion in 1960 to 0.2 billion in 1980. Consequently, major companies like Toei, Toho, and Shochiku, which had been producing about a hundred movies annually, curtailed their output, some even going bankrupt, such as Shin Toho in 1961 and Daiei in 1971. Nikkatsu, which was close to bankruptcy in 1971, managed to survive by specializing in soft-core porno films, called *"roman"* porno, as against the cheaper "pink" films, which had been flourishing since 1960. Although film critics ignored Nikkatsu's *roman* porno at first, they later recognized the artistic value of some after Tatsumi Kumashiro came out with *Sayuri Ichijo—Moist Desire* (*Ichijo Sayuri— Nureta Yokujo,* 1972). In all Kumashiro's different types of films, men and women sacrifice everything for the sake of sensual

244

pleasure. Even prostitutes, a frequent subject of his, are portrayed as lovable human beings because of their love of pleasure. In *The Four-and-a-Half-Mat Room in Back—Soft, Secret Skin* (*Yojohan Fusuma no Urabari—Shinobi Hada*, 1974), Kumashiro's main character is a youth who is raised in a brothel and goes about gratifying the sexual needs of the prostitutes. Since he is so likable, he is an interesting variation of the *nampa*-type of juvenile delinquent—the skirt-chaser.

The opposite of the *nampa* was the *koha*, or ruffian, and this dichotomy of social deviancy was strictly maintained until the influence of postwar Americanism. It is thus a demonstration of the tenacity of feudalistic attitudes toward sex in Japan. The *koha* delinquent, like the *tateyaku* and the samurai, regards sex as a necessary evil and ignores women, preferring to fight morning, noon, and night. He is often also a rightist. The *nampa*, like the *nimaime* and the townspeople, believes love to be the greatest joy in life and is constantly in search of the forbidden pleasures of love and sex. He looks down on the *koha* and is more liberal in his politics.

Kumashiro's lovable youth who gives sexual satisfaction to prostitutes is probably the first presentation of the *nampa*-type of juvenile delinquent as an ideal. He is the symbol of the old townspeople's culture, a culture expressed in *nimaime* performances in Kabuki plays about lovers' suicides—an extreme manifestation of sensual pleasure—and in erotic *ukiyo-e* paintings of the feudal age. It continues to be a vibrant tradition and is the extreme opposite of samurai culture.

Another expression of this tradition can be found in the male lead of Oshima's *The Realm of the Senses* (*Ai no Koriida*, 1976), a film backed by French interests and based on an actual incident that occurred in 1936. The sexual excesses of Kichizo and his sweetheart, Sada Abe, culminate in her strangling him to death at the height of sexual ecstasy and castrating him afterward. Contemporary Japanese were interested in this incident because of Sada Abe, a woman with an amazing appetite for sex, and her murdered lover elicited only pity as a comical sacrifice. Oshima, however, portrays Kichizo as a man who did not mind being killed if he could sexually excite and please the woman he loved. In this way, he represents a development of the *nimaime* tradition, and through him Oshima's film becomes a beautiful tragedy rather than a simple tale of sexual indulgence.

Oshima's film was made possible by an important development in the 1970s, the rise of independent producers. Until 1960, the market was almost monopolized by three to six major companies, and while this state of affairs stabilized production, it was also extremely difficult to produce films that did not please studio heads. This monopoly collapsed with the decline of the industry in the 1970s. Although film production in general became more difficult, film-makers with originality could produce and distribute, at their own risk, different kinds of movies. Three directors who did this were Imamura, Seijun Suzuki, and Kurosawa.

Imamura's *Revenge Is for Us* (*Fukushu Suru wa Ware ni Ari,* 1979), about the life of a clever con man who commits a series of brutal murders, is an examination of his innermost feelings. Suzuki's *Zigeunerweisen* (*Tsuigoineruwaizen,* 1980) begins with a recording of violinist Pablo de Sarasate playing his own composition ("The Gypsy Melody" of the title), and then delves into the bizarre lives of five men and women whose existence takes on a ghostlike quality. As the director himself says, "It is a film where living people are actually dead and the dead are actually alive." Kurosawa's major period drama, *Kagemusha* (*Kagemusha,* 1980), is the story of a double for a famous general who died in 1573.

These three masterpieces all have the common theme of protagonists who do not know who they really are, or whose outward appearance and inner subjectivity are so different that they have illusions about which is their true self. In previous Japanese movies, directors only portrayed people who knew exactly who they were. Many of them had no doubts at all about the feudalistic moral system, for example, loyalty toward one's superiors, and only a few revolted against it. There were those who strove against poverty to make a happy home, and the defeated who failed in these endeavors. They all knew what they were seeking, or what they lacked. At the end of the 1970s they are replaced by characters with identity problems, who cannot apprehend what it is they are seeking.

These characters are an honest reflection of the situation confronting the modern Japanese. The greater part of their tradition, in particular loyalty toward one's superiors, was annihilated by

246

defeat in World War II. The hundred-year-old goal of catching up with the West so as not to become a colony is now achieved, but the values and ideals associated with pursuing that goal are lost, or uncertain. American-style democracy lost a lot of credibility due to the Vietnam War and the abnormal increase in crime there in the 1970s. For leftists, both the Soviet Union and the People's Republic of China became fallen idols in the 1960s and 1970s. The advanced countries of Western Europe, from which Japan traditionally imported new ideas, new learning, and art forms, no longer exert the same influence. In short, since the Japanese are at a loss for suitable models, they must discover themselves by themselves. The present Japanese cinema has reached the position where people at least recognize that they do not know who they are, and we should watch closely for what they will create next.

APPENDIX I

A Chronology

1896
Edison's Kinetoscope is imported.
1897
The Lumière brothers' Cinématographe and Edison's Vitascope are imported. Films are shown in Japan with a narrator (*benshi*), a system that continues until talkies replace silent movies.
1899
The first Japanese films are shown. Performances by Kabuki actors Danjuro Ichikawa and Kikugoro Onoe in *Maple Viewing* are recorded on film, and this is the oldest extant Japanese film. It was shown to the public four years later.
1900
With the Boxer Rebellion in north China, the first newsreels are made.
1902
The American movie *Robinson Crusoe* is imported, marking the first public showing of a feature-length film in Japan.
1903
The first permanent movie theater is built in Tokyo.
1904
Newsreels of the Russo-Japanese War prove very popular.
1905
Japanese film producers venture on extensive film tours of Southeast Asia, with the result that the word *nippon* (Japan) comes to mean "movies" in Thailand.
1906
The first "color" movie, with color painted onto the film, is shown to the public.
1907
Osaka's first permanent movie theater is built.

1908

A Kyoto Kabuki manager, Shozo Makino, begins making period drama movies with Kabuki actors. He nurtures so many superstars in that genre that he is dubbed its father.

1909

Matsunosuke Onoe, Japan's first movie star, appearing in over 1,000 films, makes his debut in Shozo Makino's *Tadanobu Goban* (*Goban Tadanobu*). Onoe came from Kabuki and specialized in playing heroic warrior roles.

1911

The French detective film *Zigomar the Eelskin* scores a big hit. Some Japanese youths imitate its criminal behavior, leading to the beginnings of a form of censorship.

1912

The first major film company, Nikkatsu, is established, and the Japanese film industry begins mass production.

1913

Several Japanese crime movies modeled on *Zigomar the Eelskin* are made.

1914

The Japanese film *Katusha*, based on Tolstoy's *Resurrection,* draws large audiences. The heroine is played by the *onnagata* Teijiro Tachibana, since film followed the theater in having men play all female roles. Teinosuke Kinugasa, the renowned director, begins training as an *onnagata* with a Shimpa troupe.

1915

American action serials gain popularity.

1916

The Italian historical drama *Cabiria* is a big hit. Intellectuals still prefer foreign to Japanese films, which attract the common people.

1918

America's "Bluebird Movies," sentimental love stories centering around farm life, win over Japanese audiences, as do Charlie Chaplin's films. Sentimental contemporary Japanese dramas (Shimpa) are also popular. Norimasa Kaeriyama starts a reform movement with two experimental films, *The Glow of Life* (*Sei no Kagayaki*) and *Maid of the Deep Mountains* (*Miyama no Otome*), both of which he produced, wrote, and directed. One of the movement's objectives is to replace *onnagata* with actresses, another is to reduce the role of the *benshi* by inserting subtitles. The more famous *benshi* would insist that studios make movies with long shots so they could talk as much as they wanted, and this often angered directors who were trying to improve Japanese film technique

250

by increasing the tempo. Until then, as many as four *benshi* would deliver the lines in one movie. As *benshi* are more popular than movie stars, they cannot be dismissed so easily, and the practice of one narrator per film is agreed on. The two movies by Kaeriyama encourage young progressive film-makers and fans, but as films they are mere imitations of Western models.

1919

Griffith's *Intolerance* and Chaplin's *A Dog's Life* are hits. During World War I, Italian, Swedish, and Danish films ceased to be imported, American films taking their place. Japanese film is still immature and scorned by Japanese intellectuals, but youths such as Ozu, who were deeply impressed by American movies, come to lead a movement to improve Japanese cinema.

1920

Amateur Club (*Amachua Kurabu*), styled after American comedies, is produced with Junichiro Tanizaki writing the script and former Hollywood actor Thomas Kurihara directing. Japan's second major film company, Shochiku, begins production. It uses actresses instead of *onnagata*, and introduces new techniques under the guidance of former Hollywood cameraman Henry Kotani. Nikkatsu also begins using actresses, and *onnagata* vanish completely from the film world in a few years.

1921

Director Kaoru Osanai, a leading figure in Japanese theater who introduced modern European drama, forms a film research center, which produces Japan's first artistic experimental work, *Souls on the Road* (*Rojo no Reikon*). Although immature and imitative, two of the young men involved—Minoru Murata and Yasujiro Shimazu—soon became leading film directors and set a standard of artistic quality.

251

1923

Young period drama actors such as Tsumasaburo Bando appear in film and are very popular. In contrast to Matsunosuke Onoe's formalized swordfighting style, Bando's is violent and fast. The characters portrayed by Bando are not Kabuki heroes but nihilistic outlaws who rebel against traditional society. These new heroes are well received among the young and remain popular until the early 1930s, when such films are suppressed. Sumiko Kurishima, who plays the leading roles in Shochiku's sentimental dramas, is the first actress to attain star status.

1924

Minoru Murata directs *Seisaku's Wife,* a tragic antiwar love story set in a farming village.

1925

Censorship by the Ministry of the Interior becomes standardized, with the objectives of maintaining the dignity of the imperial family and the authority of the military, of excluding leftist thought, and of cutting out kissing scenes and other "erotica." Even foreign news films on scandals among European royalty are prohibited. In the late 1920s leftist movies become popular but they are frequently cut so much they are unintelligible.

1926

Teinosuke Kinugasa directs one of his masterpieces, *A Crazy Page,* an avant-garde film about the delusions of the insane in a mental hospital. While not a commercial success, its artistic level, comparable to foreign films, is encouraging. Swordfighting films (*chambara*) on the struggle between the followers of the emperor and the shogunal supporters just before the Meiji Restoration become popular and form the most important genre of period drama until 1945. With the emperor's supporters shown as the "good guys," these films encouraged ultranationalism in the form of emperor worship. *The Woman Who Touched the Legs (Ashi ni Sawatta Onna),* a successful, slightly erotic light comedy modeled on American films, is made by Yutaka Abe, a former Hollywood actor.

1927

Abe's brand of American modernism becomes increasingly popular with the release of *The Five Women Around Him (Kare o Meguru Go-nin no Onna).* All three parts of Daisuke Ito's period drama, *A Diary of Chuji's Travels,* become hits, as young movie-goers support its outlaw hero (Denjiro Okochi) in his fight against the authorities.

1928

Ito continues to make successful period dramas with Okochi as his main lead, among them the *Sazen Tange* series about a one-eyed, one-armed nihilistic super samurai. Despite this, period dramas generally endorse feudalistic thought. Pro Kino (standing for the Japan Proletarian Motion Picture League) gains support from progressive intellectuals, students, and film-makers. Founded by leftist film critics such as Akira Iwasaki and Genju Sasa, it records May Day demonstrations and strikes with 16 mm cameras. One screening at Yomiuri Auditorium in Tokyo draws such a crowd that many are turned away, resulting in an impromptu illegal demonstration.

1929

At the Shochiku studio in Kamata on the outskirts of Tokyo, under studio head Shiro Kido, directors such as Ozu, Shimazu, and Gosho create the new film genre of "everyday realism" (*shomingeki*), portraying the lives of common people with humor and pathos. Shochiku is dubbed "The Actress's Kingdom" because of the number of actresses, such as Kinuyo Tanaka, it fostered. Mizoguchi's leftist film *Metropolitan Symphony* (*Tokai Kokyogaku*), reputedly a masterpiece, is only shown publicly after being severely cut by the censors.

1930

Shigeyoshi Suzuki's leftist film *What Made Her Do It?* (*Nani ga Kanojo o so Saseta ka*) is a hit. The leftist movement is now at its peak and since such films make money, the studios encourage their production.

1931

Gosho's *The Neighbor's Wife and Mine* (*Madamu to Nyobo*), with a jazz musical score, is Japan's first successful talkie. Political suppression puts an end to Pro Kino and the popularity of leftist films wanes, while a fad for militaristic movies starts.

1932

The first golden age of Japanese cinema begins. Ozu directs *I Was Born But. . .* , depicting the servility of the petit bourgeoisie in times of hardship. Such films on the lives of average city-dwellers gain popularity.

1933

Ozu directs *Passing Fancy*, a masterpiece about the lives of the common people.

1934

Shimazu directs *Our Neighbor Miss Yae* (*Tonari no Yae-chan*), a masterpiece of the "home drama" genre.

1935

The third major film company, Toho (formerly PCL) starts operation. One of its big stars of slapstick and musical comedies is Ken'ichi Enomoto (Enoken).

1936

Hiroshi Shimizu directs *Mr. Thank You* (*Arigato-san*), the first of a series of lyrical masterpieces shot in impromptu fashion entirely on location. Mizoguchi's *Osaka Elegy* and *Sisters of the Gion* establish realism in Japanese film. Mansaku Itami directs *Kakita Akanishi* (*Akanishi Kakita*), a masterly intellectual comedy. Sadao Yamanaka directs *Soshun Kochiyama*, a period drama rich in emotions. Ozu makes *The Only Son*, an example of Japanese "neo-realism." Sotoji Kimura directs *Older Brother, Younger Sister* (*Ani Imoto*), a powerful neo-realistic drama about the love-hate relationship of a working-class brother and sister. Under the Bureau of Propaganda many beautiful and poetic documentaries are directed by Kozo Akutagawa in Manchuria, trying to justify its colonization. The finest is *Forbidden Jehol* (*Hikyo Nekka*).

1937

With the beginning of the Sino-Japanese War, the government demands the cooperation of the film industry and bans films depicting the military comically or the cruelty of battle realistically, or portraying "decadent" pleasure-seeking. These demands are unopposed as leftist and liberal antiwar elements have already been suppressed. Yamanaka makes *Humanity and Paper Balloons,* a pessimistic masterpiece showing a samurai as a pathetic, servile man who is out of work.

1938

War movies are made in abundance. The first famous one is Tomotaka Tasaka's *Five Scouts,* which wins a prize at the Venice Film Festival. Kajiro Yamamoto directs the semidocumentary *Composition Class (Tsuzurikata Kyoshitsu),* a depiction of everyday life of the lower classes, based on the compositions of a poor girl in primary school. Hisatora Kumagai directs his period drama masterpiece *The Abe Clan,* examining the samurai spirit. Tasaka makes *A Pebble by the Wayside (Robo no Ishi),* about a poor youth fighting adversity. As the Sino-Japanese War threatens to continue for some time, the government intensifies its demands for more patriotic and nationalistic films to counter the individualistic and liberal influence of American and European movies.

1939

The Motion Picture Law is passed, placing the film industry completely under government control until the end of the war in 1945. All scripts have to be passed by censors, and actors and directors have to take an examination for a license to work. Mikio Naruse directs *The Whole Family Works,* a low-key realistic treatment of the hardships of the working class. Hiroshi Shimizu makes *Four Seasons of Children (Kodomo no Shiki),* the best lyrical film about country children. Kozaburo Yoshimura's *Warm Current* is favorably received and students especially are moved by his modern, Westernized version of romantic love. In *Earth,* Tomu Uchida realistically depicts the lives of the poorest farmers. Mizoguchi directs *The Story of the Last Chrysanthemums,* the tragedy of a woman in the feudalistic world of Kabuki.

1940

Fumio Kamei directs the documentary *Fighting Soldiers,* superficially in support of the war effort. When the censors note its antiwar ideas, Toho withdraws it and Kamei is arrested the following year. Shiro Toyoda directs *Spring on Lepers' Island (Kojima no Haru),* about a woman doctor's devotion to her leper' patients.

1941

With the start of the Pacific War, all American and European (except German) films are banned. Kajiro Yamamoto makes *Horse (Uma),* a beautiful, poetic portrayal of country life, part of it directed by his assistant, Akira Kurosawa. Yamamoto had arranged for the Imperial Army to order his studio to make it, and in return he provides a patriotic movie, in which the colt raised by a poor farm girl becomes an army horse in the end.

1942

In *The War at Sea from Hawaii to Malaya,* a "National Policy Film," Yamamoto makes heroes of the pilots who attacked Pearl Harbor.

1943

Kurosawa directs his first film, *Sanshiro Sugata.* Hiroshi Inagaki directs *The Life of Matsu the Untamed,* one of the most humanistic war-time films. A 1958 remake of it later wins the Venice Film Festival's Grand Prix.

1944

The subject matter of all films is the war effort.

1945

Defeat. Lack of equipment results in the film industry being very inactive. Motion picture companies are placed under the Occupation forces, which prohibit films with themes of revenge or antidemocratic principles.

1946

As swordfighting scenes are banned, the superstars of period dramas begin brandishing pistols instead of swords in movies modeled on American gangster movies. Kissing scenes, encouraged by the Occupation forces, are very popular. Fumio Kamei's *A Japanese Tragedy* (*Nihon no Higeki*), a documentary criticizing the imperial system, is confiscated. But the Occupation censors' most urgent concern lies in preventing the public from knowing the extent of the damage of the atomic bomb explosions. Labor disputes occur in every motion picture company. At Toho the union is strong enough to obtain the right to participate in film planning and almost to have the studios under its own management. Thus only a few powerful works were made there, such as Kurosawa's somewhat leftist film *No Regrets for Our Youth,* and production of B-grade entertainment movies virtually ceases. Some at Toho opposed the union and broke away to form a new company called Shin Toho.

1947

Toho continues under the control of the labor union and works of "democratic enlightenment" are produced, for example, Kinugasa's *Actress.*

1948

Toho's management tries to dismiss a number of union members, a strike ensues, and union members occupy the studios. To disperse them, both the police and the U.S. Army are mobilized, the latter using tanks and airplanes, and the union is defeated and its leaders driven from Toho. The U.S. motive may have been that the Toho union was one of the most powerful bases of the Japanese Communist Party, which had developed rapidly with the end of the war. The cold war era was beginning, and it was probably a necessary show of suppressing unions influenced by the Communist Party. The strike and its result led the public to believe the U.S. Army would forcibly crush a leftist movement. During this year, the harsh realities of postwar Japan are depicted in the following: Kurosawa's *Drunken Angel*; Mizoguchi's *Women of the Night*; Shimizu's *Children of the Beehive* (*Hachi no Su no Kodomotachi*); and Ozu's *A Hen in the Wind*. Inagaki directs *Children Hand-in-Hand* (*Te o Tsunagu Kora*), a masterpiece on the education of the mentally retarded.

1949

Ozu directs *Late Spring*, a masterpiece on the peaceful life of a middle-class family that makes audiences feel for the first time that peace has finally come to Japan.

1950

Tadashi Imai directs *Until the Day We Meet Again*, the first successful antiwar movie. Melodramas showing maternal love and sacrifice (*haha mono*) become popular. Kurosawa directs *Rashomon*, an innovative period drama with sexual and psychological themes and avant-garde techniques. The Korean War begins. SCAP headquarters orders the major motion picture companies to expel all communists and communist sympathizers. Film-makers such as Kamei, Imai, Gosho, Satsuo Yamamoto lose their jobs in this red purge.

1951

256

Film-makers dismissed in the Toho labor dispute and the red purge form independent production companies and begin making movies again. The first is Imai's *And Yet We Live*, which was strongly influenced by De Sica's *Bicycle Thieves*. *Rashomon* wins the Grand Prix at the Venice Film Festival, the first time a Japanese film becomes known internationally. Mikio Naruse directs *Repast* (*Meshi*), a masterpiece on the home life of a clerk and his wife. With Japanese Fuji color film, Keisuke Kinoshita makes *Carmen Comes Home* (*Karumen Kokyo ni Kaeru*), Japan's first feature-length color movie.

1952

The second golden age of Japanese cinema begins with the release of masterpieces such as Mizoguchi's *The Life of Oharu*, Kurosawa's *Ikiru*, and Naruse's *Mother*. The Occupation ends, and the theme of revenge is immediately restored to period drama, as well as plenty of swordfighting scenes. Most representative of this is Masahiro Makino's *Jirocho: The Record of Three Provinces* series of nine films made from 1952 to 1954. In *Children of the Atom Bomb,* Kaneto Shindo treats a previously taboo subject.

1953

Imai is invited to make a film at a major studio; the resultant antiwar movie about high school girls who die in the battle for Okinawa, *The Tower of Lilies,* is a big hit. Mizoguchi's *Ugetsu* and Ozu's *Tokyo Story* are made. The love melodrama *What Is Your Name?* establishes a new box-office record. In *Before Dawn (Yoake mae)* Yoshimura presents the Meiji Restoration from the viewpoint of the common people, with the hero going insane when he realizes the new government will not necessarily bring happiness to the masses.

1954

Kinoshita's *The Garden of Women* depicts the struggle against the feudal structure of a woman's college; he follows it with his great success, *Twenty-four Eyes,* a sentimental pacifist film. Kurosawa makes *Seven Samurai,* one of the greatest period dramas. Yoshimura's masterpiece *Cape Ashizuri (Ashizuri Misaki)* portrays youths in the gloomy prewar period. Naruse directs *Late Chrysanthemum (Bangiku),* a masterful drama on the psychology of middle-aged women. Mizoguchi makes *Sansho the Bailiff,* based on a medieval Japanese legend. The monster film *Godzilla (Gojira)* is a big hit and becomes a series.

1955

Two masterpieces about a woman's steadfast love for a worthless man —Naruse's *Floating Clouds* and Toyoda's *Marital Relations (Meoto Zenzai)* —are criticized by progressive critics as being "retrogressive." Tomu Uchida directs *A Bloody Spear at Mt. Fuji,* a fine period drama with lyricism, humor, and violent emotion. Kinoshita directs *You Were Like a Wild Chrysanthemum (Nogiku no Gotoki Kimi Nariki),* a beautiful and nostalgic love story. In *Record of a Living Being,* Kurosawa looks at the possibility of nuclear war. Gosho directs *Growing Up (Take-kurabe),* a nostalgic film about Meiji Japan.

257

1956

Kon Ichikawa directs *Harp of Burma (Biruma no Tategoto),* an antiwar film with a religious theme. In *Darkness at Noon* Imai takes up a murder trial in progress, attacks the court for its judgment, and both the trial and the film become social issues. The defendants are eventually found not guilty. Thereafter criticism of the courts, previously taboo, was pursued. A series of successful movies is made on the delinquent behavior of the "sun tribe," based on the sensational works of the young novelist Shintaro Ishihara. Although some public opinion against these films is strong, their popularity continues and they become an established genre, replacing love melodramas, which had been the most popular genre previously.

1957

The most profitable movies are the period dramas made by Toei, a company that turned swordfighting scenes into spectaculars with such box-office success that Toei becomes on a par with the major film studios. Kurosawa makes *Throne of Blood,* a period drama based on *Macbeth* that includes Noh modes of expression. Miyoji Ieki directs *Stepbrothers,* a criticism of the feudalistic nature of a military household in prewar Japan. Yuzo Kawashima's *Sun Legend of the Shogunate's Last Days (Bakumatsu Taiyo Den)* adds a new depth to traditional humor.

1958

Yasuzo Masumura directs *Giants and Toys,* a satirical comedy about the senseless competition among Japanese businessmen. Yujiro Ishihara becomes popular as a James Dean–type of rebellious youth; in the 1960s, he is the leading star. In this year the average Japanese went to twelve or thirteen movies, an all-time record. The Japanese film market is monopolized by the six major studios—Toho, Shochiku, Daiei, Shin Toho, Nikkatsu, and Toei—each producing about one hundred films annually.

1959

Parts 1 and 2 of Masaki Kobayashi's *The Human Condition,* a tragedy set in Manchuria during the latter part of World War II, are released. When Part 6 is completed in 1961, it becomes the longest Japanese film, with a total running time of about nine hours. Nobuo Nakagawa directs *The Yotsuya Ghost Story on the Tokaido (Tokaido Yotsuya Kaidan),* based on the classic thriller. Kon Ichikawa directs *Fires on the Plain (Nobi),* about starving Japanese soldiers in the Philippines who consume human flesh. Satsuo Yamamoto directs *The Song of the Cart,* about a woman living in a feudal farming village. Kihachi Okamoto directs *Desperado Outpost (Dokuritsu Gurentai),* a satire on the Imperial Army.

1960

Nagisa Oshima creates a stir with the portrayal of youths rebelling against established morality in *Cruel Story of Youth,* and by depicting a disruptive dispute within the leftist student movement in *Night and Fog in Japan.* Young directors who also made their first films at Shochiku are dubbed "Shochiku's *nouvelle vague*" since they advocated reform. Kinoshita directs *The River Fuefuki (Fuefukigawa),* a masterpiece of realism on the medieval wars seen through the farmers' eyes. Kon Ichikawa makes his nostalgic *Her Brother.* Kaneto Shindo makes *The Island (Hadaka no Shima),* without dialogue and with an incredibly low budget and a cast and crew of ten or so. Despite being shown at small public halls rather than movie theaters, it wins the Grand Prix at the Moscow Film Festival and becomes the model for small, autonomous film production companies.

1961

In *Pigs and Battleships* Shohei Imamura humorously depicts the mores of the "colonized" Japanese living near a U.S. naval port. In *Bad Boys* Susumu Hani uses real delinquents as actors, filming their story entirely on location. Kurosawa makes *Yojimbo,* a period drama brimming with showmanship.

1962

In *A Band of Assassins* (*Shinobi no Mono*) Satsuo Yamamoto sees feudal times through the eyes of rebels and peasants. Kiriro Urayama directs *A Street of Cupolas* (*Kyupora no Aru Machi*), the story of a young boy and girl growing up healthy and sound despite their poverty. Yoshishige Yoshida directs *Akizu Hot Springs,* about a passionate, self-destructive love affair. A hit comedy about a shrewd opportunist who advances in the business world, *The Age of Irresponsibility in Japan* (*Nippon Musekinin Jidai*), reflecting Japan's economic success, is turned into a series that lasts several years. Previous movies about white-collar workers often showed them as pathetic figures, and so this cheerful, optimistic film is unusual in the genre. Masaki Kobayashi directs *Harakiri,* a powerful, orthodox period drama. In *The Story of Zatoichi* (*Zatoichi Monogatari*) actor Shintaro Katsu plays the blind masseur who is also a famed swordsman. It is so successful that it becomes a series, lasting about ten years, with two or three films released annually. Zatoichi recalls the *Sazen Tange* series, which was extremely popular from the late 1920s throughout the 1930s, attesting to the popularity of a physically handicapped hero in period drama.

1963

259

The fad for modern *yakuza* movies begins. Swordfighting movies featuring *yakuza* (outlaws) as their main characters have been an important subgenre in period drama ever since the 1920s, but these modern *yakuza* movies are distinguished by their contemporary settings, a formalized Kabuki-like aesthetic intensified by the use of color, and the cruelty of the killings. Their popularity lasts about ten years and traditional period dramas almost vanish entirely from the screen. Beginning with *A Glorious Life* (*Hana no Shogai*), television (NHK) begins producing long period drama serials. The main characters are usually political leaders, and the view of history is seen from the upper class— a direct contrast to Mizoguchi's postwar period dramas on the lives of the lower classes. Extremely low-cost pornography, "pink" movies, are made. Imamura directs *The Insect Woman,* in which he observes the life of a prostitute as microscopically as a scientist studying an insect.

1964

Imamura makes *Intentions of Murder,* a masterpiece that portrays the tenacity and vitality of a woman from the lower classes. Masaki Kobayashi directs *Kwaidan (Kaidan),* four magnificently executed ghost stories. Hiroshi Teshigawara directs the avant-garde *Woman in the Dunes (Suna no Onna),* a symbolic depiction of life in marginal circumstances. Uchida directs *Hunger Straits (Kiga Kaikyo),* a powerful crime movie. Eiichi Kudo directs *The Great Melee (Dai Satsujin),* a period drama resembling a modern *yakuza* movie that also reflects the student movement of the time. Masahiro Shinoda directs *Assassination (Ansatsu),* a portrayal of a charismatic country samurai. Movie audiences continue to decline in the face of competition from television.

1965

Ichikawa's *Tokyo Olympiad (Tokyo Orimpikku)* and Kurosawa's *Red Beard* are released.

1966

In the following works sex is the central theme: Imamura's *The Pornographers: Introduction to Anthropology (Jinruigaku Nyumon),* Oshima's *Violence at Noon,* Masumura's *The Red Angel,* and Seijun Suzuki's *Violence Elegy.*

1967

Oshima directs *A Treatise on Japanese Bawdy Song,* on sexual repression, but which is also an investigation of fantasy. Imamura directs the documentary *A Man Vanishes (Ningen Johatsu),* in which a woman's private life is investigated through a hidden camera. Koji Wakamatsu directs *Violated Women in White,* a masterful, sado-masochistic "pink" movie.

260

1968

Kosaku Yamashita directs *Big-Time Gambling Boss (Socho Tobaku),* one of the best modern *yakuza* movies. Propelled by Oshima's avant-garde, antiestablishment *Death by Hanging,* the Japanese Art Theater, ATG, begins production of successful low-cost, experimental films, which have continued to this day. Imamura directs *The Profound Desire of the Gods,* a masterpiece set on an outlying island and recounted from a cultural anthropological viewpoint. In the tragicomedy *Human Bullet (Nikudan),* Kihachi Okamoto examines the psychology of young *kamikaze* pilots. Shinsuke Ogawa directs the feature-length documentary *Summer in Sanrizuka: The Front Line for the Liberation of Japan,* on the farmers' opposition to building Tokyo's international airport at Narita. As the New Left becomes more active, there is an increase in the number of independent productions of social documentaries concerning student, political, antipollution movements, etc.

1969

In the late 1960s the youth movements undergo a transformation throughout the world, and in *Diary of a Shinjuku Thief* Oshima depicts Shinjuku, which was the center of this transformation in Tokyo. In *Double Suicide* Masahiro Shinoda presents classical Kabuki with avant-garde dramaturgy. Yoji Yamada directs *It's Tough To Be a Man,* a comedy and the first of the only consistently successful series during the following twelve years of decline in the Japanese film industry.

1970

Yoshishige Yoshida directs *Eros Plus Massacre,* an avant-garde master-piece concerning the problem of sex and revolution among anarchists in the 1910s. Imamura directs the feature-length documentary set in a U.S. naval port, *History of Postwar Japan as Told by a Bar Hostess,* an unflinching portrayal of Japan's slavish devotion to America and its postwar lust for money. Oshima depicts the schism between concept and reality in *The Man Who Left His Will on Film* (*Tokyo Senso Sengo Hiwa*), where sex and violence become abstractions of the anguish of the human soul. Akio Jissoji directs *This Transient Life* (*Mujo*), a powerful, sensual treatment of incest.

1971

Noriaki Tsuchimoto directs *Minamata: The Victims and Their World,* a documentary concerning the victims of mercury poisoning and their indictment of the commercial enterprises that cause it. Shuji Terayama directs *Throw Away Your Books, Let's Go into the Streets* (*Sho o Suteyo, Machi e Deyo*), a somewhat grotesque but cheerful and comical avant-garde film. In *The Ceremony* (*Gishiki*) Oshima summarizes postwar Japanese history in his depiction of the family of a provincial man of status. Nikkatsu studios avoid bankruptcy by specializing in low-cost films, so-called *roman* porno movies.

261

1972

Tatsumi Kumashiro's *Sayuri Ichijo—Moist Desire,* on the anarchistic life of a stripper, wins critical attention; afterward he continues to make nihilistic porno films full of life and freedom.

1973

The popularity of modern *yakuza* movies ends, to be replaced by gloomy violent films of gangster battles, but only Kinji Fukasaku's *Battles Without Honor and Humanity* series produces any box-office hits.

1974

Shuji Terayama directs *Pastoral Hide and Seek* (*Den'en ni Shisu*), an avant-garde film of erotic folklore. Kumashiro directs *The Four-and-a-Half-*

Mat Room in Back—Soft, Secret Skin, a masterful porno film rich in emotion, anarchy, and nihilism.

1975

Fukasaku directs *The Graveyard of Honor and Humanity (Jingi no Hakaba),* a masterpiece in the genre of violent film. Satsuo Yamamoto directs *Annular Eclipse (Kinkanshoku),* an exposé of Japan's leading politicians, none of whom make any protest.

1976

Oshima directs *The Realm of the Senses,* a masterpiece of hard-core pornography. The film was developed in Paris, and the version shown in Japan was cut by the censors. Kazuhiko Hasegawa directs *Young Murderer (Seishun no Satsujinsha),* a drama about a young man who kills both his parents.

1977

Yoji Yamada's *The Yellow Handkerchieves of Happiness* scores a hit. Its presentation of wholesome love between an average man and woman stands out in an age of cinematic sex and violence. Actress Sachiko Hidari directs *The Long Single Road Ahead (Toi Ippon no Michi),* a powerful film about workers produced by the National Railway Workers Union. Kaneto Shindo directs *The Solitary Travels of Chikuzan (Chikuzan Hitori Tabi),* about the life of a wandering blind shamisen musician.

1978

Yasuzo Masumura directs *Double Suicide at Sonezaki (Sonezaki Shinju),* based on a Kabuki play about passion that ends in death.

1979

Imamura directs *Revenge Is for Us,* a semidocumentary about a man who commits a series of murders.

1980

Kurosawa directs *Kagemusha,* an epic elegy on grand medieval battles. Suzuki directs *Zigeunerweisen,* a ghost story told with aesthetic decadence.

1981

Kohei Oguri directs *Muddy River (Doro no Kawa),* about childhood friendship and premature awakening to adult realities. Yoshitaro Negishi directs *Distant Thunder (Enrai),* concerning a young farmer who bravely persists despite the decline of agriculture in industrialized Japan. Both these young directors win critical acclaim, as does Suzuki for *Heat Shimmer Theater (Kageroza),* a beautiful, modern ghost story.

APPENDIX II

An Interpretive Biography
by Gregory Barrett

The sentiments expressed in Japanese film strike a responsive emotional chord in Tadao Sato for they are the result of the common experiences of men like himself who lived through World War II and witnessed Japan's postwar collapse and its subsequent recovery. His background is a strong influence on his critical judgment, and so a brief account of the important junctures in his life would enable us to better understand his point of view, since he continually relates personal experiences to film, thereby augmenting his comprehension of both. A summary of his social and political concerns is also in order as they affect his critique of Japanese film.

Tadao Sato was born in the provincial city of Niigata, northeast Japan, in 1930. He was the eighth and youngest child of a shopkeeper who dealt in equipment for fishing boats. The first critical juncture in his life may have occurred when he failed the entrance examination to high school because he forgot to bow while a poem by the emperor was being recited by one of the examiners, and was accused of disloyalty to the emperor and the nation.

Sato has jokingly admitted that his life-long hatred of authoritarianism stems from this single incident; although at the time he was plagued by guilt for this "sin of disloyalty" and, to erase it, turned "militarist." He enrolled in a Naval Air Cadet pretraining school and became an apprentice seaman in the Imperial Navy in 1945.

Yet in doing penance for one sin Sato committed another, for he joined the navy against his mother's wishes. The subsequent guilt he felt toward her probably played a large part in his surmisal, in Chapter Four, that cinematic images of suffering women have a strong hold on Japanese men largely because they induce guilt. In this respect, Sato concurs with the University of California's psychological anthropologist, George A. De Vos, who, on the basis of extensive research, concluded that the Japanese mother induces guilt feelings in

263

her children by her "quiet suffering," or moral masochism, and a child's failures and rebelliousness are interpreted by the child as one cause of her suffering.

Sato became thoroughly disillusioned with militarism even before the war ended with Japan's defeat. In Chapter Five he reminisces on his own experiences in the pretraining school in order to show how they contrasted with the pristine screen image shown in *The War at Sea from Hawaii to Malaya.* "Each day was filled with brutal punishment. We were subjected to repeated slaps on the face and to the torture of endless calisthenics, and the NCOs constantly hit us with staves and ropes, often for personal gratification." Thus, the young Sato saw through the sham of discipline and recognized his naval training for what it was: the brutal exercise of power over young men who were, in effect, being trained to die.

When the war ended Sato returned to Niigata, first working in a factory and then as a clerk with Japan National Railway. At that time, like many other young Japanese, he was attracted to communist thought for several reasons: he belonged to the working class, the proletariat; and in communist literature, which flourished in the immediate postwar period, he found an answer to the most perplexing question for Japanese then—namely, why did Japan fight in and lose the war? In the Imperial Navy he had been indoctrinated to believe that he was fighting to liberate Asia from Western imperialism and had thought that such a moral course of action could not fail. Books published after the war, however, pointed out the relationship between military expansion and capitalistic expansion, and thus the moral basis for the war was removed.

Another reason for communism's appeal was that it restored Sato's faith in being Japanese. Defeat for the nation had dealt both a material and a moral blow to the Japanese. Now that the grand claim of liberating Asia had been exposed, Japan's militarism was reduced to a brutal exercise of power, the epitome of authoritarianism. For an idealistic youth like Sato, there was nothing worthy of respect in those who submit to it, and since he was Japanese himself, he felt he had nothing of value to identify with. When the communists were released from prison by SCAP, Sato, and many others, saw them as heroes because they had at least resisted militarism and fascism, and in their courage Sato was able to regain his pride in being Japanese. Actually, the Occupation authorities themselves intended to foster such feelings by lending encouragement to films about Japanese who resisted the old regime. And lastly, communist thought appealed to Sato because he saw in it the ideal of a classless society where everyone is equal.

264

In 1949, with the surplus of young workers, Sato was laid off by Japan National Railway and got a job as a telephone repairman with Nippon Telegraph and Telephone Public Corporation. Since a high school diploma was important, he enrolled in a night school but seldom attended classes, deciding instead to educate himself by reading books on subjects that interested him—psychology, literature, sociology. This eventually led him to develop his own theory of *dokugaku*, or self-education, as opposed to academic training, and to become a theorist on education also. He read, went to movies in his spare time, and had his essays on them published by magazines such as *Eiga hyoron* (*Film Criticism*) and *Shiso no kagaku* (*The Science of Thought*). In 1956, his collection of essays was published as *Japanese Film*, and Sato joined the editorial staff of *Eiga hyoron* and moved to Tokyo, the next important juncture in his life.

For most Japanese the move from the provinces to the capital is an unsettling, if not traumatic, experience. Family and friends are left behind, and the uneventful but familiar is replaced by the eventful and uncertain. As Tadao Sato says, in Chapter Three, "Motion pictures began to cater to the solitary bachelors in the big cities. Most of them, myself included, came to the city alone from the provinces and were without family connections. They empathized with the *yakuza* hero, an orphan in the universe."

While coping with loneliness in Tokyo, Sato also became disenchanted with communism, for 1956 was the year of the suppression of Hungary and Khruschev's speech denouncing Stalinism. As early as 1950 Sato had become disillusioned with the Japan Communist Party, which had split into the international faction (*kokusai-ha*) and the main faction (*shuryu-ha*) as a result of Comintern's criticism of its policy on peaceful revolution. The former followed the new Soviet theory and the latter adhered to the old one. During that same year the Korean War broke out, and as Japan was still under Occupation, MacArthur ordered the dissolution of the Japanese Communist Party. In the ensuing red purge the movement was forced underground and no one knew of its precise activities; however, there were rumors of an internecine war with each faction accusing the other of being a puppet of imperialism, and these rumors forced Sato to review his thoughts on communism. In the examining process Sato began to suspect a growing contradiction between the ideal Soviet Union and the real one.

In 1954 Sato was strongly influenced by a book written by Shunsuke Tsurumi, *Taishu geijitsu* (*The Art of the People*), which maintained that, contrary to what communist leaders and intellectuals believed—that the

Japanese masses desired a revolution—in reality the people are conservative and do not like even the idea of revolution. From this Sato concluded that communist leaders only interpreted for the masses to suit their own aims. Moreover, he wondered if university graduates could really understand how the common people felt. Their plan, it seemed, was first to enlighten the people ideologically and then lead them; however, it was more important for Sato to understand their sentiments first. Thus, in his essays on films he endeavors to understand the sentiments of the common people rather than negate them as the communist intellectuals had done.

When the tyranny of Stalinism was revealed in 1956 when Soviet tanks moved in to crush the Hungarian revolt, there was no doubt in Sato's mind about the strong hold the Soviet regime exerted over its satellite states. Sato realized that while the left and the right were ideologically incompatible, when it came to the exercise of power they were no different. The Soviet Army presence in Hungary was not any different from the old Imperial Army in China, and worship of the emperor or of the Soviets could be equated with submission to power.

Sato's disillusionment with communism probably made him more receptive to the films of the new directors of the late 1950s. His previous concern for social justice made him applaud the leftist humanism of older directors like Tadashi Imai and Satsuo Yamamoto, and the sympathy shown for the weak by Akira Kurosawa and Keisuke Kinoshita. He claimed that these directors belonged to the generation that was intellectually initiated during the Marxist domination of Japanese thought in the late 1920s to early 1930s, when artistic expression tended to be based on the idea of social justice.

In contrast, the new directors seemed more concerned with the intricacies of individual egos, which drew them to Sato, who did not hold much store for social justice. As editor-in-chief of *Eiga hyoron*, he devoted a special issue to new directors in 1958, and the essay by Yasuzo Masumura stated their case best. Masumura rejected the socially realistic films of the past, claiming that the detailed delineation of social realities served only to overemphasize the pressures of society on people, thereby rendering the individual's defeat almost inevitable. Masumura intended to ignore this to draw attention to the human ego, expressing himself by exaggerating it.

As Sato stated in Chapter Eleven, directors like Masumura belonged to the postwar generation, which had witnessed the exposure of the limitations of various schools of thought. From this experience, their self-assertion took precedence over social justice, and they soon progressed toward opposition to oppression in any shape or form.

Thus, Sato, who had similarly witnessed the defects of communism, identified with these new directors, this postwar generation. He particularly admired Masumura because the latter, by ignoring external conditions, also ignored the power of authority. However, ignoring it was not enough; one has to oppose it. And the new generation did not progress toward opposition to oppression in any shape or form until Nagisa Oshima came along.

Sato has been a friend of Oshima's since the latter's assistant director days at Shochiku studios. He praised Oshima's first film in 1959 and has been a sympathetic critic of his works throughout Oshima's career. What attracted Sato to Oshima was Oshima's uncompromising, antiestablishmentarian themes, evident from his first film, which coincided with Sato's own loathing for authoritarianism and revived the leftist film tradition of the early 1930s, in which the establishment was attacked.

This antiestablishmentarianism is not only directed against conservatives. Leftists also have their own establishments, like the Japan Communist Party, which can oppress minority factions and individuals just as much as rightist establishments. In *Night and Fog in Japan* Oshima indicated that tyranny not only exists in the Stalinist-type leadership of the student movement of the 1950s but also among the leaders of the movement in 1960, when the film was made.

In Oshima's films oppression is not limited to the political sphere; it can also occur as the result of an established social order, such as the family system, education system, etc. He is against any form of oppression, and in Oshima, Sato found a kindred spirit.

This "opposition to oppression in any shape or form" was also evident in the New Left, and faith in it replaced Sato's disillusionment with the old Left. Thus, he welcomed the student revolt in Japan in the late 1960s, when activists occupied university buildings throughout Japan. Although in some cases the cause of a particular campus revolt seemed insignificant (such as a rule revision that restricted student freedom), the prerogatives of the university still came under the category of "opposition to oppression." Regardless of the causes, Sato was impressed by the fact that student activists would not accept the excuse that although the system was evil the people who administered it and made a living from it were themselves innocent victims of the system. If the university was evil, said the students, then those who administered it and their teachers were also evil. It seemed that Sato felt that by pinning the blame on the people in the system, people recognized their responsibility for it and the system could be changed. In the past, while people admitted that the system was bad, their conclusion was always that it was impossible to change it.

One result of campus revolts was that some courses would be determined by students, some of whom asked that Sato, the working-man critic, be allowed in 1971 to teach at the University of Tokyo, the citadel of academic elitism. He used some of the essays in this collection as his text then, and the following year he taught at the same university's school of journalism. Thereafter, he returned to free-lance writing. He had left *Eiga hyoron* in 1961, and after serving as the editor-in-chief of *Shiso no kagaku* in 1962, had had no official position.

Sato's admiration for student activists lasted until the early 1970s, when the movement degenerated into internecine strife and violent battles that took a toll on student lives. Sato felt that the radical student leaders were regarding themselves as a privileged class, which had the right to commit acts of violence against others, and as such, they did not differ from those who had seized power and had become corrupted by it. Those who had pointed an accusing finger at the administrators in the system and their own teachers had lost their "innocence." In accounting for the change in Oshima's films in the late 1960s, when he seemed to have become taciturn, Sato says, in Chapter Eleven, that Oshima could no longer judge others with the premise that he alone was innocent, and this can also be considered Sato's assessment of what happened to the Japanese student movement.

The degeneration of student activists reveals that oppression is also perpetuated by the pleasure human beings find in exercising control over others, in other words, they really lust for power. In the character of the poor drayman in *The Song of the Cart,* Sato pointed out (Chapter Eight) that given the chance to exercise power a poor man would oppress others just as much as a rich man.

268

Disillusionment with the student movement was coupled with disappointment with the new socialist nations, such as Cuba and Vietnam, Sato had once admired. Despite their internal reforms their foreign policy is pursued through the use of power, which is, in effect, a form of oppression. Disenchantment with socialism, however, has not led Sato to embrace the capitalist camp, for he doubted whether capitalism could contribute more to people's happiness.

However, Sato was not left with a gloomy social and political outlook. When asked about his political view in an interview, Sato said that he no longer believes in ideology but he would welcome something like China's cultural revolution if it happened spontaneously. However, as that movement resulted in the deification of Mao Tse-tung, which can be equated with the prewar worship of the Japanese emperor, it is far from the ideal of any egalitarian society.

Sato's ideal of a classless society has also led him to formulate a new theory on education, as the present system is creating a new class society based on elitism. Modeled after Sato's own experiences, he proposes that all students, after graduating from high school, engage in physical labor, as Sato himself did, from age 16 to 26. Then, with the decline in physical strength in middle age, they can either do clerical work or go to college. In Sato's theory, as in Mao's, there will not be a special elitist class, only different periods in the lives of all members of society—times when they either worked with their hands or their minds.

As Sato abhors the exercise of power and, unlike Mao, he will not force his theory of education on the people but rely on Japanese youth to follow his example. He has propagated these views in ten books on education and has found some receptivity.

The overriding purpose of all the books Sato has written on film and other aspects of the popular culture of Japan has been to clarify the sentiments of the people. When he reviewed film genres that were beneath the dignity of college-educated critics, he attempted to explain the feelings of the so-called lower classes. His recent book on *Chushingura,* the epic that appeals to all social classes, examines the structure of sentiments in the whole of Japanese society. A truly egalitarian society would not be one based solely on the interests and sentiments of the working class, but on those of all the social classes.

Sato does not really believe that an egalitarian society can be brought into existence through political revolution. Political change usually boils down to a change in power, and violence commonly begets violent reactions rather than subtle changes. Thus, Sato is most interested in the small changes in the everyday life of the people. An example of these changes is that more and more young couples today live with the wife's parents and, consequently, there is much less friction between the young wife and mother-in-law, which has affected the personalities of Japanese women, both young and old. Such shifts in the continuum of Japanese sentiments are revealed in popular culture, and Sato's attention has recently been drawn to the daytime television dramas for the housewife.

In Chapter Twelve Sato observed that the television image of the middle-aged woman in family dramas was quite different from the old one of the suffering mother. She has evolved into a strong-minded, attractive woman who acts as though she can enjoy life now that her children are grown-up. This change can mean that middle-aged Japanese women are happier than their counterparts in the past, now that friction with younger women has been reduced and there is less need for maternal sacrifices because economic conditions have improved so much. However, in *Josei bunka no jidai ga yatte kita* (*The Age of Feminine Culture Has Come,* an essay appearing in *Fujin koron* [*The Consensus of Women*], April, 1978), Sato finds it more significant that these television family dramas are now generally written by women scenarists for a predominately housewife audience. The old movie image of the drab but courageous mother, who gives her all for her kids, has been fashioned by male scriptwriters and male directors for an audience that included many men, and this reflected their guilt feelings toward their own mothers.

In addition to the change in image of the middle-aged housewife, Sato, in *Terebi dorama to Nihonjin* (*TV Dramas and the Japanese,* an essay appearing in *Drama,* No. 1, July, 1979), has noted that compared with the movies of the past, there has been a larger number of stories about women running small businesses or in various occupations, and even some concerning leaders in the Japanese Women's Liberation movement. As early as 1966 there was an excellent television drama about the antiwar poetess, Akiko Yosano, who lived in the Meiji era (1868–1912). Then, in 1977, the life of Itsue Takamure (1894–1976), a feminist and researcher in the history of women, was portrayed in *Hi no Kuni no Onna* (*Woman from the Land of Fire,* the fire referring to her native area of Kumamoto, where the famous volcano Mt. Aso is found). In this drama her self-centered husband gradually recognized her superior ability and, in effect, became her househusband so that she could complete her research. Her most famous book, *Bokeisei no kenkyu* (*Research on Matriarchy*), was published in 1938. On April 6, 1979, there was a two-hour drama entitled *Ameyuki-san,* concerning Waka Yamada, a marriage consultant and social critic who severely criticized the male-oriented Japanese society of the 1920s and 1930s. Rescued from prostitution in Seattle by one man, who later committed suicide, she married another man who loved and respected her, even though she had been a prostitute. The drama seemed to suggest that she became great through the sacrifices of these men, and thus reversed the old theme of male success based on female sacrifice.

270

In these recent television dramas Sato detects a change in the depiction of male-female psychology in Japan. In the old movies a man occasionally sacrificed himself for a woman, and as this image was directed toward an audience including many males, it was an atonement for the sins of a male-dominated society. Now that television drama is aimed at a predominately female audience, this sort of action can be accepted as a natural expression of love. In other words, an alternate mode of behavior in male-female relations is being presented on television, one quite different from the traditional mode where love is measured against guilt. This can become a model for future behavioral patterns, thereby affecting Japanese society. Although few men watch these dramas, the middle-aged mothers who do may transmit to their daughters different expectations in marriage from those of old, and young men who approached these ideals would be more liked than those who did not. In this way, Japanese male behavioral patterns can be said to be affected at least indirectly by the influence of female-oriented television dramas.

The present-day television dramas are also a manifestation of what Sato calls the "feminine culture." The new culture itself is the expression of a new social class, which he describes in *The Age of Feminine Culture Has Come*. It consists of women, children, and old people and can be called a consumer class, since they consume the products usually made by men; however, Sato thinks that this is a negative view of the relationship. In the consumption of products he sees the reproduction of human beings, spirit (*kokoro*), and life itself. He views children as beings who are in the process of forming their spirit, and old people as those who have completed this formation. The housewife gives birth to children and protects and cares for the aged, her own or her husband's parents, and, in a way, "manages" their spirits or hearts (*kokoro*).

When manufacturing products is the central concern of society, men are thought of as the producers and women, children, and old people only as consumers. However, when we consider the fact that products are only made in order to reproduce life and spirit, then the consumers can be called reproducers. Sato sees the gradual replacement of a production society by a reproduction society, where women would occupy the most important position.

For Sato, both capitalistic and socialistic societies are based on production. The struggle between them is not only based on the ideal of freedom *versus* the prevention of exploitation but also on competition for producing the most goods. In both there is the belief that social justice can only be realized in an affluent society. Recently, however, this common belief has hit a few snags on the problems of pollution and limited natural resources. Moreover, in the product-oriented societies of both capitalist and socialist countries children and the aged are oppressed. This is particularly true of modern Japan, where the young are forced to study for increasingly difficult school entrance examinations in order to get a higher wage in the labor market, and where old people tend to be considered useless because they no longer produce anything. Along with women, they both form a new oppressed class, for in the light of recent wage increases, it is difficult to call the Japanese working class oppressed. Sato believes that as the caretaker and protectress of children and the aged, the woman is in a position of leadership in this new oppressed class. She can either press forward for liberation or subordinate herself to her husband and charges.

The above views of Sato bear some correspondence to those of American social scientists. The feminist sociologist, Arlie Horschild, stated in a lecture attended by the translator that in a capitalistic society the labor of women as housewives and caretakers of children is undervalued because it carries no wage, and that conversely the "productive" labor of their husbands was validated by wages. In *Socialization for Achievement* (Berkeley: University of California Press, 1973) De Vos states that in America, the women's role is seen as less worthy because, as housewives, they are not given the same status as men in an economically oriented society. However, De Vos believes that their role was valued in traditional Japan because the production of children insured the all-important continuity of the family. The maternal role was validated by the exacting training received for it, and even the role of housewife was considered an important one requiring a great deal of planning and a sense of organization.

Because of urbanization and the nuclearization of the Japanese family, Sato believes that the role of housewife and mother has lost some of its old value and is in need of revalidation. The typical modern Japanese housewife lives in a city or suburban apartment and her husband is often a white-collar worker. His or her parents may come to live with them at some time or other; however, most of the time she has only one or two children to take care of. Housekeeping does not take as much time as in the past due to modern appliances and the small size of the typical apartment. The rural and urban housewife of the past, on the other hand, usually had more children, a bigger residence to keep up, and the aged to care for. She had to work in the rice paddies or on the farm, and entertain more at home because in the old neighborhood society her husband's residence and work place were often the same. In contrast, the modern Japanese housewife seems to have too much free time and, in a culture where hard work is valued more than in most, she even appears lazy.

Sato's interest in the new feminine culture sums up his present social and political concerns. As he is opposed to occupational discrimination, he welcomes television dramas about career women. Moreover, he wants to revalidate the role of the modern housewife. In this respect he concurs with Itsue Takamure, who formed a bypath in the Japanese Women's Liberation movement by stressing the importance of child-raising over the need to get more jobs for women. Finally, by speaking out against the oppression of women, the aged, and the young in a product-oriented society, Sato has demonstrated his own "opposition to oppression in any shape or form," a stance which reflects his life-long enmity toward authoritarianism.

INDEX

286

287

288

定価4,300円

in Japan